Melancholy and Society

Melancholy and Society

Wolf Lepenies

Translated by Jeremy Gaines and Doris Jones

Harvard University Press
Cambridge, Massachusetts
London, England
1992

This book was originally published as *Melancholie und Gesellschaft* by Suhrkamp Verlag, copyright © 1969 by Suhrkamp Verlag.

Preparation of this translation has been aided by a grant from Inter Nationes.

This book is printed on acid-free paper, and its binding materials have been chosen for strength and durability.

Library of Congress Cataloging-in-Publication Data

Lepenies, Wolf.
    [Melancholie und Gesellschaft. English]
    Melancholy and society / Wolf Lepenies; translated by Jeremy Gaines and Doris Jones.
        p.   cm.
    Translation of: Melancholie und Gesellschaft.
    Includes bibliographical references (p.   ) and index.
    ISBN 0-674-56468-5 (alk. paper)
    1. Melancholy—Social aspects.   2. Boredom—Social aspects.
3. Melancholy in literature.   4. Social history—17th century.
5. Social history—18th century.   I. Title.
HM291.L41613   1992
302'.17—dc20   91-27928
                                                        CIP

Contents

Foreword

by Judith N. Shklar

"Fear and sorrow without a cause": Robert Burton's definition of melancholy can hardly be bettered. It covers the whole range, from clinical depression to the enervating ennui that afflicts entire social groups. We can recognize it in ourselves easily enough, but melancholy can be expressed in so many ways that it is simply an inexhaustible subject of reflection. There are articulate as well as wordless sufferers. Some people broadcast their blues; others bear them in utter silence. And some manage to do both simultaneously, by writing about their misery, either directly or obliquely. In his brilliant study, Wolf Lepenies tells us most about writers whose works express the melancholy of entire social classes, especially hereditary or self-created aristocrats. These people have been cast aside by historical change, and the affliction that they have to endure is ennui, rather than acute emotional pain. This literature is therefore not always very moving, though the sentimental novel has its place in it. Public melancholy is a matter more of boredom than of real depression. We are confronted not by Dürer's desolate female face, but with relatively tolerable social distress.

Lepenies' main argument is that at certain historical moments, social circumstances reduce whole groups of people to melancholy. They are not among the silent victims. Like Hamlet, they understand quite well why they are in the state they are in, and they often say so. They do not think of themselves as aberrations or as interruptions of a well-functioning, integrated society. They know that they are not mere exceptions to the social norm. On the contrary, they are the necessary expression of a world that is always awry in countless different ways. When we consider them, we do not wish that they might have had access to modern psychiatric remedies. For they are not isolated individual sufferers. They belong to a class that has lost its public significance, and they feel as useless as they are.

One response to the full self-awareness of this kind of melancholy is to dream of utopian societies in which melancholy would be perfectly impossible. Indeed, one might well say of many literary utopias that they are cities in which people such as their authors could never exist. Utopia is a response to a sense of disorder, and it offers an inverted mirror image of a disoriented mind. In utopia everything is in perfect order. More significantly, utopia does not call for action. Quite the contrary, it is the work of a resigned consciousness and of a social lesson learned by those whom social futility has reduced to the melancholy of chronic inactivity. The author of a utopia plays with perfection because it is impossible and therefore positively invites the passive acceptance of the imperfections of the world as it is. It is to the interplay of these two opposed but yoked states of mind, the desolate and the utopian, that the following pages are mostly devoted. Lepenies has drawn a new sociological map of the melancholy sources of fantasies about the flawless, wholly planned social order, and of the resignation that it implies.

The melancholic's contemplative utopia is certainly not the only vision of social perfection. If one thinks of utopias as blueprints for communal enterprises like the ones that sprang up all over America in the nineteenth century, then these imaginary societies would seem like ambitious plans of social action, and hardly passive. Such rural utopias were not regarded as impossible, even though almost all of them did in fact fail quite quickly. Whatever Fourier's intentions may have been, his disciples in America meant business, and they went out to create little paradises with every expectation of success. These failed enterprises did not mean the end of the reforming spirit, however, and many of their participants went on to take up other significant social causes. These men and women were not classical utopians. They were social activists who tried to improve their own lives and that of their country by following a doctrine. Their short-lived communes were utopias designed for immediate action in their own country. The word "utopia," however, means "nowhere"—outside time and place. Originally a utopia by its very nature could never exist, not even briefly. The classical utopia, to which the name really applies, should therefore not be confused with efforts to actually create perfected communities.

The best-known literary utopia was also the first: Sir Thomas More's perfectly rational community, which was not marred by any of the many personal vices and social evils that were most conspicuous in the England of his age. Its message was critical but implied no urge to act. The story was, after all, explicitly about nowhere. Among the significant aspects of life in this purely imaginary world is the psychological effect of a wholly planned society. Utopia's inhabitants would never have any occasion to be depressed, bored, or egocentric. They would lead sensible and satisfactory lives. The inventor of such a social scheme may not be so calm, and may be forced to learn to become more resigned and possibly also melancholy. As a lesson in passivity, there can be no hint of a suggestion that "nowhere" could ever become "here and now," or lead anyone to social action. It is not a program of any sort. For all its critical implications, utopia is melancholy's twin: an active spirit is reduced to quiescence in the face of the inevitable failures of fallen humanity.

Until the French Revolution, whether they were located on the moon or some other planet, on an obscure continent or island, in the remote past or never at all, utopias were a myth designed to instruct the unregenerate and to make them aware of all their failings. Though often written by devout Christians, utopias were generally driven by reason. The faults that they eliminated were no longer manifestations of original sin, but expressions of irrationality. Utopia was in many ways the humanists' replacement for paradise. Irrationality and immoderation sufficed to explain our unalterable misconduct and our endless social failures. It was not a more cheerful view than the Christian sense of sin; it simply offered a different, but no less hopeless, diagnosis. Indeed, it offered none of the traditional religious forms of comfort and solace. The new awareness of the mass of unalterable social vices induced mere resignation, and utopia as a literary genre was itself a symptom of the paralysis of melancholy. Thus, Robert Burton's *Anatomy of Melancholy* contains a little utopia, which might seem incongruous in so complete an account of every sort of depression, both personal and social. Utopia seems to be somehow intellectually necessary to a full intellectual psychology of the subject. It is the melancholic's political fiction.

Classical utopian fantasies are thus neither random nor socially insignificant; neither are they marginal phenomena simply because they inhibit rather than release social energies. The peculiar form of melancholy that is involved in their creation is, moreover, not only a personal state of mind. It may be a social response to quite specific social changes. Melancholy and boredom can be social phenomena caused by historical changes. Not only the occasional individual but discernible classes of similarly situated people may fall prey to depression, and they do so for recognizable public reasons. People who have been deprived of their political functions or who have been denied any significant place in public life are not only likely to feel frustrated in their enforced futility, but may fall prey to permanent melancholy and boredom.

Literary accounts of melancholy are as numerous as they are often illuminating, and Lepenies draws on many. An elite that has become sick of itself and of its culture offers a rich choice of characters. Who could possibly give us a better sense of their misery than the long-suffering characters in Chekhov's plays? Each one of these lost souls is a recognizable individual, but they are the people who make up the Russian gentry on the verge of collapse and at the end of their moral and political tether. To think of *Ivanov, Uncle Vanya,* and *The Three Sisters* is to know not only the boredom of rural life without a future and without even a past worth remembering, but also the very essence of ennui. Vanya and his kind were not the first to have had to endure such a condition, though only Chekhov can make us live it over and over again. The idleness of these lives is a political disease without a cure, and it is made only worse by the victims' dream of going to another place where everything will be not just different, but the perfect opposite of their daily reality. They talk of going to Moscow or to Paris, but actually they can go nowhere. When Ivanov commits suicide, it amounts to a simple statement of that fact.

In Lepenies' view, the extremity of melancholy may even lead to gestures of rebellion, such as the Fronde. This ill-organized uprising against the newly consolidated absolute monarchy of seventeenth-century France, he argues, was not meant to succeed. It was merely a spasmodic effort to escape the boredom that political futility had imposed upon the old nobility. With nothing to do, these men tried to dispel their mental uneasiness by a random and completely pointless bit of violence. Even though this was not all there was to the Fronde, Richelieu and later Louis XIV did take steps to contain the boredom of the privileged orders. The officer corps was closed to all who could not offer proof of several generations of noble birth, thus guaranteeing the aristocracy a monopoly on the one form of employment that was regarded as sufficiently honorable. Then there was the court to keep them busy. As any reader of the recollections of the Duc de Saint-Simon knows, there was plenty to do at court. Constant ceremony, ritual, attendance upon the king, fierce competition for precedence and for the king's attention were designed less to dispel than to positively outlaw melancholy. To seem cheerful was one of the obligations of all courtiers. Searching for ways to occupy their time, they found that getting properly dressed for the court took many hours. There were also spectacles, games, endless gambling. The last was often of truly pathological proportions.

The second class among which Lepenies finds a comparable melancholia is the German bourgeoisie, which was long denied any place
in the public realm. In doing so he reminds us that the longest and
intellectually never wholly completed struggle in European social history has been that between the aristocracy and the bourgeoisie. Since
the Middle Ages the bourgeois, whether he is a merchant or a lawyer,
has been the object of hostile humor. And the bourgeois who, like
Monsieur Jourdain, tries to rise above his proper station was the particular object of ridicule and contempt long before he was finally
immortalized by Molière. We should likewise not forget that the
bourgeois artist, too, might take his revenge on the aristocracy, which
treated him like a domestic servant. The aristocrat who does nothing
and sports all the vices of idleness was no stranger to the stage of the
eighteenth century. The voice of Figaro would have been heard even
without Mozart's help. Each class not only used its social power to
reduce the other to futility, but then abused its victims for the faults
inherent in the condition to which it had condemned them. Their
mutual antagonism seems, moreover, to have survived every degree
of social change.

If we still find the complex play of ennui and antagonism in full
bloom in the pages of Proust's novel, it may well be because this is a
theme that has an irresistible power over the literary imagination.
The novel and the daily papers kept the European aristocracy alive
long after the industrial economy had pushed them aside. The truth
of the matter is that social power is not everything. The aesthetic
imagination has found more in the decaying aristocracy than in its
eternal enemy, the bourgeoisie, especially the prosperous and vic-
torious bourgeoisie. There are even self-created literary aristocrats
who adopt the melancholy of the caste with which they have come to
identify. Henry Adams, heir to a republican ideology and citizen of a
representative democracy, was so consumed by his sense of displace-
ment that he turned it into a theory of education. Social change, he
decided, had become so swift and so devastating that education was
simply impossible. Nothing that one learned in one's youth remained
valid. It was, to be sure, only his aristocratic sensibility, in the very
midst of a democracy, that was to make *The Education of Henry Adams*
such a perfect expression of nostalgia. And nostalgia, as Proust's
novel reminds us, is at the core of melancholy.

Nostalgia, boredom, and ennui are what the bourgeois and the
aristocrat inflict upon each other. The bourgeois is, however, by far
the more common object of literary assault. Karl Marx's expectation
that the proletariat would eventually deliver the final blow to a self-

destroying bourgeoisie was only a continuation of this literary aristocratic resentment. For Marx's proletarians bear a truly remarkable
resemblance to the self-image of the old nobility. Inspired by abun-
dant physical courage, intensely class conscious, and far too independent to endure the discipline of commerce and industrial production,
they were to vindicate at last the old aristocratic ethos against the
domination of the eternally despised capitalist and bourgeois. It has
not quite turned out that way, but the boredom of underemployed
blue-collar workers is manifest, not least in Europe. The whole
scenario of aristocratic melancholy is not unlike the rituals of the
violent sports fans who attend matches all over Europe at present.
They, too, foment riots against order and discipline to interrupt the
socially created tedium of their daily lives; and although the stadium
is neither so expensive nor so well organized as the royal courts, the
riots do provide ritualized antidotes to the endemic boredom that
cannot be entirely controlled now—as it was not, in fact, fully eliminated at any time in the past.

It is probably only scant comfort to melancholy individuals to know
that they are the source of their own malady, even if their social
experiences have done much to encourage it. "Our fate is not in the
stars," and Saturn has nothing to do with our emotional life, even
though astrology did seem to comfort at least some Renaissance
melancholics. The acceptance of a less mysterious world does not,
however, preclude a considerable diversity of responses. Members of
the same class cope with their common situation in quite different
ways. The politically imposed uselessness of the defeated French
nobility after the failure of the Fronde found expression in the half-
cynical, half-melancholy writings of the Duc de la Rochefoucauld,
especially his *Maximes.* In contrast, his close friend Madame de
Lafayette, in her incomparable novel *La Princesse de Clèves,* gave way
to moral nostalgia, to the memory of a personal ethos of honor that
clearly was a defiance of the new monarchy and its world. As such, it
was a relatively robust protest. In either case, these aristocrats were
able to create a place where melancholy and boredom could be
openly displayed, namely the aristocratic salon. Since one was obliged
to be cheerful at court, the salon became an alternate world in which
the real feelings of the displaced aristocracy could be shared without
disguise. It made for an incomparable intimacy.

The aristocratic salon did not last long. By the middle of the
eighteenth century it had been displaced by salons that were meant
to dispel melancholy and boredom. Far from being socially homo-
geneous, they were composed of aristocrats, rich bourgeois, magis-

trates, and, above all, men of letters. The atmosphere was permissive, and the salons were quite consciously alternative societies. They were the source of public opinion, itself a new notion; and as Voltaire had it, "opinion is the queen of the world, and whoever rules the queen rules the world." These salons were hiding places not for a subversive boredom, but for an aggressive alternative to a court that was now accused of being dull. That may have been bourgeois sour grapes, to be sure, but it was not so entirely. Courtiers could be found in the salons as well, and there is every reason to believe that they found their mixed company entertaining. Indeed, the too close relationship between the Court and the Town, between courtiers and men of letters especially, was a source of anxiety to those who were beginning to generate genuinely radical ideas. Both d'Alembert and Rousseau saw this new, indiscriminate salon society as deeply corrupting to men of letters. In the event, these salons in their pursuit of entertaining ideas and people were the incubators of the ideas that put an end to all the boredom of the ancien régime. Whatever the failures of the French Revolution, it was not boring. It replaced social ennui with political activity, and melancholy with genuine grief.

In Germany the French Revolution came to generate its own wave of melancholy, as a pervasive sense of futility gripped a bourgeoisie that was firmly barred from political life and social dignity. This bourgeoisie found its literary representation in Goethe's *Werther,* whose lovesick hero commits suicide, not least because he lacks the energy for anything resembling an active life. Bourgeois melancholics longed not for overplanned utopias, but rather for isolation in nature or for passionate activity, one might even say for disorder. For their melancholy was rooted in an all-too-well ordered daily life. Here the cure for melancholy is no longer, as it was in earlier ages, a desire for order in daily life that would somehow restore the world of the nursery. The clock had by then won its victory, and imposed all the order anyone ever might have longed for. There was no incentive to invent those utopias in which there was a rule for every contingency of human life and in which nothing unforeseen could possibly happen. The perfectly planned society was not what the Werthers of the age would or could dream of. What they did long for was a less disciplined world.

This generation of melancholics, as Lepenies shows, thought of themselves as creative geniuses trapped in little towns where nothing ever happened. They were Prometheus-like giants fettered to a mediocre shop, pulpit, or newspaper. They might be tutors or teachers, and they were never within sight of an escape to the stormy, sublime, and natural order of their dreams. They yearned not for aristocratic society but for heroic activity. Locked into confined spaces, they longed for a utopia of total disorder rather than for its overdirected opposite.

There was always also the alternative of a retreat into solitude, as prescribed by Rousseau. This might seem a promising escape from enclosure, boredom, and melancholy, but Rousseau's experiments with solitude had been notably unsuccessful and offered little encouragement, even though they were imitated. The fantasies of German *Sturm und Drang* and its various successors were, moreover, not mere fantasies. They were often meant to reveal an actually corrupt and corrupting court cabal that not only excluded but also systematically demeaned most of the society that it dominated. Sincerity became their supreme virtue, not only because truth is a public as well as a personal duty, but because the ethos of self-revelation is classless. It becomes a virtue when we assume that we all have an identical and on the whole good "inner" self, but that it is covered by layers upon layers of social convention and personal dissimulation which destroy our nature and render us deceitful, to the disadvantage of our fellows. A sincere society would consist of equally self-exposing individuals who would not disfigure their inner being by accepting alien norms and hurt each other by inflicting false images upon one another. The future was not, however, beckoning for all, and there was an appalling amount of sentimentality dispensed by the melancholy for the benefit of the bored. The prevalence of *Weltschmerz*, a sentimentality that clogged the emotional arteries with treacle, was truly extraordinary. Writers claimed not only that genius was doomed to suffer in a mean society, but that every "man of feeling" had a duty to suffer ostentatiously and tearfully.

What, if anything, is wrong with this sort of sentimentality? Why does it seem so distasteful? After all, there is nothing morally reprehensible about people who enjoy schmaltzy tunes. On the contrary, some of the most brutal and destructive people on earth have been known to have the most refined aesthetic tastes. Yet we do condemn sentimentality as a false and unworthy show of feeling. Is it a form of dissembling, a pretense to feel something that one does not in fact feel? Or is it a show of emotion that is not required, a waste of moral energy, as when people cry over the death of a character on a TV soap opera but remain coldly indifferent to the misery in their midst? Or do we suspect that sentimentality is simply self-pity indulged in as a pleasure and not for any specific cause? Certainly, in the early nineteenth century, an easy ability to shed tears and a readiness to express melancholy were regarded as virtues and marks of a fine spirit in America no less than in Europe. Sentimentality was a moral taste shared by the useful and busy no less than by the futile and idle members of society. Social theory might indeed argue that it was a rebellion against order, such rebellion being as characteristic of melancholy as is the longing for an orderly utopia. Melancholy may express the longing both for order and for disorder, reacting against whichever seems to prevail. Apparently, too few rules upset us no less than too many.

The literary versatility of melancholy guaranteed its survival. Lepenies tells us just how it outlived the defeated French aristocracy and the disenfranchised German bourgeoisie. It lives on as the ideological boredom of self-created aristocrats, who protest against the dullness of bourgeois society at its peak. The dandy is not an aristocrat by birth; rather, he is an artist who creates an aristocratic persona for himself in a rage against the drab city, its commercial mentality— "the Belgian spirit," as Baudelaire called it. Physical beauty becomes an ideology, so that not only must the dandy excoriate the appearance of the actual world as both disgusting and boring; he cannot afford to grow old and lose his looks. If his waistcoat no longer fits perfectly, he must commit suicide. Oscar Wilde's *Picture of Dorian Gray* is a radical admission of the futility of all human effort, not in the face of Saturn but in the face of ordinary mortality.

Most of all, the dandy missed the old royal courts, with their rigid etiquette and theatricality. Their passing left him bereft of a socially congenial milieu. He could not accept a world in which there was no audience for court jesters. Wilde could still entertain with his stylized and often campy comedies, but he could not find a place where there was a daily audience to applaud his clever *mots* and antics. No bourgeois public, however easily entertained, could make up for what one might have received at court. Indeed the music and dancing masters say as much in the beginning of Molière's *Bourgeois Gentilhomme*. The courtiers not only appreciated the arts; they were genuine connoisseurs. The enemies of courts had created a vacuum. There was neither the right kind of patron, nor the theatrical rigor of decorum and etiquette that made the comedian both a licensed subversive and a participant in one of the best rehearsed and most expensive of all shows. So, at least, it may have seemed to the bourgeois artist in a bourgeois world, which treated melancholy as a deviant private disorder and boredom as a moral failing of the idle. They deserved to suffer.

It is not likely that the displaced aristocrat, the excluded bourgeois, and the isolated artist are the only people to be reduced to melancholy by social changes that they cannot control in any way. Work, as we all know, is one of the great cures for melancholy and boredom. In America it is also the source of social standing and respect. And unemployment can come swiftly to both blue-collar workers and middle-class people. Many give up looking for new employment too quickly as they become despondent. But serious as their melancholy is, it may be far less extreme than the anguish of the newly liberated workers of Eastern Europe, especially in Germany. The loss of social order has brought them a melancholy and a collective sense of helplessness. The sudden collapse of a planned society will probably not give rise to new fictional utopias of planned order, but random violence is not unlikely.

Nostalgic aristocrats—or, to be quite exact, intellectuals who profess to be exiled nobles of the spirit, whatever their social origins might be—can always find ways of legitimizing their melancholia. There is literary fame and fortune for writers who can turn dissatisfaction into a story or a philosophical system. These refined forms of *Weltschmerz* are, however, mischievous when they serve to hide the reality of ordinary suffering. Intellectuals tend to be frivolous. The many people who suffer from debilitating, socially induced melancholy are in no position to dream of an aesthetically satisfying past. Gender as much as class is a locus of melancholy. That this is not a private matter is no longer news: women are melancholic because they are systematically taught to be helpless and then blamed for their incompetence. If a politically degraded aristocracy was melancholy, it is hardly surprising that women, who have been far more completely exiled and condemned to futility, should suffer even more severely. And if work and public recognition cheered up the men of the German bourgeoisie, there is no reason to suppose that women would not also respond similarly. To entertain such a thought requires neither utopian fantasies nor a complex sociology of knowledge. Neither does it constrain us to look back with longing or anger.

The last word about melancholy will probably never be written. To be sad because one is sad is ultimately too fundamental a human experience to be understood by even the most imaginative social science. It is, nevertheless, important to see melancholy in its many contexts, not because it is a comforting exercise but because it is an act of recognition. The melancholy of others does not reduce one's own, but it at least makes it comprehensible, both in its resignation and in its defiance.

Melancholy and Society

1 Introduction

> Do you not know that a secret society exists here on earth, known as the melancholy company?
>
> Jens Peter Jacobsen, *Mrs. Marie Grubbe: Pictures from the Seventeenth Century*

In this book we investigate the origins of designations extrinsic or intrinsic to the object to which they refer; we ask not whether someone is melancholy but what it means when someone claims to be melancholy. Likewise, melancholy will not be studied as a sign for some "social" or "national" character; what the French call *la maladie anglaise* the English refer to as "French boredom," and we could counter Roepke, who makes a similar remark about the Germans, with Schopenhauer, who labeled the English the most melancholy people. Yet in 1821 Stendhal traveled precisely to London to find a means of combating his spleen.

What is offered here is neither a conceptual history that attempts to be exhaustive nor a reflection on views of the individual's temperament and their possible significance for a science of "social action," which might hope to render its hypotheses on action more precise by assigning individuals to different classes of temperament. This is the method followed by "popular" doctrines of the temperaments, from Theophrastus to La Bruyère; they are intended to enable a person with the correct knowledge to behave suitably in every situation insofar as he or she can accurately assess the other actors. They are, in other words, aids for orientation.

We shall not refrain from incorporating "history," meaning historical reflection on the genesis of self-evident truths; indeed, all our statements will be shaped by such a reflection. The discussion will focus not on the German character but on the melancholy of the German bourgeoisie—melancholy that emerged in the eighteenth century and had its roots in Luther. Neither will our inquiry deal with "French boredom." Rather, we shall look at the "ennui" of the aristocrats who failed in the Fronde, and then turn our attention to the *maladie du siècle*.

We shall draw on a variety of different sources: novels will appear alongside utopias, sociological analyses alongside aphorisms. The subject matter forces such disparate domains on us, for neither melancholy nor utopian thought or boredom can be assigned to one single discipline and discussed in its terms. If one has a sociological interest in these topics, then one must be prepared to tolerate our occasionally cursory presentation of source material, indeed to view this approach as an advantage, as a chance to be naïve and thus to pose basic questions. Literary statements are, accordingly, taken seriously in this book and are not just introduced as trimmings for the dry material. If it is true that people really act when they define a situation as real (W. I. Thomas), then scholarly analysis must begin to acknowledge the importance of secondary realities (literature, expressions of popular culture, phenomena from everyday life that initially seem irrelevant). Such detours give us an opportunity to avoid dogmatism: they help us see the relevance of that which at first glance appears remote; they also enable us to look beyond a closed canon of compelling domains of interest and, as we work in proximity to other sciences, lead us to perceive less a danger to our own independence than a welcome chance to raise interdisciplinary questions.

2   Order and Melancholy

So long as no one complains, it can be assumed that
everything is taking its due course.

Fichte, *Der geschlossene Handelsstaat*

Melancholy as Dis-order in the Work of R. K. Merton

We shall begin our analysis not by describing a "melancholy of the
current age" but by examining one contemporary writer's effort to
construct a sociological theory in which melancholy, though appearing only as a marginal concept, is at least clearly embedded in the
overall framework of sociology. We shall describe this positioning of
melancholy and assess the status of that writer's theoretical approach;
then we shall inquire into the implications of the historical ante-
cedents of such a description of melancholy (if any exist). The theo-
rist in question is Robert K. Merton, who presents his ideas in his
book *Social Theory and Social Structure,* particularly in the chapters entitled "Social Structure and Anomie" and "Continuities in the Theory
of Social Structure and Anomie."[1] Although he initially mentions the
concept of melancholy in the latter chapter, the two must be seen as
a unit: the first provides the basic prerequisites for assigning melancholy a place in Merton's "system."[2] The attempt to describe "types
of individual adaptation" forms a crucial part of the analysis, and
Merton stresses that he is referring "to role behavior in specific types
of situations, not to personality." Merton's inclination to "play it
safe"—seen in the way he reduces the firm link between individual
and society to a concept of sociological theory (namely, role) that is
more arbitrary in nature than clearly delineated—persists in his emphasis that his observations refer to American society and, more
specifically, to economic activity. In this "typology" Merton differentiates among the various types of adaptation according to whether
they accept or reject cultural goals and the institutionalized means
of attaining them. He distinguishes five modes of adaptation: "con-

formity," "innovation," "ritualism," "retreatism," and "rebellion." There would be little need to call attention to the awkward translation of such terms into German if one did not have particular misgivings with regard to "retreatism," which is a crucial concept. In this case, the German rendering of the term, *Rückzugsverhalten*, cannot be considered acceptable, for it is basically too saturated with action to be applied to this phenomenon. There remains an element of action in *Rückzug* (meaning "retreat"), which is frequently and aptly conveyed by the military term "orderly retreat."[3]

Conformity involves the acceptance of goals and means readily available in a culture; innovation entails accepting goals but rejecting means; with ritualism, goals are rejected and means accepted; in the case of rebellion, both means and goals are rejected but are immediately replaced with new ones. Evidently retreatism, which is of special interest to us here, is diametrically opposed to both conformity *and* rebellion—in other words, to forms of behavior that, when compared with each other, can be situated at opposite ends of a continuum.

Merton initially defines "retreatism" in quantitative terms: it is the rarest form of adaptation. According to Merton, people who behave in this manner—that is, who reject goals as well as the socially sanctioned means for attaining them—live in their society but do not belong to it; by definition, people in a state of anomie cannot make up society. Clearly, such behavior is subsumed under the concept of anomie, which provides a structure and a framework that are then fleshed out with terms such as "retreatism." Merton's phrasing also shows the influence of the apt definition coined by Ralf Dahrendorf, who characterized the "enduring state of tendential anomie" as "unsociety."[4]

This analytical category in Merton's theory is filled out with empirical, behavioral material that resembles a catalogue of vices: he includes in it psychotics, autists, pariahs, outcasts, vagrants, vagabonds, tramps, chronic drunkards, and drug addicts. In addition, it embraces escapist forms of behavior such as defeatism, quietism, and resignation. If we consider the common, everyday understanding of the term "retreatism," we can already see it as an approximation of what could be perceived as "melancholy." Retreatism is subject to social condemnation, because it calls society into question without attacking it; its deviance is based on pure passivity. According to Merton, "deviants"—who are condemned in actual life—find compensation in the realm of the imagination. Yet they always remain isolated. Their passivity does not allow them to lead a life as part of a group, but rather grants them a private, individual existence.

In the second of the two chapters mentioned above, Merton summarizes a further analysis of retreatism under the heading "Anomie and Forms of Deviant Behavior."[5] Here he develops the idea, already intimated in the preceding chapter, that retreatism is a form of real behavior that occurs outside society rather than inside it.

Drawing on Zena Smith Blau's study,[6] Merton defines "retreatism" as a longing for the past and apathy in the present. Retreatism appears as "intensification," even when compared with "alienation." Merton concedes that such forms of behavior have hitherto been neglected by sociology, since they neither lend themselves well to statistical analysis nor appear to be interesting objects of study, given that their effects tend not to be obvious.[7]

> Yet the syndrome of retreatism has been identified for centuries, and under the label of accidie (or variously, acedy, acedia, and accidia) was regarded by the Roman Catholic church as one of the deadly sins. As the sloth and torpor in which the "wells of the spirit run dry," accidie has interested theologians from the Middle Ages onward. It has engaged the attention of men and women of letters from at least the time of Langland and Chaucer, down through Burton, to Aldous Huxley and Rebecca West. Psychiatrists without number have dealt with it in the form of apathy, melancholy, or anhedonia. But sociologists have accorded the syndrome singularly little attention. Yet it would seem that this form of deviant behavior has its social antecedents as well as its manifest social consequences, and we may look for more sociological inquiry into it of the kind represented by Zena Blau's recent study.
>
> It remains to be seen whether the kinds of political and organizational apathy now being investigated by social scientists can be theoretically related to the social forces which, on this theory, make for retreatist behavior.[8]

This is the point in Merton's description of social structure and anomie at which the concept of melancholy first explicitly surfaces. Although it is used as a psychiatric metaphor for "retreatism," it takes on broader meaning through Merton's historical retrospective and his references in passing to literary works.

Before examining the concept that Merton ultimately labels "melancholy," we should look at two passages in his argument which do not refer directly to the concept of melancholy and yet are closely related to it.

In his analysis of ritualism, that form of deviant behavior in which a person rejects culturally prescribed goals while upholding the socially sanctioned means for attaining them (means which then remain nonfunctional—that is, do not "get" the person anywhere), Merton pinpoints a sequence of ritualistic behavior which spans the increasingly unmanageable "struggle for existence" (he terms it "ceaseless competitive struggle"), status anxiety, the lowering of goals, routine action, and fear of action itself. In this connection Merton cites Pierre Janet's essay "The Fear of Action," which appeared in 1921. Seven years later Janet published another essay with much the same title which was based on a lecture given at the 1928 Wittenberg Symposium. He called it "Fear of Action as an Essential Element in the Sentiment of Melancholia."[9]

We shall return to Janet's two essays below. Here, though, it should be mentioned that the concept which Merton introduces in the framework of his description of ritualistic, deviant behavior is actually used by Janet to explain the melancholic experience of the world. In his approach to the phenomenon of melancholy, Merton exhibits a disinclination to treat the topic—which is precisely the fault he imputes to sociologists.

This link between fear of action and behavioral anxiety, however, need not remain confined to *one* form of deviant behavior. Merton himself points out that in role sequences various forms of deviant behavior can follow one another, that conformity can give way to ritualism and eventually "culminate" in retreatism. This line of argument also seems plausible from another, more anthropologically oriented perspective. The sequence of deviant behavior Merton outlines can be described as a progressive loss of that which is taken to be self-evident in a culture—a loss accompanied by an increasing fear of action. Action once oriented to goals *and* means loses its goal orientation in the transition to ritualism. Yet the claim to certain values is necessary, "if only for purely pragmatic—and in the more profound sense, anthropological—reasons, namely: to make action possible in the first place, to set a goal or goals for the human 'besoin de faire quelque chose'" (Claessens).[10] In the transition from action inspired by conformism to ritualism, the necessary claim to certain values or goals shifts under the ever-growing pressure of anxiety. Rather than actually attaining the goals prescribed as culturally suitable, the individual transposes his claim onto the means of action, which then "get him nowhere." The progressive "deterioration" of the impulse toward action, to use Vilfredo Pareto's term, ends in retreatism and passivity. The fact that this may happen does not mean the claim that there is an anthropological need involved here is wrong: it is precisely the loss of the capacity for action that causes melancholy to become diverted into psychopathological phenomena.

The detour into an anthropological line of argument, which we shall discuss below, shows how the point of departure taken in Merton's description could, of its own accord, be developed into an interpretation of melancholy that goes much further and is far more theoretically sound than that which the author himself puts forth.

At another point Merton notes, "Presumably in every society in history the heroes of the culture were regarded as heroes precisely because they had the courage and vision to give up the norms of their group at the time. As we all know, the rebel, revolutionary, non-conformist, individualist, heretic or renegade of an earlier time is often the hero of the present."[11] Merton, who makes an admittedly fragmentary survey of historical views of melancholy, could have linked this approach to the syndrome of melancholia. For there is considerable discrepancy among theorists' views with regard to the culturally specific valuation of the syndrome. The fact that the development of views of melancholy has been far from straightforward stems from a controversy centering on two opposing conceptions; these can perhaps best be described as the psychopathological, medically oriented, negative view and the cosmological, philosophically informed, positive view. The issue of the "nobilitizing" of melancholy relates directly to Merton's comment regarding the hero who was once condemned because his actions did not conform with the norms, yet who is praised for those actions today.[12] Whereas Merton's description of varieties of deviant behavior could form the basis of an in-depth theoretical contemplation of melancholy, a historical survey which Merton himself calls fragmentary ("a few among the many accounts of accidie") precludes such a study. Merton's selection centers on the theological notion of acedia. As a result of this limitation, his concept of melancholy is divorced from all developments in classical antiquity and the Middle Ages. Likewise, the literary references Merton cites scarcely do justice to the subject: this is precisely where a sociologist could have indicated which views of melancholy represented conceptions held by societies as a whole—for example, the "Werther syndrome" in eighteenth-century Germany or the *mal du siècle* in nineteenth-century France.

But melancholy is only a marginal concept in Merton's work, even though it relates directly to his goal: namely, to determine the sociologically relevant causes and effects of melancholy. We shall follow his method here, albeit in reverse order. Before turning to an investigation of current forms of "political and organizational apathy," we will look at the historical genesis of the concept of melancholy—not by providing a history of the concept, which we rejected above but rather by exploring the sociological conditions and links between various views of melancholy in retrospective, "restrained speculation" (Norbert Elias). Before taking such a step "backward," however, it seems necessary to reduce Merton's view of melancholy, which contains myriad implications, to one key concept. The description of melancholy as a deviant form of behavior among many forms of behavior suggests that we can find some concept to use as a reference point in determining what is to be understood by "deviance." Merton is interested in describing the emergence of deviant behavior; a stable society serves as a point of orientation for deviance—a society whose stability is guaranteed by conformity, that is, by the acceptance of cultural goals and the institutionalized means for realizing them.

Although Merton claims that his theory is oriented toward contemporary American society and its economic activity, his definition of the concepts of "stable society" and "conformity" seem devoid of all content. Such a lack is a prerequisite for the development of analytical concepts. Taking this as a standard of measurement, the parameter on which Merton appears to base his description is not a society of any given type—which would impose itself, by definition, as the content—but instead the concept of *order*. Order, stripped of any shape in terms of content, refers to the state of a society which continues to exist and to "function" because its members behave *in such a way that* it functions. It is hardly possible to criticize such a description for being based on formulas devoid of content, precisely because it seeks to have as little content as possible.

Despite this absence of content in its formulas, the concept of order establishes the underlying parameter for any description of society. We shall not consider here those problems arising from the fact that substantive notions of order may emerge and then claim to be "correct" vis-à-vis other notions. The claim to be "correct" can, of course, be brought into play only against conceptions of order which are themselves defined by content. One can then assert that formulas devoid of all content and purely analytical in nature can, in principle, be filled with anything, are manipulable and also susceptible to ideology.

As already mentioned, our discussion will not treat this issue. What remains decisive is that in Merton's analysis a formal concept is separated from the concreteness of "the concentrated experience of concrete human order" (Voegelin).[13] The concept of order has an affinity with that of the system: the system must function, just as order can be preserved only through conformity. Society and partial phenomena of that society are then not *evaluated* against that order—

because no universally accepted value is given—but rather *measured,* because the concept of order provides a *standard of measurement.*

Taking the standard of order as a unit of measurement, forms of behavior appear as appropriate or inappropriate, depending on whether they promote order or dis-order. Unfitting phenomena, in the sense that they do not fit in, are described as insubstantial: as forms of dis-order. Merton's observation that retreatists live in society (content orientation) but do not belong to it (formal order orientation) is typical of such a stance. Melancholy as a form of the retreatism that Merton describes can thus be understood, in terms of a more dynamic description (which connotes the possibility of role sequences), as a loss of order, and, in terms of a static description, as nonorder, nonconformity, dis-order.

In Robert Burton's utopia, which will be the subject of the next section, we find a notion of melancholy similar to Merton's. Since both writers are concerned with views of melancholy that relate to the order/dis-order syndrome, it is only natural that they make explicit reference to the concept of anomie. Merton himself mentions the origins of the concept, and Burton seems already to have considered its significance, or at least that of its implications. This serves to explain the "catalogue of vices" that appears in both authors' descriptions of melancholy; it is a function of the broad scope covered by the parameter "dis-order." But the concept of anomie, above and beyond that, holds myriad possibilities for various forms of argument which could all be related to aspects of the study we are undertaking here. Thus, in seventeenth-century theology "anomy" already means "disregard of law, lawlessness"; but in the same period (1689) another source says, "You Presbyterians distinguish between the Action and the Anomy, or Irregularity of it." [14] In other words, the sources make reference not only to the "dis-order" of "anomy" but also to its close link with the concept of action (very nearly inhibition of action). The stabilizing effect of subcultures in anomic situations (Richard Cloward), an effect that has been described again and again in theories of anomie, points to mechanisms which permit the "practice" of melancholy without insisting on distantiation from society. Equally strong is the emphasis placed on the link between anomie and introspection, meaning a withdrawal from social contacts. Moreover, this reinforces our suspicions that the object determines the nature of the description: supposed introspection, which in the sociologists' view (as we shall see below) can hardly appear other than as a catalogue of vices, preforms theories in the direction of psychology. Merton criticizes R. M. MacIver for developing a psychological "approach" despite the fact that "the psychological con-cept . . . [is] . . . a counterpart of the sociological concept of anomie, and not a substitute for it."[15] Albert Cohen, in turn, accuses MacIver of psychological reductionism: "Within the framework of goals, norms, and opportunities, the process of deviance was conceptualized as though each individual—or better, role incumbent—were in a box by himself."[16] Thus, in psychologistic terminology, introspection becomes something for which theories attempting to explain this very phenomenon are then criticized: a science of anomie becomes an anomic science.

MacIver's work exhibits many such tendencies. He describes Dada and existentialism as philosophical ideologies of an anomic situation in which boredom promotes anomie. He emphasizes the importance of the role of "unquiet introspection" and ultimately maintains that anomie (he spells it "anomy") is "a disease of the civilized, not of the simpler peoples."[17] This touches on thematic issues that become sig-nificant in the context of boredom and melancholy. If, in addition, we consider the importance of the question of legitimacy—a question strongly emphasized by Gordon Rose, who proposes using the term "legitimacy loss" instead of "anomie" (in sociology)[18]—then the con-nection alluded to above becomes even stronger. Burton's *Anatomy of Melancholy* appears as an intriguing precursor of such attempts.

Robert Burton's Anatomy of Melancholy

Merton's interpretation of the concept of melancholy, in which he admits its sociological importance but nevertheless treats it only mar-ginally, leads to its reduction as a concept: in his work, melancholy appears as a loss of order or as dis-order, and the concept of order is rendered formalistic in nature. According to this scheme, one can also describe deviant behavior with respect to societies which possess different sets of culturally self-evident truths. The formal concept of order merely needs to be equipped with the specific "contents" of the culture in question.

A historical perspective serves, among other things, to demonstrate the formal similarity between the concept described above and the concept of melancholy advocated by Robert Burton in his *Anatomy of Melancholy*, which first appeared in 1621. Our recourse to Burton's work is not arbitrary. Aside from the fact that his utopia affords us a chance to explore the presuppositions and implications of numerous conceptions of melancholy, Burton's *Anatomy* also provides further avenues that can be explored when considering melancholy and resigned behavior from a sociological viewpoint.

The fact that Merton mentions the seventeenth-century "anatomist" but otherwise gives no information about his person or his work justifies a slight digression here. Lord Byron wrote in his diary on November 30, 1807, "The book which in my opinion is most useful for someone who wishes as quickly as possible to gain a reputation for being well-read is Burton's *Anatomy of Melancholy*, the most entertaining and edifying potpourri of quotations and classical anecdotes that I have ever read."[19] Friedrich Engels considered the *Anatomy* to be "one of the most serious psychological treatises of the eighteenth century"; though initially he said, "It fills me with horror," he later found it a "constant source of pleasure."[20]

This air of amused surprise is displayed by all Burton's interpreters and even admirers. Whoever writes about melancholy and takes pride in his knowledge of literature, or at least is not ashamed of it, is under considerable pressure to doff his cap to Burton. When a well-known English *homme de lettres*, namely Harold Nicolson, was sent by his friends on a journey to Java, he employed the leisure hours he suddenly had in compiling an "investigation into groundless melancholy" and stated with programmatic certainty, "I share with Dr. Johnson, Tristram Shandy and Charles Lamb a warm affection for Robert Burton"[21]—even though the *Anatomy* seemed to him to be fairly "cluttered with anecdotes and quotations." Samuel Johnson reprimanded Burton for the same reasons, charging that the *Anatomy* was "overloaded with quotation"; yet it was the only book that could induce him to get up two hours early.

When Walter Jens's *Dialogue on the Novel* ultimately took shape as a plan for a novel about melancholy people, "Burton's famous tractatus" played a part.[22] Yet this and other evaluations, which surely are more than mere expressions of fashion, contrast grotesquely with the constant neglect of those aspects of Burton's work which have stood the test of time. These include his specific description of melancholy and his notion of utopia as a counterbalance to the rule of melancholy—an old theme, for Saturn already appears in Greek comedies as closely linked to melancholy, in his role as the "lord of Utopia."[23]

Robert Burton was born on February 8, 1577, in Lindley, Leicestershire, and went to school in Sutton Coldfield and Nuneaton; at the age of sixteen he went up to Brasenose College in Oxford, and from there to Christchurch College in 1599, where he took his first and second degrees in 1602 and 1605. He became a tutor in Oxford, vicar in a small country town, and in 1626 librarian of Christchurch. His life scarcely ever changed. He never pursued a career, and was subject to melancholy from childhood onward: "Robert Burton was, by all accounts, a child insufficiently loved, before becoming a tyrannized school pupil, a confused student, and a dissatisfied bachelor. All of his frustrations led him in the direction of melancholy—a boy who perhaps was congenitally disposed to be melancholic, given that his maternal uncle, Anthony Faunt, had been . . . borne away by a fit of it."[24]

The first edition of the *Anatomy* came out in 1621; later ones followed in 1624, 1628, 1632, 1638, 1652, 1660, and 1676. Burton continually revised the text of the treatise, amending individual parts to different degrees. In the space available here, we cannot hope to do justice to a work in which thousands of other authors are quoted (usually apocryphally and unreliably), which in the octavo edition comprises 1,036 pages, and which has been called—with little exaggeration—"an encyclopedia of learning."[25] The superficiality to which we are thus forced can, however, be justified: the preface "Democritus to the Reader" is a key passage in Burton's oeuvre and is anything but a mere preface; indeed, it is a veritable utopia.

The fact that in seventeenth-century editions "Democritus to the Reader" was paginated separately declares this utopia to be a work in its own right, as Burton himself emphasized. Likewise significant is the fact that in the course of the different editions the text of the utopia grew threefold—a growth considerably larger than that of the *Anatomy* as a whole.[26]

It remains to be noted that—in paradoxical contrast to the influence of the overall work—Burton's utopia was virtually forgotten. In 1964 Jean Robert Simon was moved to inquire, "Why is it . . . that Burton's utopia has been ignored by historians of utopian literature?"[27] Pierre Mesnard blamed this neglect on readers, who "ignore on occasion the 'satirical preface,' which itself comprises over 100 large octavo pages."[28] And J. Max Patrick wrote that "the prime cause of neglect was Burton's failure to incorporate his account in an imaginative narrative framework; for ideal societies which are described coldly or with little or no narrative . . . tend to be overlooked."[29]

This suppression of Burton's utopia is all the more incomprehensible if one considers that this part of the *Anatomy* is the first original utopia written in English. More's *Utopia* and Hall's *Mundus Alter et Idem* were translated from the Latin, by Robinson (1551) and Healey (1609), respectively. Interpreters and biographers of Burton are perpetually astonished at the fact that he has been ignored by "social historians" and continue to emphasize his utopia's sociological relevance:[30] "Its ideals are not those of the philosopher or the theologian, but of the social scientist."[31]

The list of those who have seen fit to omit mention of Burton itself justifies according him great importance in the context of our study, an importance that stems not least from his specific approach, which links utopia and melancholy. Burton does not deny his tendency to be eclectic, even in the title of his utopia. The choice of the name "Democritus" was a convention of the day. In 1607 Samuel Roland published *Democritus, or Doctor Merry Man: His Medecine against Melancholy Humours;* and nine years after Burton's death a work entitled *Democritus Ridens: Sive Campus Recreationum Honestarum; Cum Exorcissimo Melancholiae* appeared in Amsterdam.[32]

The key passages in the utopia, which Burton presents through a mouthpiece named Democritus Junior,[33] can be summed up briefly without losing their main points. Burton is one of those authors who ornament their thoughts with such a plethora of quotes, whether in support or disagreement, and with such numerous opinions, whether attributable or apocryphal, that the thread of the argument must first be laboriously extricated from the general tangle. This, admittedly, is an element of his style. Burton writes to dispel his own melancholy: "I writ of melancholy, by being busy to avoid melancholy. There is no greater cause of melancholy than idleness, *no better cure than business*."[34] He soon abandons this egocentric approach, however, and proceeds to describe a melancholic society: "But whereas you shall see so many discontents, common grievances, complaints, poverty, barbarism, beggary, plagues, wars, rebellions, seditions, mutinies, contentions, idleness, riot, epicurism, the land lie untilled, waste, full of bogs, fens, deserts, &c, cities decayed, base and poor towns, villages depopulated, the people squalid, ugly, uncivil; that kingdom, that country, must needs be discontent, melancholy, hath a sick body, and has need to be reformed." And in another description he writes: "The State was like a sick body which had lately taken physick, whose humours were not yet well settled, and weakened so much by purging, that nothing was left but melancholy."[35]

Burton's conception of melancholy and the reformist and utopian approach he derives from it are already evidenced here. They conceal more than just the expression of some literary disgruntlement accentuated by the metaphor of melancholy. Yet there is a problem inherent in transposing melancholy onto the state, a problem that can be clearly defined by examining the history of the concept.

If we ignore the cosmological speculations of late classical antiquity, in which melancholy is linked to Saturn—the planet of "high contemplation, the star of the philosophers, magicians and hermits who live to the pleasure of God"[36]—then two important strands can be discerned in the development of the concept, both of which were to prove important for Burton. One is associated with Hippocrates, the other with Aristotle. "We first encounter the term 'melancholy' in the *corpus hippocraticum,* initially in the essay 'On Air, Water, and Topography,' which is generally considered to be among the oldest of the Hippocratic writings dating from the last third of the fifth century, though it is doubtful whether they were in fact a product of Hippocrates' own hand."[37] The melancholy type first appears in the third book on epidemics, and not long after this the term "melancholic" is used to refer to a disturbed mental state. Finally, in the essay "On the Nature of Man," believed to have been written by either Hippocrates or his son-in-law, one comes across the new hypothesis that "even a healthy person has black gall within him, albeit in correct proportion to the rest of his humors."[38] Aristotle's name is associated with the linking of melancholy and genius, even if, according to Hellmut Flashar, the decisive passage in the *Problemata Physica* (which, with the *Historica Anima* and the *Metaphysics,* is the most comprehensive text in the *corpus aristotelicum*) "assuredly does not stem from Aristotle's hand."[39] In part 1 of Chapter 30 we read: "Why do all men of extraordinary ability in the field of philosophy or politics or literature or the arts all prove to be melancholics?"

We lack a "formula for the answer," as Flashar says, but the assertion has become the basis for all speculative attempts to link melancholy and genius. Melancholy appears here not as an illness but as nature. The shift to a position which conceives of this link as normal can be found in Plato, whose "original antinomies . . . [are] those of *mania* and *amathia,* of madness and unteachableness . . . In his work 'Melancholikos' he discusses the *unteachable* temperament, not the black-galled temperament treated in Hippocrates' writings."[40] Thus, until medieval times two conceptions of melancholy and genius prevail. One, influenced by medicine, views melancholy as something negative; the other takes up the pseudo-Aristotelian *Problemata* and makes melancholy something noble—and here the early Florentine Renaissance played a decisive role.[41]

Burton thus inevitably had difficulties characterizing the melancholic nation, since melancholy was an illness ascribed to individual types of person. This view was anchored in physiology and was selective in nature: only certain human organisms could be described as melancholic. The second, diametrically opposed opinion worked in a similar way: the linking of melancholy and genius also had a selective effect, although this now served to confer distinction on the individual.

Both conceptions actually contrasted with Burton's, for his was not selective but universal in scope: he saw melancholy neither as a singular illness nor as one of many characteristics of the genius. Strangely, Burton's interpreters have shown little awareness of this complex of problems. When they are interested in his melancholy they forget the utopian element, and when they describe the utopia they fail to mention that it is based on the prior existence of a specific notion of melancholy. It was possible to conduct an inquiry into the conditions fostering such "political melancholy" even before ascertaining that "il y a une mélancolie politique, qui tient comme l'autre à des humeurs malignes" ("There is a political melancholy which, like the other, results from malevolent humors").[42] Burton had to contend with both the medical-psychopathological theory and the "genius" theory.

From the moment the concept of melancholy is conceived of as universal in nature, the first of the two theories no longer prevents the concept's being expanded. Burton thus does not only define melancholy as a constant human quality: "And who is not a fool? Who is free from melancholy? Who is not touched more or less in habit and disposition?"[43] Such a definition robs the concept of its edge by expanding it. If all are mad, then madness is but a quality all can be accused of having—that is, the accusation has little effect. Equally, if all are melancholic, then melancholy can no longer really be regarded as a disease. For the expansion of the concept not only applies to humans; it is now something more than just an anthropological quality: plants, animals, and even minerals can also be melancholic. Taking Boterus as an example, Burton says that "kingdoms, provinces and Politickal Bodies are subject in like manner to this disease."[44] Burton thus weakens the selective effect of a conception of melancholy oriented toward psychopathology and medicine. Human beings, animals, plants, and minerals are diseased, but so are kingdoms and political organizations as a whole. It is here that the question arises as to how the concept of melancholy, if it is expanded, can still function as a stimulus for utopia, given that what is normal is described as anomalous and what is generally widespread is called illness.

Before answering this question, we must first adumbrate Burton's exposition of the concept of genius, which we can do swiftly. Burton reduces this conceptualization to the theme of the melancholic king: "For as the Princes are, so are the people; *qualis rex, talis grex:* and which Antigonus right well said of old, *qui Macedoniae regem erudit, omnes etiam subditos erudit,* he that teacheth the King of Macedon, teacheth all his subjects, is a true saying still."[45] It is not until the classical notion of melancholy is modified with a view to its universal applicability and fused into a single concept that one can use it both in the realm of politics and as a suitable device for describing an antimelancholic, utopian counterproject.

Prior to constructing this utopia, Burton drew up a differentiated description of the melancholic state. If we did not intend to juxtapose Burton's notions of utopia and melancholy, we would be obliged to pay closer attention to this description. In it, Great Britain is compared with ancient Greece and Italy is compared with France, Germany, and the Netherlands. It has been claimed, by J. W. Allen among others, that hardly any other author of Burton's day took so little notice of the political or religious controversies of his age[46]—a view supported, among other things, by the fact that he provides only a partial account of English society under James I's reign (1603–1625), being interested more in "aristocrats of old stock, *parvenus*, and intellectuals."[47] Yet his in-depth comparison of countries is one of the elements of his utopia that best reflects reality. As J. Max Patrick wrote, "He was the first utopian to use a scientific, comparative method as the basis for his sociological theories: in this connection he preempted modern sociological methodology. He was a pioneer in affirming a secular, non-communist, planned society. His utopia most certainly deserved a better fate than that of being neglected."[48] Unlike Allen, Patrick points to the way in which Burton, perhaps unwittingly, mirrored reality in his work. W. R. Mueller notes this as well: "The reign of Charles I was in theory the closest approximation to Burton's utopia that England ever knew."[49]

It is not our task here to determine how close to or how far removed from reality Burton's utopia was; rather, we are trying to establish and draw attention to the manner in which a particular conception of melancholy underlies the notion that utopia is a remedy for a melancholic state. Just as we offered only a brief description of Burton's concept of melancholy, one that attempted to relate it to the tradition of melancholy in antiquity, we shall likewise reduce Burton's utopia to a few axioms. Initially Burton adopts a measure of poetic license for the description of his utopia: "I will yet, to satisfy and please myself, make an Utopia of my own, a new Atlantis, a poetical Commonwealth of mine own, in which I freely domineer, build cities, make laws, statutes, as I list myself."[50]

Burton's utopia lies on the forty-fifth parallel in the middle of the temperate zone, and is subdivided into twelve or thirteen provinces that are carefully demarcated. Each province is circular and twelve

Italian miles in diameter, no village being permitted at a distance of
more than eight miles from a town. Burton is sharply critical of any
utopian egalitarianism: Campanella's City of the Sun and Bacon's
New Atlantis are to him "ingenious fictions, but mere chimaera," and
he finds Plato's Republic to be "lacking in piety, absurd and ridicu-
lous" in many respects, "devoid of any glory and splendor." Instead,
Burton wants his utopia to include various levels of hereditary nobility, as well as other ranks and positions that may be hereditary, or
subject to loss by vote, or even given away as gifts. Burton is an anti-
egalitarian, but he connects "inequality of conditions" with "equality
of opportunity."[51] Utopian government takes the form of a monarchy, there being "few laws, but those securely kept, plainly put down,
and in the mother tongue, that every man may understand."[52] Only
a "set number" of attorneys, judges, lawyers, doctors, and surgeons
are allowed, and this number must not be exceeded. In particular,
the number of laws and lawyers should be kept to a minimum:
"Where they be generally riotous and contentious, where there be
many discords, many laws, many law-suits, many lawyers, and many
physicians, it is a manifest sign of a distempered, melancholy state."[53]

Our description of Burton's utopia need not go further, since we
can now make a sufficiently accurate comparison between Burton's
notion of melancholy and his utopian approach. The basic outline of
his utopia predetermines his conception of melancholy: given that
his utopia is the counterpart of a country sunk in melancholy, melancholy is accordingly the negative duplicate image that we can extract
from the utopia through enumerating the contrasts. If we add the
comments his interpreters have made to the above brief summary,
then Burton's enterprise may also be characterized as "pedantic" and
"correct in its application,"[54] "a careful classification,"[55] the wish to
"shape" life "more simply and effectively" and to be a cure for "com-
plication and confusion," a utopia in which "scientifically ascertained
weights and measures are given uniformly for the whole country"[56]—
in short, "a colossal machine, the cogs of which transfer all movements prescribed by the central powers to every inch of the country."[57] And all of this is described in a book whose three parts "are
divided into sections, which are in turn divided into chapters, which
are themselves then subdivided into subchapters."[58]

No better word can be found as a superordinate category for these
concordant characteristics than "order"—a concept which we contrasted with Merton's notion of marginal melancholy. With his
utopia, Burton counters his concept of prevailing melancholy.
Whereas the latter notion, when used to refer to a nation or state,

takes the form of a "catalogue of vices" similar to Merton's list of melancholic individuals, Burton's utopia reflects an efficient monarchical state that places great importance on smooth functioning and is planned down to the smallest details. This state holds up a perfected order in opposition to the dis-order of melancholy—a perfected order that leaves no room for surprises, since all eventualities have long been foreseen. Any deviation is rigorously punished: almost all interpreters of Burton's work, even his friends and literary disciples, have expressed astonishment at the legislative system he devises. It does little to make amends for injustice inflicted on some victim or to educate the guilty party; rather, its purpose is that of "fulfilling a form of cold and abstract revenge . . . The punishments are of such a cruelty that today one would term them sadistic, and they function as though they were the juristic blessing for the bloodiest of instincts."[59]

Even if we must fault such a judgment for remaining so close to its own self-evident cultural truths, we cannot overlook the discrepancy between Burton's ideals, infused with a spirit of humanism, and the inhumane severity of his punishments. Of all the nuances and facets entailed in the Burtonian utopia, the theme of a few, severe, easily surveyed laws most clearly reflects their creator's wish to devise a counterpart—namely order—to the dis-order of melancholy. This trait is not restricted to Burton but is typical of the utopias of the Renaissance and is characteristic of utopian thought overall. Paul Foriers expressly points this out in his essay "Les Utopies et le droit."[60] The theme, already evident in More's work (clearly distanced, however, from the barbaric legal methods of his time, which is perhaps the reason Erasmus called him the "best advocate"), is also to be found in the writings of Bacon, Campanella, Morelly, and Robespierre (as well as in those of Tacitus, Hobbes, Rabelais, Montesquieu, Fichte, Möser, and Comte). Likewise the aversion to advocates is present not only in More's utopia but also in Cruce's writings: "That is why tribal peoples ranging from Spain to India are right to beseech their king not to bother them with any advocates. For unrefined people living in the country are more at their ease than those who use subtle deception."[61]

The idea of linking the concept of order with that of melancholy would seem to suggest itself quite naturally. Having arisen from a "knowledge of order" (as Eric Voegelin puts it)—that is, from the Pythagoreans' and then Empedocles' speculations about the nature of cosmological elements—melancholy already appears as dis-order in classical antiquity's pathology of the humors. The correct and orderly distribution of the body's fluids *(humores)*, the "well-balanced mixture of qualities,"[62] is judged to constitute health. Dis-order, meaning the predominance of one of the three humors—mucus (phlegma), yellow gall, or black gall (cholos)—is manifested as illness. Phlegm, yellow gall, and black gall were originally the *humores viciosos.* Thus, at a later date, once illnesses had come to be designated by terms drawn from the classification of temperaments, there was no name given to sanguine persons, for blood was not considered harmful. A sanguine nature was referred to as *complexio temperata.*[63] In like manner, cosmological speculations can be linked to the problems arising from a notion of dis-order: this pattern turns up again in the relationship between melancholy and Saturn.[64] The reference to dis-order is clear in the work of Hildegard von Bingen, who connects *humor melancholicus* with the Fall; the latter is the origin of dis-order and in Christian theology was caused by humankind.

This conception of melancholy—geared as it is to the difference between order and dis-order—is transposed by Burton's method into an intermediate domain, which is neither as universal as the cosmology of antiquity or the Middle Ages nor as micrological as the medicine of antiquity or of the Arabic and medieval worlds.[65] Burton calls his intermediate domain (and it is in this context that he speaks of melancholy) the "state," although the term "society" would fit better. His distinction between "kingdoms," "provinces," and "politick bodies" would seem to suggest this. Here, as elsewhere, Burton shows himself to be "in every way a moderate man, a middle-of-the-road man."[66]

The description of melancholy and the melancholic nation of his day serves Burton as more than a pretext for developing an anti-melancholic, utopian counterpart—quite apart from the fact that he had already fulfilled this function in his introduction, after he had described utopia. The *Anatomy of Melancholy* was published at a time when the "Elizabethan Disease" had become a general complaint, at least among intellectuals.[67] This climate also influenced Burton: the *Anatomy* gives us the impression that it is part of an immense portfolio on melancholy. Erasmus in his *Laus Stultitiae* (1509) and Sebastian Brant in his *Narrenschiff* (Ship of Fools), which appeared in English in Barclay's translation in 1509, had earlier dealt with the theme of universal folly. Timothy Bright's *A Treatise of Melancholie* was printed in 1586, and in 1599 appeared du Lauren's *A Discourse of the Preservation of Sight; of Melancholike Diseases; of Rheumes, and of Old Age.* In 1601 Thomas Wright wrote on melancholy (*The Passions of the Minde*), as did Thomas Adams in 1616 (*The Diseases of the Soule:*

A Discourse Divine, Morall, and Physicall). The first edition of Burton's *Anatomy* went to print in 1621, eleven years after Jacques Ferrand's *Traité de l'essence et quérison de l'amour ou de la mélancolie érotique* had appeared in Toulouse.

At the same time, systems devised by "harmonizers"[68] slowly took shape—a clear indication of a society's forward movement and of its intellectual mobility. Caleria sketched out his *Concordantiae Poetarum, Philosophorum et Theologorum* at a very early date (he died in 1474). Casmannus wrote the *Cosmopeia sive Commentationum Disceptationum-que Physicarum, Syndromus Methodicus et Problematicus* in 1598, and the *Nucleus Mysteriorum Naturae Enucleatus* seven years later. Johannes Alstedius drew up his *Physica Harmonica* and in 1610 compiled an encyclopedia, "a methodological survey of all the sciences."[69] The age was long past when Thomas Aquinas had been able to unify in one *summa* something that now—despite the richness of the vocabulary used—could only with difficulty conceal the disparate potential of the intellect. It would nevertheless be too superficial to view the pessimism that arose in the sixteenth century as something caused merely by the plethora of competing attempts to find intellectual solutions to scientific questions. For the Europeans of that time were confronted, in J. W. Allen's words, by "orthodox Platonism, a religion that was in agreement with Plotinus, a form of atheism based on Proclus, a purified Aristotle, the heretics Averroes and Alexander, an epicureanism that denied Providence, and a form of stoicism that nevertheless arrived at a Christian ethics in a roundabout way."[70]

The above should be taken not as the causes of general pessimism and a proclivity for melancholy, but rather as the symptoms of an unstable society. In *The Civilizing Process*[71] Norbert Elias drew attention to the decisive importance of this age. Likewise Arnold Williams countered Allen's argument quite plausibly by pointing out that opposing systems existed even in medieval times, although it was still possible for a stable society to avert the centrifugal tendencies of such systems.[72]

Burton has been called the "gargoyle sited between the two spires of England's intellectual Cathedral," the two spires being Bacon and Hobbes.[73] Let us remember that "viewed sociologically," Bacon's attempt "to replace the aristocratic organon with a *Novum Organon* in which thought factually played the role of a tool [corresponded to] the social and economic shift that occurred among the Germanic-Romanic tribes once the work of the burgher class caused towns to flourish while knights and monks lost their significance." We must also keep in mind that in Hobbes's doctrine "the Christian-Augustinian opposition between *civitas terrena* and *civitas dei*" is finally abandoned.[74] Seen in this light, Burton can truly be considered the representative of a late, transitional epoch.

Burton's utopia shares with other utopias the fact that it is a theory of power projected into the future and held to be realizable in some distant practical application. Yet Burton is comparatively vague in his description of the institutions of power. That precision is to be found in the *concept* of institution, in the *law*. Theories of power are, however, (to use the words of Helmuth Plessner) "the late products of a form of thought that no longer has a close natural relationship with a notion of the state as an institution."[75] Utopia falls prey to the fact that reflecting on what is self-evident in cultural terms—that is, becoming cognizant of what is "merely" socially mediated naturalness—already entails the loss of what is considered self-evident and natural. With reference to the old, from which it wishes to free itself so that it can prepare itself for what is desirable as the new, the concept of utopia already exhibits a resignative trait. And in relation to the future, a resignative stimulus remains in the form of melancholy—as was the case in Burton's work. It is the inadequacy of melancholy that releases utopian desire.

The melancholic air shapes utopia and betrays the personal displeasure of its creator, who pulls himself together sufficiently to describe the ideal system in which everything is supposed to be better. Georges Duveau wrote in connection with More the utopian: "In laying down the laws for his utopia, he compensated for the melancholies that he had considered necessary for creating a sound body of legislation for England," yet then attributed this resignative trait to utopia. "There is a slight sense of defeat in the utopia: the missing embrace, kisses without an echo ... A body of literature is the expression of a society; yet a society expresses not only its gratifications, its successes, but also its needs, its dreams, its aspirations."[76] Emile Dermenghem wrote of More in a very similar vein: "Despite that gaiety that borders on exuberance, the man was—and not contradictorily, but rather completely—inhabited by a sort of melancholy which was not true sadness and which had nothing morbid about it."[77]

In Burton's work, melancholy as the metaphor for displeasure with the state is inextricably linked with utopia that has been brought into the system as the antimelancholic hope for government. This provides another explanation for the severity of utopian legislation: the state, freed of melancholy, holds the deviant and the lawbreaker to be symptoms of an impending relapse, which must be countered with strictness—"to avoid confusion," as Burton continually emphasizes. Once overcome, melancholy proves the hypertrophy of the desire for happiness—a process that culminates in eugenics.[78]

Following our discussion of Merton's notion of melancholy as deviant behavior and as based on a formal concept of order, a survey of the reception of Burton's work has served to clarify the suggestion that order-oriented thought is linked to a conception of melancholy. The great difference between the two avenues of thought precludes any attempt to pursue the comparison of this (admittedly decisive) common trait. Yet it must be stressed that Burton's aversion to melancholy is not content with formally devaluing melancholy as "dis-order" but is capable of fleshing out the concept of order with content—in the form of an antimelancholic utopia.

Utopia as a Projected Order

In Burton's work, the reduction of law, which is aimed at achieving controlled transparency and demands that order be reestablished, is also the basis for prohibiting melancholy. This syndrome does not constitute a phenomenon particular to Burton; rather, it is characteristic of an action-saturated society and a form of utopian thinking that is geared to totally planned action. Mühlmann[79] speaks of possible "prophecies of wrongness" which are either pessimistically conservative or euphoric in their future orientation—characteristics which can also be applied to the utopias inasmuch as they are designs for order. The actual utopia is thus already implicit in Burton's description of melancholy in the England of his day, even if allocated to some euphoric realm in which no melancholy can prevail. Utopias are, of course, only possible if *ordo ordinans* and *ordo ordinatus* are contrasted and kept separate; utopia and utopian thought are not possible until the concept of order is splintered, again revealing the former to be the later product of the process of thought.

"Utopia" in this context is understood to include only those designs for society in which humans are compensated for everything that they miss out on in their earthly existence. The land of milk and honey belongs in this category but not *1984*, although it would be interesting to consider what significance should be attached to this shift of melancholy from reality to utopia. One is inclined to suspect that there is an aversion to utopia—an aversion, moreover, that suggests an affirmative buttressing of the status quo: thus, here as well, we find the prohibition of melancholy, projected back to the earth. Paradoxically, this type of pessimism resembles the courtly

prohibition of melancholy—just as cultural critique raises itself to
the level of a prophecy of doom, and all too willingly dons an aristocratic air.

The ban on melancholy is not limited to utopia. In his description
of the civilizing process, Norbert Elias mentions a standard rule of
behavior ("A young man should be gay and lead a joyous life. It does
not befit a young man to be mournful and pensive")[80] that insti-
tutionalizes the ban on melancholy and appears to be typical of a
society that was based on the eccentricity of affects, and on rapid and
decisive action: "A life where the structure of affects was different
from our own, an existence without security, with only minimal
thought for the future. Whoever did not love or hate to the utmost
in this society, whoever could not stand his ground in the play of
passions, could go into a monastery; in worldly life he was . . . lost."[81]

In Campanella's City of the Sun we encounter a form of minimal
planning that extends even to the domain of sexuality and is truly
addicted to order: "Those who commit sodomy are disgraced and
are made to walk about for two days with a shoe tied to their necks
as a sign that they perverted natural order, putting their feet where
the head belongs . . . Tall handsome girls are not matched with any
but tall brave men, while fat girls are matched with thin men and
thin girls with fat ones, so as to avoid extremes in their offspring."[82]
This is linked with the previously mentioned theme of the few, transparent, easily understandable and rigorous laws: "The laws are very
few, all of them being inscribed on a copper plate placed on a column
at the temple door, on which the definitions of all things are briefly
set down—what God is, what an angel is, what the world, the stars,
man, etc.—these are all set down with great wisdom, as are also the
virtues."[83]

It follows that Campanella's view also includes the characteristic
ban on melancholy already mentioned in connection with Burton:
"since theft, murder, rape, incest, adultery—crimes of which some
among us are guilty—do not exist" in the City of the Sun, the
inhabitants accuse each other of being lazy and sad, and make an
effort to "feed on dry articles (in winter), and in autumn they eat
grapes; since these are given by God to remove melancholy and sadness; and they also make use of scents to a great degree."[84]

The ban on melancholy is also implicit in the color symbolism:
"The people dress in undershirts of white linen . . . They abhor black
as though it were something foul; consequently, they despise the Japanese for favoring this color."[85] At another point Campanella speaks
of black mourning dress as befitting the times: "This color is also the

allegory of a theory driven to its peak which makes us blind, melancholy, and mean . . . I see a time ahead in which people will start wearing the white tunic again."[86]

The ban on melancholy means more than the legal condemnation of gloom *(Schwermut)*: it is a rigorous internalization of the norms anticipated by the utopian view of a future society, a view that directly affects the psyche and makes mourning impossible or at least nurtures an aversion to it. There are no qualms about relying on other devices to achieve that goal—as Campanella's reference to the Japanese would indeed suggest. Here, national stereotypes already have to be devised in order to generate and perpetuate that mood so conducive to the state, namely, a love of externally directed aggression, untempered by resignation.

This aim is combined with the method of "controlling knowledge from the 'inside,' which we shall term the 'utopian method.' In this connection, 'from the inside' signifies that the utopian method is not a social technique, but rather a method of thinking."[87] The intellectual rigor underlying Campanella's ban on melancholy is a telling sign of the form which the planned state will take; as with Burton, a utopia swollen with action and anticipated in all its parts presupposes an aversion to melancholy. To an even greater degree than Burton's utopia of the new England, Campanella's City of the Sun is foisted on a society whose members are no longer in a position to allow themselves to be sad—for the open display of their emotions would ultimately reveal the failure of total planning. At this point suspicion turns again to the psyche of the person who harbored suspicion: "Himmler was wondering: 'He [Ohlendorf] must suffer from liver and gall ailments. His reports are always gloomy; he has such a pessimistic view of the world that there must be some bodily reason for it. After all, it is known that liver and gall bladder problems can have that effect on the mind."[88]

The syndrome of action systems designed in utopian thought and the institutionalized renunciation of melancholy that, as in Campanella's model, goes so far as to determine the emotional structure of the human being is not limited to the sixteenth and seventeenth centuries, which we have concentrated on thus far. It is also found in its pure form in Edward Bellamy's *In the Year 2000: A Retrospective on the Year 1887.*[89] The author's preface already documents the importance of the problem of order, for he speaks of "living as we do in the closing years of the twentieth century, enjoying the blessings of a *social order at once so simple and logical* that it seems but the triumph of common sense" (p. 5, italics added). This state of simple, transparent order is taken up again in the already familiar symbol of an absence of attorneys: "We do without lawyers, certainly . . ." (p. 141). In the Boston of the year 2000 the general duty to work is so rigorously internalized by the utopians that the character Julian West is led to wonder: "But how could I live without service to the world? you ask. Why should the world have supported in utter idleness one who was able to render service?" (p. 2). Mandatory labor and control over any form of private leisure are total: "It is certain, Dr. Leete replied, that no man in his right mind and able man today can get out of having to share in the work and efforts of the others, regardless of whether he happens to call himself a student, which is a nice way of putting it, or simply admits to being a lazy bum!" (p. 106).

In the Boston of the year 2000 precautions are taken to ensure that no one is bored; every house has a telephone, distracting anyone who might otherwise be inclined to have silly ideas (such people are always the ones who harm the system): "And with the receiver at your ear, I am quite sure you will be able to snap your fingers at all sorts of uncanny feelings if they trouble you again" (p. 79). Sports are manipulated into being a need in the same way: "Even if the people of that period [the nineteenth century] had enjoyed larger leisure, they would, I fancy, have often been at a loss how to pass it agreeably. We are never in that predicament" (p. 138).

In this utopian atmosphere of smoothly functioning institutions, of the general duty to work, and of regimented leisure as a palliative against the boredom that threatens the system, it is only natural for melancholy to be absent as well. When Julian West mentions it, this emotional state seems strangely out of place in the context of the system he has described thus far. It seems as if his psyche had rejected the environment: "I never could tell just why, but Sunday afternoon during my old life had been a time when I was peculiarly subject to melancholy, when the color unaccountably faded out of all the aspects of life, and everything appeared pathetically uninteresting" (p. 206). Yet this state of emotions heralds the end of utopia; the next morning West finds himself back in the old world: "All that about the twentieth century had been a dream. I had but dreamed of that enlightened and care-free race of men and their ingeniously simple institutions" (p. 216).

It is relatively insignificant that the sudden intrusion of reality in Bellamy's case ultimately turns out to be a bad dream—a sleight-of-hand that serves just as much to irritate the reader as it does to reveal the insecurity of the utopian designer—and must in the end give way again to life in the year 2000. The important thing here is that melancholy is likewise not part of Boston in the year 2000 and does not reappear until the present once again becomes the topic of the book.

The idea of a ban on melancholy is not only an element of utopias that explicitly refer to themselves as such; it is also to be found in what one might call "utopian programs"—that is, trends and artistic movements which, by virtue of a group's thrust and conviction, appear to have an affinity to systems similar to that of the lone creator of a utopia.

In the Futurist Manifesto, which Filippo Tommaso Marinetti had drawn up on his own and finished at the end of 1908, "despite the fictitious claim that it was a collective effort"—the same Marinetti who said of himself that he owed "his great willpower characteristic of the sanguinist (!) and superhuman"[90] to his father—one reads:

1. We want to sing of the love of danger, familiarity with energy and daring.
2. Courage, boldness, and rebellion will be the fundamental elements of our poetry.
3. Until today, literature praised immobility weighed down with thought, ecstasy, and sleep. We want to praise movement thirsty for attack, feverish insomnia, the running pace, the *salto mortale*, the slap in the face, the punch . . .
. . . . .
9. We want to glorify war—this the only form of hygiene for the world—militarism, patriotism, the destructive act of the anarchists, the beautiful ideas for which one dies, and contempt for woman . . .

From Italy we catapult our manifesto full of engaging and inflaming passion into the world, and with it today we establish *Futurism,* for we want to free this land from the cancerous tumor of professors, archaeologists, tourist guides, and antique dealers.[91]

Later Marinetti makes a programmatic plea for the "glorification of instinct and of the tracking sense in man the animal, the cultivation of a divining intuition."[92] In the Futurist political program of October 11, 1913, signed by Marinetti, Boccioni, Carrà, and Russolo, we find the metaphor with which we are already familiar from our investigation of utopias: "*A minimum of professors, very few lawyers, very few doctors.*"[93] Nor does the manifesto on the "fundamental insights" of

Futurism, signed seven years later by Marinetti, Settimelli, and Mario Carli, fail to include an explicit reference to the ban on melancholy: "*In life a Futurist is:* . . . One who is cheerful, who always takes action with a view to tomorrow (!), without qualms of conscience, without pedantry, without a false sense of shame, without mysticism, and without melancholy."[94]

The peculiar relation here between the emphasis on action, the preference for planning, and the ban on melancholy can be cross-checked—in Surrealism. A "preference for the ugly as opposed to the beautiful, for the dream, dreaming, melancholy, nostalgia, and yearning for 'paradises lost'"[95] are all linked here with an express disinclination to act: "As we see, the Revolution is in ideas. The surrealists' conception of it permits them to scorn all pragmatism, all concrete material activity. Further: they find this activity *shameful.*"[96]

This is why André Breton writes an "Introduction to the Discussion on the Minusculity of Reality" in the first (and also the last) issue of *Révolution Anarchiste,* October 1, 1927, and why Pierre Naville "puts forward what is 'actually a very logical concept, namely, pessimism' as a common denominator for the action of the Surrealists and of the political revolutionaries."[97] "Above all, people must be made to despair of themselves and of the order of society"[98]—this phrase can be found in the program, published in 1928, by a group of young followers of Surrealism, whereas Futurist Aldo Palazzeschi in his text "The Counter-Pain" develops a program to reeducate the "late-bloomers, *those who have incurably succumbed to melancholy*" or, failing that, to eject them from society.

One can therefore assume that the described syndrome of thought geared to action and total planning, in the process of which melancholy is banned as an integral part of the thinking, is a general characteristic of utopia. This assumption will be reinforced below, with additional references. It is a question of utopian thinking aimed at establishing a system, Duveau's "pensée utopique,"[99] and thus it is also a question of the system which would emerge if utopian thinking were ever to become implemented in reality.

In connection with studies on utopian thought, it is again Duveau who speaks of a desire to find the "archetypes of human thought"—this being the "great ambition of the sociologist," as he puts it. Without wishing to argue here whether there can be a good or a less good sociology, it can be said that Duveau's project does not come up to his own expectations. The wish to discover archetypes or to turn up a priori positions is repressed. This means not that their existence is denied, but that it is assumed to be unrecognizable: "There is probably an absolutely necessary and valid a priori—only we can never know what it is. For the criterion that it allows us to recognize would itself already have to possess that quality of absoluteness to which it is first supposed to lead us." [100] Yet refraining from inquiry as to what is a priori does not preclude consideration of the issue of how resignative behavior arises, the reasons for which have already been generally outlined in the encounter with utopian thought, at a "deeper," "more fundamental" level: namely, at the level of anthropology. Such a consideration must be deferred until the end of our study, however. As a logical consequence of the attempt to establish a link between order and melancholy, a second step is necessary in order to complete that attempt: we must examine how melancholy and disorder are described, and how it is possible for melancholy to be engendered by order.

3 Surplus Order, Boredom, and the Emergence of Resignative Behavior

On the Use of Literary Sources

Let us now explore the relationship between order, boredom, and melancholy, as a counterproject to the conception that defined melancholy as dis-order. In the first part of our investigation the lion's share of the analysis relied on literary documents, and in what follows they will be given even greater weight—irrespective of whether we concern ourselves with La Rochefoucauld's significance, the salons, the sentimental inclination of German literature in the eighteenth century, Kierkegaard's "interior," the *mal du siècle,* or Marcel Proust.

When Vinet pondered de Bonald's aphorism that literature was the expression of society ("la littérature c'est l'expression de la société"), he was in a position to then write: "I know of no law that could be more absolute, and of no truth that bears more the sign of constituting an a priori."[1] Note that this was the statement of a literary scholar, and a Frenchman at that—and that he wrote it over a hundred years ago. Nowadays no one would so casually label things as being a priori, particularly not trivialities. Indeed, anyone who does not want to renounce his literary interests while attempting to analyze society scientifically can refer to Kant, who in his early work *Anthropology from a Pragmatic Point of View* mentioned "although obviously not as sources, but nevertheless as aids for an anthropology: world history, biographies, indeed plays and novels."[2] Clearly, Kant's shamefaced "indeed" contained the seeds of that aversion which allows itself to approach literature with a sociological probe and to graft literature as a whole onto a particular branch of sociology—namely, the sociology of knowledge. It is to the latter that a literary sociology belongs. At the same time, this prevents literature from being used as a source by sociology. The answer was not long in coming: the "literary world," afraid for its territory, has long since raised its more or less open aloofness vis-à-vis sociology to the status of a method. "Just like the sociological variant, the medical observation of art sharpens one's eye for facts of a secondary order and dulls it to the main matter at hand," claims Walter Muschg.[3] It is unusual to hear, from sociologists, pronouncements such as the one that claims novels are not just, as Krysmanski puts it, "products of prevalent conditions, and not only have a reciprocal effect on these conditions, but, by becoming a source, gather time within themselves and become its reservoir."[4] Such statements are not aimed at the application of sociological questions in the domain of literature with the sole purpose of paying due regard to the self-estimation of sociology as a discipline. The difficulty lies not in analyzing novels sociologically but in using them concomitantly as sources. This means, for example, thinking not only of the Protestant work ethic and of a capitalist mentality when discussing the bourgeois' great affinity for acquiring money that accrues interest, but also bringing Honoré de Balzac's *Comédie Humaine* to mind.

What is and remains a favorite objection is the claim that sociology as a science oriented toward the present can dispense with literature. From this standpoint, which helps kill two annoying flies—history and literature—at the same time, nothing remains of history and all that is left of literature is the permission to use the occasional beautifully crafted quotation or ironic aperçu. Whoever tolerates literature as a source must go beyond these boundaries, and must be careful not to fall prey to that evasive pose which immediately devalues the thing it wishes to protect by conjuring up the good old days in the world of literature: "Novels are one of the sociologist's true sources: even if one considers a book as full of *esprit* as Simone de Beauvoir's piece on the mandarins in French literary circles, one still does not get the sense that it achieves that degree of microscopic precision and illuminating superiority which transforms Emile Zola's novels into invaluable sociological sources."[5]

The rejection of literature, on occasion covert, as an important source, a rejection that is quite compatible with "literature" having a status as an object of sociological knowledge, usually goes hand in hand with an equally stringent animosity toward history. Conversely, pleas for the scientific value of literature as a source are at the same time a recognition of the need for a historical approach. Eric Voegelin, for example, who strictly opposes an anthropology devoid of history that construes "humankind as a nontranscendental being immanent to the world," simultaneously accords literature an outstanding role: "In terms of material, . . . taken in isolation the institutions of the time provide little access to the reality of knowledge. People in Germany who want to acquaint themselves nowadays, for example, with the great problems of systematic, ordering thought would do better to concern themselves with novelists such as Robert Musil, Hermann Broch, Thomas Mann, and Heimito von Doderer or with dramatists such as Frisch and Dürrenmatt instead of reading professional literature on politics."[6] A confession that is all the more fresh if one reminds oneself that the author is a professor of political science!

In a vein similar to Voegelin's emphasis on the special value of literary sources for problems of order and systematic thought—and this is of particular importance for the approach espoused here—Leo Lowenthal insists on the significance of history and believes that "when we turn our attention to the problem of how a literary character dissents from a social order or how he seeks to justify it, then we have descriptive material of prime importance."[7]

Statements like those quoted above, however, always seem to be apologies for a bad conscience. Whoever insists that La Rochefoucauld, for example, is of value for psychology—and perhaps also sociology—is probably revealing less an insight into science than the love of an author who he or she feels should not be relegated to purely private use.

Melancholy and Rulership

The question raised in the *Problemata Physica,* attributed to Aristotle, as to why all outstanding philosophers, politicians, poets, and artists are (chronic) melancholics already incorporates the paradigm according to which the ruler is the prototype of the melancholic; it thus seeks to explain problems of rulership in relation to the issue of melancholy. This complex has been maintained, in connection with boredom, all the way to Walter Benjamin and Theodor Adorno:

> But the concept of this boredom, elevated as it is to such unpresumed dignity, something which Schopenhauer, with his antipathy toward history, would be the last to concede, is thoroughly bourgeois. It is a complement to alienated labor, as the experience of antithetical "free time," either in that this is merely supposed to reproduce the expended energy, or that the appropriation of alien labor is a burden, a mortgage it has to bear. Free time remains the reflective reaction to the rhythm of production which is imposed heteronomically onto the subject, and is also compulsively main-

tained in the tired breaks . . . The boredom of those, however, who do not have to do any work is not all that different. As a totality, society imposes on the controlling authorities that which they do to others, and what the latter are not allowed to do, the former will hardly allow for themselves.[8]

Kierkegaard, who ranked gloom among the cardinal sins and declared his allegiance to a tradition that had condemned acedia, chose a ruler—Nero—as the embodiment of the melancholic. Other writers consider Tiberius, Rudolf II, Charles V, and Philip II as melancholics. Tirso de Molina is said to have modeled the hero of his play *El melancolico* (1611) on Philip II.

Dürer's engraving "Melencolia I" was made for Emperor Maximilian, who was said to be fearful of Saturn.[9] Huizinga reported how melancholic behavior in the Middle Ages became standard behavior at the court: "The note of despair and profound dejection is predominantly sounded not by ascetic monks, but by the court poets and the chroniclers—laymen, living in aristocratic circles and amid aristocratic ideas. Possessing only a slight intellectual and moral culture, being for the most part strangers to study and learning, and of only a feebly religious temper, they were incapable of finding consolation or hope in the spectacle of universal misery and decay, and could only bewail the decline of the world and despair of justice and of peace."[10]

Du Laurens took this assumption so far as to contend that the melancholic dreams of being a ruler by stepping into this "role," so to speak, in his dreams: "If an ambitious man become melancholike, he straightway dreameth that he is a King, an Emperor, a Monarke."[11] Finally, William Ireland attempted to show that he had "traced a hereditary neurosis . . . appearing in various forms and intensities as epilepsy, hypochrondria, melancholia, mania, and imbecility, till at length it extinguished the direct royal line of Spain."[12] This strict conception of melancholy as a disease brings our discussion full circle.

The Mechanism of Kingship

The foregoing remarks were meant only to indicate that the problematics of rulership and melancholy are interconnected and that such a viewpoint has a long tradition. The clear orientation "backward into the past" and the initial structure of a conception of melancholy which links it directly to the problematics of order (and order is understood here not merely as a formal regulator juxtaposed to melancholy, as was the case in the above descriptions) are both found in the outline of that complex splicing apparatus which Norbert Elias termed the "mechanism of kingship."

The "civilizing process" which Elias traces entered its decisive stage at the point when the monopolization of power made possible the staging of long chains of actions, the refinement of one's emotions, and a large measure of rationality. Elias has shown how in every instance of individual rule—including the rule of an absolute monarch—the central ruler and the central apparatus were dependent on and tuned into each other, so that the particular position of the former consisted in being both referee and player in this interplay of forces. The stability of the situation was guaranteed if approximately equally strong groups faced one another within society, groups that struggled among themselves to a greater or lesser degree without being able to destroy one another and in this manner permitted the king to continue playing his role as referee.

What was crucial for developments here was a situation in which the differentiation between a military and a moneyed nobility (*noblesse de robe*) granted the institution of kingship the greatest—namely, absolute—power. The social strata confronting one another were by no means purely antagonistic groups, for "minimal differences" were decisive:[13] "The highest goal of individual bourgeois is, as we have mentioned, to obtain for themselves and their family an aristocratic title with the attendant privileges. The representative leading groups of the bourgeoisie as a whole set out to seize the privileges and prestige of the military nobility; they do not want to remove the nobility as such, but at most to take their place as a new nobility supplanting or merely supplementing the old."[14]

Occasional alliances between aristocratic groupings and bourgeois strata failed—for example, the Fronde, which Elias termed a "sort of social experiment" and of which Sainte-Beuve said everyone had viewed it as "armed jesting." The significance of the moneyed aristocracy increased with the growing importance of money: "Under Henry IV, and still under Louis XIII, court positions, like the majority of military appointments and, still more, like administrative and judicial offices, are purchasable and thus the property of their occupant."[15] In this situation the king, who himself was a descendant of the aristocracy, tended again to help the military aristocracy; under Louis XIV people who were not aristocrats had only a minimal chance of gaining access to the court, which was "given its clear role as an asylum for the nobility on one hand, and a means of controlling and taming the old warrior class on the other. The untrammelled knightly life is gone forever."[16] This, if only in outline, is the historical background against which our second approach to the complex of melancholy develops. In the *Requestes et articles pour la rétablissement de la noblesse,* which was addressed to Louis XIII by the old aristocracy and which is cited by Elias, there is already an indication of the focus which the consideration of melancholy was to gain thereafter. The *Requestes* suggest that the aristocracy is "in the most pitiful state that it was ever in . . . overwhelmed by poverty . . . *idleness* is making it licentious . . . and oppression has all but reduced it to despondency."[17]

The example of Louis XIII clearly shows what dangers were imminent if the individual ruler neglected his function as balance and referee. The aristocracy suffered on account of the leisure forced upon it, leisure composed of nothing other than the depressing feeling that one had been excluded from all relevant decision-making processes and action. This impaired willingness to act required a valve in order to let off steam, and this was found from the time of Henri III onward in courtly ceremonies, which prescribed in pedantic detail even the manner in which the king was to be helped on with his shirt, and who could do so, and when. Louis XIII would seem to have paid insufficient attention to the value of this "secondary order" that had emerged in the ceremonies of court. As a consequence, there was talk of "the melancholic theater of the inner court." Contemporaries agreed that Louis was "the hypochondriacal king par excellence,"[18] and at the beginning of his memoirs La Rochefoucauld declares that Louis' "indisposition increased his sorrows and the faults of his temperament [*humeur*]."[19]

It was court ceremony that thwarted the ambitions of the old aristocracy, which was deprived of power and jealous of the increasingly important moneyed aristocracy, but incapable of taking any action against the king without reaching an agreement with the parvenus. These ceremonies dazzled the old aristocracy by creating a world of rules that extended to the very minutest details, a world in which there was an appropriate place reserved for each and every person. The king did not recognize that his complete disinterest in the daily affairs of court was a danger not only to the atmosphere among the aristocracy but also to the balance of power as such. He forgot that it was insufficient to merely demand vaguely that order was to govern the court if one was no longer prepared to lay this order down in all its details and strive to adhere to it.

The powerlessness of the aristocracy, maintained through the balance of the antagonistic power groupings, began to be expressed at the moment when boredom set in and was no longer intercepted and channeled through the system of a secondary order, which, in the inflexibility of its principles and the high degree of its obligatory character, had to accord with the real loss of power of its members. Etiquette was, after all, a means of passing the time; the lack of it made people conscious of time and of the fact that there was nothing to do because they were not allowed to do anything. Louis XIII, however, "hardly looks for avenues with which to relieve the boredom that afflicts his household. Almost always foreboding and silent, he does not understand that his court thirsts to be kept in movement, to feel joy, to be offered parades, and that good politics would be to distract the court in order to keep it from conspiring." [20]

Thus, satire first developed out of the boredom of the aristocracy barred from all action; this was followed by conspiracies and finally by the Fronde. It is again La Rochefoucauld who describes what a great influence this feeling of boredom must have had on behavior. In Paris, Queen Anne (of Austria) had finally decided to keep the king beyond Richelieu's sphere of influence, when the king moved to Versailles and Richelieu followed. People begged her to accompany the king, writes La Rochefoucauld, "and not to expose him in such a situation to his own insecurity and the cardinal's designs; but the fear that she would be bored and badly lodged in Versailles seemed to her to pose an insurmountable obstacle to her going and caused her to reject such necessary advice. The cardinal knew how to exploit this opportunity skillfully." [21]

The relation between the first- and second-tier orders was of decisive importance for the boredom of the old military nobility, boredom that grew ever more pronounced under the reign of Louis XIII and finally exploded in the Fronde in one last despairing convulsion. The first-tier system of order entailed the institutionalized distribution of real means of influence and power—for example, the balance that Norbert Elias referred to as the "mechanism of kingship." The second-tier system of order was a derivative of this first order, comprising highly formalized, inflexibly binding, and hierarchical rules, regulations, and privileges, like the ones that were summarized in etiquette.

Both systems of order were independent of and yet mutually determined each other: the first system of an order of forces that were played off against one another could be maintained by the king—who held the balance between different power groups—only if he succeeded in giving this balance permanence and diverting the pressure of unsatisfied needs into the second-tier system of order, which readily offered the formal power otherwise denied in reality. The second-tier system was in this sense derived from the first;[22] it transposed relations of super- and subordination onto a plane of "powerless" behavior, if we understand power primarily as the capacity not only to influence something but also to decide something. This, however, was the prerogative of the absolute monarch.

As the example of Louis XIII shows, conflict arose precisely when the holder of real power neglected to keep the second-tier system of order in operation. The consequences were, first, a weakening of the impetus to act among those strata who were dependent on the functioning of the second-tier system of order; then a growing awareness of the fact that opportunities for action were being curbed; and, finally, boredom. At this juncture in the "mechanism of kingship," "ennui" meant a loss of opportunities for development in the second-tier system of order and the gradual realization of this loss. If no wars were being waged that shifted internal conflicts outside society and thus reduced internal tensions, then a high degree of reflection was provoked among the aristocracy, who now had nothing to do— and even the first system of order was drawn into the wake of ensuing cataclysmic considerations. Relieved, in the sense that at such a time the obligations of etiquette brought relief: the obligations that one was permitted to take upon oneself constituted free spaces. Admittedly, attempts were initially made to restore to the second-tier system of etiquette, whose significance was neglected by the monarch, something that the aristocracy itself was no longer in a position to restore of its own initiative; this game functioned only if the referee, too, abided by the rules. Just as we have seen that the king and the powers he held in balance were linked with one another in a matrix of interdependencies in the first system of order, we also find that they were linked in the second-tier system. The high degree of interdependence of the two systems made it impossible for the functions of the one to be upheld if those of the other had been curbed.

The Court and the Salon

The salon represented an attempt to construct a new system of order so as to dispel boredom, while excluding the person who was actually responsible for creating it—namely, the king. The Fronde, by contrast, was the final and ill-fated attempt to repair by force the loss of power which had become manifest owing to the failure of the second-tier system of order. Stable, closed societies such as those of an absolutist nature are characterized by a fictitious, unconscious, second-tier system of order which disguises the real, first system of order. To the extent that the mechanisms of the second system are no longer self-evident and become consciously perceived by their participants, the first system is likewise threatened. The two systems form a matrix of communicating lines in which the fluid social movements of one also influence those of the others.

Thus in seventeenth-century France, the aristocracy's willingness to act, no longer motivated by etiquette, "backed up" into the domain of the first system: the curtailment of etiquette gave rise to boredom, and boredom, in turn, gave rise to action. Hegel formulated this interlinked structure in terms of what he called, in his *Phenomenology,* the "foolhardiness, which, like boredom, invades the status quo." The Fronde, as an expression of such action, failed; La Rochefoucauld himself described it as "a sorry farce." The reasons for this are of less interest to us here than the consequences of that failure. Let it suffice to note how all historians of the subject have characterized this uprising: as a unique fusion between a powerful compulsion to act and a lack of planning, "a movement without ideas, in which financial difficulties, the poverty of the people, and the vain ambition of those on high played roles in a game whose object was not clear to anyone";[23] "a unique moment in modern history, especially in terms of the combination of men capable of action, who were forced to act almost without principles, and of men of intelligence who had enough wits about them to see through this action and analyze it."[24]

Statements of this type clearly show that in the Fronde no one knew exactly what he wanted, but that each person had a reason to change the existing state of affairs. No one could predict or describe the future he wanted to help create, but everyone wanted to flee the past, barely put behind him. It was not until the Fronde failed that a perfect balance was established between the two sides.

The concept of the "mechanism of kingship" devised by Elias and adopted here contains both dynamic and static moments: it refers to the process of balancing diametrically opposed forces, as well as to the state of balance then achieved. This balance was upset by the Fronde. The nobility attempted, and failed, to weigh more heavily in the scales. The response was repression, and force was initially used to restore the balance. A sociological investigation of this phenomenon becomes interesting at the point where the open use of force was excluded as an option. For the monarchy and the military nobility were dependent on each other because of the existence of a third force: the rising bourgeoisie, which strove, by means of purchased titles, to conform to the old system of aristocracy. This pressure to strike a balance also explains the rapidity with which quarrels broke out and were just as quickly settled during this period: on July 2, 1652, La Rochefoucauld was critically wounded in the Faubourg Saint-Antoine; on October 21 of the same year the king returned to Paris and published an amnesty that included La Rochefoucauld's name; in November the king gave La Rochefoucauld's son, Charles, the Benedictine abbey of Molesmes.

These isolated events, however, are of less interest to sociology than the behavioral mechanisms that gradually emerged after the Fronde failed. Up to this point the "mechanism of kingship" and its use by the absolute monarch as a balance control have been described in terms of the first-tier system of order, that is, as the decision-making authority institutionally invested in one person. Courtly etiquette was regarded as the second-tier system of order. It represented the residual domain in which the nobility was granted a degree of formal power to compensate for the real power it was denied. "Boredom" was the term used to refer to the disenchantment with the second-tier system of order, and this ultimately developed into an attack on that of the first tier, the real power-balancing system. After the failure of this onslaught, characteristic forms of behavior emerged on both sides—namely, that of the king and that of the nobility—which manifested a specific ratio of etiquette, boredom, and melancholy.

The behavior exhibited by both La Rochefoucauld and the court of Louis XIV reveals the alternatives for action. These come to have a stabilizing effect and guarantee the balance between the first- and second-tier systems of order. La Rochefoucauld becomes resigned, referring to his state of mind as melancholy: "To begin with my disposition, I am melancholic, and to such an extent that no one has seen me laugh on more than three or four occasions in the last three or four years. My melancholy, it seems to me, would nevertheless be bearable and almost soothing if it were only of the type which emanates from my mood; but so much of it comes from elsewhere and it so strongly preoccupies my imagination and my mind that I usually dream without saying a word or have no relation to the words that I utter."[25]

La Rochefoucauld describes with great clarity a form of melancholy that today would be referred to as exogenous: he claims to have laughed scarcely at all in three or four years. At the time he wrote this passage, around the year 1654, he was confronting the definitive failure of his plans. Aside from a short military interlude during the occupation of Lille in 1667, La Rochefoucauld's life henceforth changed: the soldier became a writer, the world became a salon, and the salon became the world. This development was typical of his day and is exceptionally well represented in the figure of La Rochefoucauld: "The life and work of La Rochefoucauld must be regarded totally and completely as a creation of cultured society, of this small, ever so feminine and refined world; his life and works enable us to follow all phases of the development of the upper nobility from 1630 to 1670."[26]

In addition to satisfying our historical interest in the subject, our investigation permits an analysis of the resigned behavior of a social class which was no longer able to influence the real course of events. To assess the degree to which such deprivation in the social sphere— even without negative, persisting sanctions—had an effect on the individual psyche, one must bear in mind that noblemen such as La Rochefoucauld were raised first and foremost to live a life filled with action: "Instead of sitting around bored on school benches, the son of an upper-class family at that time entered the army, and thus the world, ten years earlier than he would today [1895]. He knew nothing about books, but soon knew all about actions and emotions."[27] Thus, Segrais declared that La Rochefoucauld had not engaged in serious study but had "a good head on his shoulders" and knew the world—experiences that perhaps allowed one to think up maxims without being capable of writing them down. For this reason a note of uncertainty can be detected in La Rochefoucauld's literary life—a fact that might confirm the suspicion that his fear of giving the obligatory speech was not the only reason for his never having been admitted to the French Academy. This fear, in turn, is a sign of shyness, which is an integral part of melancholy.

All of this must be taken into account if one wishes to acknowledge the extent of the limitations on action to which La Rochefoucauld was subject, and not fall victim to the erroneous assumption that this was someone who merely changed his profession—albeit under duress. No one thought any longer of rebelling against the king; there was no need to protect oneself from those "below," nor was there any need to fight for one's rank and opinion. The boredom that Madame de Maintenon wrote of became the worst enemy. This boredom took hold of everyone, the members of the salon as well as the court lizards, the former Frondeurs as well as nobles loyal to the king. The behavioral patterns that developed both in the salon and at court following the failure of the Fronde were geared in both places to coping with boredom. The balance afforded by the mechanism of kingship, temporarily upset by the uprising of the nobility, was slowly restored and became steadier than ever. In a society where initially there were no tensions to be played out among the classes holding power—the military and monied nobility, as well as the royal family—what became important was to kill time in a dignified manner, time that no one knew what to do with because there was nothing left to do. At the same time, the sense of boredom had to be repressed, both in the salon and at court. The aristocrat who betrayed his boredom was blatantly documenting his powerlessness; the king, for his part, sensed that boredom was the sign of an impending rebellion. Thus, in a completely balanced situation of this type, every effort was made to repress one's emotions and to take pleasure in exposing the lack of control in others. La Rochefoucauld's maxims clearly reveal this connection between boredom and the inhibition of inner feelings: "We often forgive those who bore us, but we cannot forgive those whom we bore" ("Nous pardonnons souvent à ceux qui nous ennuient, mais nous ne pouvons pardonner à ceux que nous ennuyons"). And in a similar vein: "One is nearly always bored by those people one is not allowed to be bored by" ("On s'ennuie presque toujours avec les gens avec qui il n'est pas permis de s'ennuyer").[28] This boredom—which stemmed directly from the position of an aristocracy both disempowered and relieved of its duties—was socially transmitted and a phenomenon of interpersonal action, as clearly shown by the maxims just cited. Ennui never appears as a "basic given" of human existence or as independent of a particular social structure. Rarely do we find boredom to be a phenomenon distinct from the society which engendered it in the first place. However, it tends to be reduced to the theme of existential analysis, beyond the scope of sociological investigation, when La Rochefoucauld speaks of an ennui so extreme that it, in turn, serves to dispel boredom: "Extreme boredom serves to drive away our ennui."[29]

Even in the virtual "privacy" of Madame de Sévigné's boredom, however, it is still possible to identify its cause, and she freely admits that there are also attitudes one can adopt:

> In this respect I am entirely on my own, my dear. I would not want to burden myself with any boredom other than my own. I shall be at the mercy of my imagination until after All Saints' Day: there is no company which will tempt me to commence my winter at such an early date. It hurts me, my dear, to spend it without you; I simply cannot get used to this separation. If I wanted to, I would assume an air of loneliness; but having recently heard Bagnols say that she was at the mercy of her reflections and felt a bit too much alone,

I am proud to say that I will be on this meadow the whole afternoon and shall converse with our cows and sheep. I have good books, above all the *Provinciales* of Pascal, and also Montaigne. What more do I need if I don't have you?"[30]

Boredom was the sign of a situation that relieved the person of all obligations. If one did nothing, one could be bored; if one was forced to do nothing, one concealed the boredom that reflected one's own impotence. Yet the salon was so close to that "world" which was present in concentrated form in the court that it could not become a complete counterpart to the latter.[31] The salon, while frequented by secular people, was not exclusively marked by that touch of the mundane associated with the word "salon" itself. Rather, the salon was also characterized by something prosaic, which is very evident in La Rochefoucauld's letters, for example, when he writes to Jacques Esprit that he will be returning to Paris again in winter, and that they will then be able to wind up their fireside chats about *belles moralités;* or when he asks the Marquise de Sablé for her opinion of maxims and at the same time asks for a "pot of carrots, a lamb, and beef ragout like the one the commander of Souvré ate *chez nous.*"[32]

In his examination of the origins of La Rochefoucauld's maxims, Gerhard Hess speaks of the "fortunate historical situation" in which society began to think about itself.[33] While this phrasing reflects the literary historian's delight at the work which thus came into being, it nevertheless obscures the compulsive mechanism which lies behind this and every other form of social introversion, and which was never forgotten in the salons of the period: La Rochefoucauld was not the only person who was well aware of his "virtual fall from grace" at court.[34]

Within the salon, diverted action flowed into a form of literature that was already organized almost in terms of a division of labor: "Every member of this circle cultivates the genre he or she prefers: at Mlle de Scudéry's one discusses the *madrigale;* at Mlle de Monpensier's in Luxembourg, *portraits;* at Mme de Sablé's, *maxims.*"[35] At the same time the salon grew so compelling that the expression of feelings or emotions became collective in nature: "In this society the friends of one became the friends of the other, by means of 'charisma,' as the Marquise said. They laughed together and grew sad together; for here, where they lived as in a community, all was not sheer happiness, and one was accustomed to sharing bitterness as well as joy."[36] In the salons it became a compulsion to share one's emotions with others and to vent them in the group. Therein lay its invaluable meaning. Despite their distinct distance from the "world"—that is, from the court—the salons did not constitute a refuge for introversion; rather, the individual's own emotional state was socially transmitted there and rendered communicable. This was not only shown by the *portraits,* in which everyone reported freely of himself ("*Découvrir l'intérieur* is referred to as the general intention");[37] it was also revealed in memoirs of the day—such as those written by Cardinal Retz—and not least in maxims, which Gerhard Hess has referred to as the "most sociable" form of aphoristic literature.

The ideal figure of the period was the same both in the salon and at the court: the *honnête homme,* of whom Pascal wrote: "Cette qualité universelle me plaît seule" ("This universal quality is the only one that pleases me"). This ideal is engendered by a "new aristocratization of society and a . . . renaissance of the old chivalrous-romantic concepts of morality" that were practiced in the wake of the definitive balance achieved by the "mechanism of kingship."[38] In a manner fully in keeping with the relationship between social structure and structure of affects which Elias described, everything was now concentrated on bringing the individual's affects under control. "Just as Minerva is superior to Mars, a discreet and anticipatory attitude is superior to a boiling and dour courage,"[39] says Fénelon in his *Adventures of Telemachus;* and Count Bussy-Rabutin wrote in his autobiography, around 1680: "From the moment I was born . . . my first and strongest inclination was to become an *honnête homme* and to earn great honors in the war. For that purpose I also sought as much contact as possible with *honnêtes gens.*"[40]

The words of this aristocrat clearly reveal the code of behavior that was binding for the period: either stay at home and dampen or restrain your affects in the long term, or go to war and let them all out. This dichotomy of behavior was subsequently institutionalized under Louis XIV: every year "one" went to war in the spring for several months and thus built up a "reservoir of action" to last for the remaining months of "ennui."[41] Testimony such as the statements just cited may give some idea of the aristocratic sources of that frame of mind which served to create a seamless mix of the myth of introversion as the "actual" form of existence and a decision-based activism.

The *honnête homme,* who oriented himself toward ideas of Castiglione and Gracián and was "absolutely a social animal" (E. W. Eschmann), was the institutionally required "product of breeding" par excellence, to use Arnold Gehlen's expression. Such a person's capacity to shift the focus of his affects as well as the compulsion to hold these in check were a function of his ability to act in the long run: the *honnête homme* was the concentrated point at which restrained affects, prudence, and higher morals all met. This at the same time corresponded to the achievement of a higher level of rationality; Georg Misch rightly points to the heritage of Descartes in this connection, and to the latter's view that only those actions "which depend on reason" can be considered human actions.[42]

There can be no doubt that a tendency toward boredom existed within such a development, at least on the inside—one might also say, in the midst—of the *honnêtes gens:* "The impetuous, exuberant noble-man of earlier days becomes the tame, well-bred courtier. The motley, ever-changing picture of the preceding period yields to a universal monotony."[43] Boredom prevailed among the *honnêtes gens;* it plagued a class relieved of its duties, regardless of whether they spent their time in the salon or at the court. The boredom of the salons has already been mentioned; but it was no less prevalent at court: "The courtiers . . . lolled in the galleries under the dimmed lights of chan-deliers, perishing from boredom and a sense of wastage."[44] Saint-Simon, most reliable witness of the period, found respite in his own curiosity: "Everyday I found myself informed about everything by means of pure, direct, and certain channels—about all major and minor things. My *curiosity,* aside from other reasons, thus received its due reward; and one must admit, regardless of whether one is an outstanding figure or not, that this is *the only source of nourishment to be had at the court* and that without it one would only be bored."[45]

Boredom arose from the secure balance afforded by the mech-anism of kingship. It was a result of the established order, with its long-term thrust. The permanent control of affects, which all too easily assumed a casual air[46] without intervening in what was going on, harbored the kinds of danger which, after all, contributed to the Fronde and which also erupted during the Louis XIV period, if only on the margins of society. The Duchess of Longueville, who had a relationship with La Rochefoucauld, withdrew to Normandy after the Fronde failed and "fell victim to a profound boredom. 'My God, Madame,' one of her lady companions said, 'boredom is eating away at you; wouldn't you like to amuse yourself? There are beautiful forests here and also dogs, would you like to go hunting?' 'I don't like hunting.' 'Would you like to work a bit?' 'I don't like working.' 'Would you like to go for a walk?' 'I don't like walks.' 'Would you like to play a game?' 'Games are something I don't like at all.' 'Well, what would you like to do to distract yourself?' 'Good heavens, what should I tell you. I don't like the innocent pleasures.'"[47]

This dialogue is of more than anecdotal value. It shows how extensive a state of boredom could be which was "only" social in nature, was regarded as such, and was not yet attributed to a basic element presumed to be an inextricable part of the human condition. Hatred of the *plaisirs innocents* was hatred of boredom, but at the same time it was also a form of inner rebellion against the established order which had already thwarted the individual and against which he or she was helpless. The rebellion remained verbal because the conditions resisted and prevented insurrection. La Rochefoucauld already had an inkling of oncoming boredom when he wrote to Lenet, "I admit that I feel very ill at ease, for I assure you I no longer know what I am supposed to do if I no longer do anything evil."[48] To be sure, these platitudes contain a certain amount of fashionable coquetry. Certainly, at that time people did things that were only intended to do justice to maxims, but the maxims also contain a fear of not being able to do anything anymore: a fear of boredom.

More than in the salon—where boredom was combated by writing instead of acting, where literature was made instead of war, and where "negative" emotions were collectively borne and defused in the group—at court it was necessary to get boredom under control. The difference between the first- and second-tier systems of order has already been discussed. Considering that the aristocracy had at its disposal less and less real opportunity to wield power, the king created a counterbalance in the form of etiquette: a system of painstakingly precise directable actions, and individual but generally binding priorities of order, which were so demanding on those who found themselves within the system that they sometimes did not even notice their real loss of power. Arnold Hauser writes that distinctions between the individual categories of the court aristocracy were blurred and that courtiers were the only people who remained at the court. Yet this statement must be revised as soon as one refers to La Rochefoucauld, for example, and his annoyance over the *tabouret* (stool) which had been awarded to his wife and then withdrawn again—in other words, the right to remain seated before the queen, "la chose du monde qui me touche le plus,"[49] as La Rochefoucauld described it; or to Saint-Simon, who never got over the fact that he had not once taken part in the king's *petits levers*, which in court slang were called the *grandes entrées*.

Etiquette as a second-tier system of order, however, could take effect and serve as a veil to disguise boredom only if the king submitted to this etiquette himself, thus suggesting that he, like any other (aristocrat), was bound to a particular convention—indeed, was especially conscientious in upholding it: "L'exactitude est la politesse des Rois," as Louis XVIII put it. This rule of the game is most crucial with respect to the functioning of the second-tier system or order, and Louis XIV, alerted to the dangers by the failure of his predecessor, Louis XIII, to domesticate the nobility, adhered to it. At this point, the difference between the behavior of the court and that of the salon became more important than the king's ability to create order and comply with this self-designed system. Saint-Simon describes with unabashed admiration how the king, for example, knew how to differentiate his greeting and adjusted it depending on the position of the person greeted and the measure of grace that person happened to enjoy at the moment: completely doffing his hat, only touching it, holding it closer or farther away from his head or ear, and so on. The difference was manifest in society's view of boredom and melancholy. It was all right to be bored at court, so long as that boredom was disguised. Yawning in the face of the powerful was invariably an affront to them. Openly displayed boredom suggested that changes were in the making. Boredom became the counterpart to etiquette, which was created to dispel boredom and yet provoked boredom: we know this especially from Madame de Maintenon.

There is something historically intriguing about the fact that, of all people, the son of the Duke of La Rochefoucauld was the most salient example of the opposition between the prescribed code of etiquette and the boredom that deviated from it. Saint-Simon tells us: "He was the only confidant in the king's love affairs, and the only one who, with his cloak covering his face, accompanied the king at a distance when he went to his first tryst."[50] Yet he was considered incapable of conducting himself properly in refined society; despite his prestigious title, he was the object of ridicule, and the few people he received were referred to by the court jokingly as "les Ennuyeux de M. La Rochefoucauld"—the bores of Mr. La Rochefoucauld. (Perhaps this ridicule served as a model for Proust's description in the *Remembrance of Things Past* of Verdurin's salon, which brands everyone it does not "get" as a "bore.")

A label such as this shows that the right to openly displayed boredom could be acquired only at the cost of one's presence at the court. Ennui was the sign of dissatisfaction with the status quo, and it was conceivable solely in someone who was "shameless" enough to display his boredom. Saint-Simon reported with disgust that he once encountered, in the salon, just such a person playing chess with his servant: "M. de Chevreuse and I who was following him were at a loss for words. M. de La Rochefoucauld noticed this and was himself dumb-founded . . . He tried to excuse what we were seeing; he said the servant played very well and that one could play chess with him. M. de Chevreuse had not come to deny that, and I even less so; we exchanged greetings and sat down, but soon stood up again so as not to disturb the game, and left as quickly as possible." [51]

If boredom was not allowed, melancholy was even less permissible: "The king hated sick people and melancholics." [52] Idleness was considered the enemy of fame, and boredom was viewed as dangerous; melancholy was not in keeping with the ideal of the *honnête homme* and was, moreover, an affront to the ruling system symbolized by the court. Distraction was not only permitted but encouraged; there are countless *allusions au jeu* in Saint-Simon's record of the period. The court was the reservoir of the *plaisirs innocents* that Madame de Longueville abhorred—as did all who had expected more from life and now had to deal with their disappointment. One could be melancholic only in the salons, and Madame de Sévigné describes the "tristesse incroyable" in which she found La Rochefoucauld. Telling her daughter about the conversations she had had with La Rochefoucauld and Madame de La Fayette, she says: "Sometimes we have conversations which are so sad that it seems we might just as well be buried." [53] Weeping, on the other hand, was permitted at the court, and in fact was even called for in the monarch's presence. Openly displayed emotions were not dangerous, because their release could be observed by all; they were subject to public control.

Réserve mélancholique appears typical for La Rochefoucauld; just as one learned "to acquire this wisdom which consists of knowing how to be bored," [54] one also learned to endure one's melancholy. The salon was a place where the world—that is, the court, meaning a gathering of those who held power or fancied themselves as holding power—was kept at a distance, but not lost. The melancholy of the salons was a reflection not of desperation but of the mournfulness over that which one once possessed. Resigned behavior in this setting was not groundless and "deep" but well founded and "superficial." According to Retz's memoirs, what distinguished people most from one another was that those who had already accomplished great things were always ahead of the others in terms of knowing how far they could go. An awareness of this fact pervaded the salon, and allowed melancholy in the salon to remain closely in touch with reality—in spite of all escapism. The individual had reason to be resigned, but was free of the resentment contained in that form of melancholy which had yet to devise its own disappointment—namely, cultural critique.

Loss of World and Proximity of World

The attention we are paying here to questions of melancholy and boredom is initially motivated by historical interest, and thus we are obliged at the outset to collect descriptive material. This material is intended to aid in drawing up generalized statements about the phenomena discussed and to prepare the way for testing such statements in terms of their applicability in the present: history helps us make hypotheses. Such a procedure rests implicitly on the conviction that the categories of human behavior are historical in nature and insists that what is supposedly the case a priori is in fact something changeable. The investigation of forms of melancholy, boredom, and reflection is not based on a concept against which these phenomena are then measured. Certain periods in history provide material on people's conceptions of melancholy and boredom in certain epochs. The real aim of the present investigation is to find what may be common denominators for such conceptions or to deny the existence of these conceptions.

Until now we have dealt with the question of melancholy in terms of two different thematic complexes. At first—drawing on Robert Burton's utopia—utopian notions appeared to suggest the existence of a particular link between the conception of melancholy and that of order. The link seemed to bring the two so close together that we appeared to be dealing with the endpoint in an analytical continuum which connected melancholy with dis-order and contrasted a utopian conception, or one that drew on the notion of thorough social planning, with a dis-order described as melancholy. This conception was developed not by referring to reality but rather by adducing statements about reality and a planned reality. A conception that—contrary to the one described—unites melancholy with a concept of order could then be thought of as the endpoint of this supposed continuum. We traced this supposition by studying an epoch in which melancholy and boredom both achieved a special significance: we looked at seventeenth-century France, at the action and counteraction of court and salon, at La Rochefoucauld and Louis XIV. We were able to confirm our suspicions that we were dealing not with a melancholy of dis-order but rather with that form of resignative behavior which arises out of a surplus of order. This principle of order is, admittedly, not inflexible. If it were to resemble the form of rule prevalent in a despotic, highly absolutist state, then analyses of the relation between social and affective structure, such as those undertaken and encouraged by Norbert Elias, would have little point, because they would simply not be considering those alternative forms of possible human behavior which could arouse sociological interest in the first place. Karl Wittfogel described the manner in which, under "Oriental despotism," blind obedience constituted the only rational form of action: those who did not obey were killed and in this way eliminated from society, thus ceasing to be of sociological interest. Yet limiting the alternatives to the dichotomy of life or death precludes all sociological inquiry. It can begin again if a continuum of possible forms of behavior is found between life and death—one of which, clearly, can itself be death, whether it be chosen by the individual or imposed by others.

The principle of order that we traced above was described by Elias as the mechanism of kingship. Saint-Simon had already spoken of the "mécanisme" of Louis XIV, which the latter had invented so as to distract courtiers from paying attention to politics and the affairs of state. The mechanism of kingship is accordingly found on two levels, which we described as those of the first- and second-tier systems of order. The first, delineated by Elias, refers to the mechanism of distributing real power and the balance of rulership; the second, Saint-Simon's mechanism, veils the first. It is here that we come upon the fiction of a power to which the king subjugates himself: court etiquette.

In seventeenth-century France, however, the salon existed alongside the court; it was a refuge for those who attempted, but failed, to bring movement into the mechanism of kingship. The Frondeurs, brought up like all members of the military nobility for a life of action, were the representatives of those forces which, weary of an order based on regal power, tried to disassemble that order. It would be wrong to conclude that we are dealing here with nothing more than a handful of power-hungry rebels. Their actions were not without a basis in tradition. The conception of a durable but nevertheless unstable balance was part of French political philosophy. In his *Grande Monarchie* of 1518, Claude de Seyssel had already described how the king was bound not only by his Christian confession and the jurisdiction of parliament, but above all by the customs *(ordinances)* that had been passed down through history, for these "are maintained for the king and until such a time as the princes lose their titles; and when he wishes to do something, he must comply in fact with their commands."[55]

This is not the same as referring to divine right—something that was also done at the time. Rather, it refers to the legitimation of rulership by a criterion of immanence (a criterion inherent in rulership itself) and thus much more susceptible to controls than any principle which originates in some transcendent realm and therefore must first be interpreted. Given such a definition, any uprising against the ruler would appear almost normal, or at least stripped of all the pathos otherwise attached to attempts to seize power by overthrowing the ruler. The nonchalance with which La Rochefoucauld and above all Cardinal Retz described the role they played in the Fronde was symptomatic for a rebellion that, as it were, still remained within the "system." This aspect of the Fronde is clearly revealed in Leopold von Ranke's description of the fate of Henri II, Duke of Montmorency:

> If provincial ideas relating to the estates were alive anywhere, then they were alive in Languedoc. People referred to old histories and discovered that the French royal house had enjoyed only very slight authority in former times, and they came to believe that it should once again be forced to abide by these original restrictions . . . It is a moot point whether the governor of Languedoc, Montmorency, really was enthralled by the idea: for a time he had been accused of showing too much lenience toward the royal court. But he now took up the histories as support for a political stance which he had decided to adopt.
>
> Henri II, Duke of Montmorency, . . . had a chivalrous, noble temperament, was generous and brilliant, courageous and ambitious, like some of the other, similar figures that the house of Montmorency had produced over the course of time. Like his forefathers, he generally concurred with the powers invested in royalty; he was on the best of personal terms with Richelieu; it is known that they loved to take dinner together.[56]

Montmorency's behavior did not fit in with the forms of action taken by other members of the Fronde. The military advance on Castelnaudari, as Ranke described it, was nothing other than a desperate attempt to act, an excess of action culminating in a fiasco that was only to be expected: Montmorency was captured and beheaded on October 30, 1632, in the courtyard of the town hall of Toulouse. He made sure beforehand that Richelieu, who had ordered his execution, was sent (to use Ranke's words again) "one of the most beautiful pictures in his collection."

Montmorency's "death wish," the end of a social type who "did *not* determine sociocultural developments,"[57] as Claessens puts it, cannot be understood if we refer only to the failure of his own actions. What is also of immense importance is the fact that he had previously already failed: in the salon. Montmorency had been the "illustrious servant" of Madame de Sablé, who eventually broke off the relationship because she suffered from the "mediocrity of his mind"![58] Montmorency's fate illustrates the link between the two avenues for action: one had to be successful either in the salon or in battle. Once Montmorency had failed in the salon he was literally left no other option but death, once defeat in the field was certain.

In his failure, Montmorency symbolizes a society in which the antagonistic parts that composed the society were dependent on one another and knew it. This dependence of the individual parts of the "mechanism" is also to be seen in the forms taken by boredom and melancholy. The court was governed by ennui but was nevertheless held in check by etiquette. Ennui held sway in the salon and was "processed" collectively, in the literal sense of the word: the literary production of the salon was processed boredom.

Nevertheless, La Bruyère's claim that boredom entered the world in the guise of laziness is anything but accurate with reference to the salons. Boredom in the salons was the boredom more of those disempowered than of those with no work to occupy them, and the difference between La Bruyère the citizen and a cosmopolitan like La Rochefoucauld is also mirrored in the categories they used to describe boredom. For the latter, power was both a yardstick to measure suitable behavior in society and a compulsion to behave accordingly, whereas for the former the "bourgeois" category of work was decisive. In this sense, La Bruyère's conception was evidently closer to those of modernity; thus, the Chevalier de Jaucourt referred to La Bruyère in his article on ennui for the *Encyclopédie*.

The case of melancholy, which is also closely connected here with ennui, is similar. To recommend work as an antidote for melancholy and boredom first becomes a possible option once the emancipation of the bourgeoisie has reached such heights that the bourgeois can emulate the behavioral patterns of the aristocracy. As we shall see below, it is precisely in the eighteenth century—which, in Germany at least, inaugurated the economic and political ascendancy of the bourgeoisie—that the desire and longing to imitate the aristocracy coincided with the necessity of having to work. One had to work in order to create a basis for sufficient "relief" from social duties in the first place; and this, in turn, was the precondition for boredom. The aristocracy is not helped by the advice that it should work because— hindered by direct legal norms, by prohibitions on their doing business, and so forth—it was from the outset neither able nor allowed to work. In the nineteenth century the typical rejection of work as a partial cure for boredom is found in Kierkegaard's writings. This rejection is justified by reference to boredom as a socially unmediated "existential" quality—a position behind which Kierkegaard the *rentier* lurks.

The boredom of the salons that resulted from a deprivation of political rights created a certain relation to a socially prominent agency of order. Revolt had become impossible, and open opposition had been eliminated as a behavioral option. The drive for dis-order, however, which grew out of people's dissatisfaction with the inflexible order of the court, paved a way for itself: the salon became a sort of "open elite"—to the same degree that the importance of the bourgeoisie increased, owing to its rising financial power and the concomitant ability to buy positions of office. Members of the bourgeoisie forced their way into the salons at an early date. Vincent Voiture, of whom Condé remarked that "if he were of my rank he would be intolerable," had access to the salon of Madame de Rambouillet; and Guez de Balzac—who, among other things, coined the concept of *urbanité*—gained entry to that of Madame des Loges. The court continued to determine fashion, yet public opinion was formed in the salon; and gradually an opposition that could not be expressed in public grew in private circles. Yet boredom did not disappear from the salons of the eighteenth century, either. Madame du Deffand wrote to Voltaire: "For heaven's sake, please save me from boredom ... I am no longer able to take interest in anything; everything bores me to death—history, philosophy, novels, plays."[59] As a consequence, at this time the salons were open to everyone—with the exception of melancholics.[60] Whereas the aristocratic salon had provided a refuge from the ban on melancholy in court, the "bourgeois" salon (Madame Geoffrin was never received at court) had no time for "bores" or melancholics: these would have endangered the salon as an institution, just as they had threatened the court in earlier times. However, there was now no place left for them to escape to— they could flee only into individuality itself. The boredom revealed in Madame du Deffand's letter was no longer in keeping with that of La Rochefoucauld. Chateaubriand was already announcing his arrival: "He is a new man ... A man of unbounded sensibilities, bathed in proper tears. He has a religious soul full of sentiments for the Church. It is a melancholy that belongs only to him."[61] This retreat arose less from a new "type," who emerged without anyone's knowing why, than from a change in society's consciousness. Society henceforth knew no refuge for melancholy other than the individual—who could choose only religion as a support. La Rochefoucauld, the "libertine"[62] and melancholic of the salons, had vanished; Chateaubriand and the "Genius of Christianity" remained. Courtly rationality, personified in the absolute state under Louis XIV, climaxed in internal calm and order—at least with regard to the strata that influenced rulership. The boredom of the epoch resulted from the feeling that nothing could be changed and nothing accomplished: the contents of the world were fixed.

In such a constellation, melancholy seized those who had attempted to change the relations of rulership, and had failed. La Rochefoucauld, who was called the moralist of the Fronde, is its melancholic par excellence. Whereas the courtiers "modeled their affects" in order either not to show boredom or to learn how to be bored in keeping with their status, in the salon the compulsion to cope with resignation led to a refinement of customs. We have already described how the behavioral forms in the salon, determined by the prevailing ideal of *honnêteté*, were based on a sublimated inhibition of affects and how simultaneously a stronger inclination toward public expression brought emotions under collective control. La Rochefoucauld's maxims were a manifestation of this control. At the same time, however, they signaled the ironization of every emotion that could be called up at random in public without a particular reason: "You cry in order to gain recognition for being soft-hearted; you cry so that others will cry for you; and, finally, you cry out of shame that you are not crying."[63]

La Rochefoucauld differentiated sharply between *honnêteté*, which took the form of concurrence between private motives and their public "presentation," and *politesse mondaine* (fashionable politeness), which paid heed only to the public and to this end made use of false emotions: here, *amour-propre* came into play. Wherever melancholy showed itself, however, whether in the form of *honnêteté* or only as "fashionable politeness," it was nevertheless compelled to conform; this was prescribed by prevailing ideals and by the pressure of established power relations. Bearing this in mind, Ivanoff expressly stated that the melancholy of a La Rochefoucauld differed considerably from that of the nineteenth century: "But if La Rochefoucauld had a reason to be pessimistic and if he was so, in effect, then one would be quite wrong to imagine that he followed the example of Byronic heroes, evading the world and detesting society."[64] Anticipating our discussion of this syndrome, we can speak here of melancholy without a flight from the world.

In its heyday, courtly rationality achieved such a degree of obligatoriness that its prescriptions held true even for those who had long since become estranged from the court: "As a measure of collective security, society had now to impose on all its members rules that no one fully believed in but that could guarantee outward peace while perpetuating lethal inner conflict."[65] Resignative behavior was also subject to this compulsion to conform. We must constantly keep in mind that the members of a society organized in terms of courtly rationality were brought up to follow the examples of the *honnête homme* and the soldier, and that resignation had no place in this system. (In this context, resignation and melancholy signify different points in a continuum of human behavior that turns away from the "world." Resignation entails a feeling of loss, disappointment, and defeat; melancholy is an enduring emotional and affective state that follows this moment of resignation.)

"The impossibility of being happy caused us to adopt a stance based on sensitiveness and to turn our attention to the philosophers."[66] Baron Grimm's statement of 1776, in fact, already held true for those who had failed in the seventeenth century. A man like La Rochefoucauld—who had been brought up to lead a life of combat, full of events and geared to ruling—had to first learn to "conduct" his sensibilities in such a manner that they helped him less to get on in the world than to turn away from it with dignity and moderation. He who appeared to be made for the battlefield could not simply dismount from his charger and enter the salon. This does not mean that such a change in behavioral patterns was impossible—the life of the courtier, as we have seen, consisted precisely of the institutionalized alternation between court and army; but having to renounce the one alternative and devote oneself completely to the other was indeed difficult.[67]

The surprising closeness to the world of the form of melancholy embodied by La Rochefoucauld rests on the fact that such people were brought up in terms of a behavioral ideal that did not lose its validity solely because ambitious plans had been shattered. The seventeenth-century melancholic accordingly remained not only "a man of the world" but "within the system," despite his distance from the center of action—namely, the court. The melancholy of a La Rochefoucauld was the melancholy of a closed culture that permitted its members only minimal deviation within a limited framework of conformity. The ideal of *honnêteté* retained its validity even in a state of melancholy, and, once learned, the ability to model one's affects and sensitize one's emotions in terms of preserving the system continued to play an influential role. The psychology of the day corresponded to this: it demanded of the individual that he or she be oriented toward society and did not, as did its counterpart in the eighteenth century, posit psyche and society as diametrically opposed entities. Such a psychology was hardly revolutionary, yet it likewise did not become embroiled in that apology for introversion that resulted from setting one's sights too high.

A closed culture, as exhibited by the court under absolutism, can also be defined as the interlinking of maximal behavioral alternatives which differ as marginally as possible from each other (namely etiquette) and show a minimum of tolerated deviation. Nevertheless, melancholic deviation functions in such a society to preserve the system, because it orients itself toward a generally accepted example. La Rochefoucauld did not start out to condemn the court but at most dreamed of himself ruling, and mourned after the *tabouret* that he never received (for his wife). The melancholy of the salon was initially still collective in reference and always oriented to the world. When the aristocracy itself began dismantling the new form of aristocratization staged by the ruler—they relinquished their distance, and the first bourgeois began streaming into the salons—there arose a form of deviation that led out of the system. Now that the salons were opening themselves to elements from "below" and the bourgeoisie were beginning to penetrate the circles of the aristocracy, the mechanism of kingship began, almost imperceptibly, to shift. It was not until the eighteenth century that there emerged a cult of introversion oriented toward the example of nature, beyond society and opposed to it. "To, as it were, transpose the salon into nature"[68] thus accords—as Helmut Hatzfeld suggests—not only with the "emotional confusion" of the Rococo but also with the trend to move the agency of power out of the system, whether into the individual alone or into nature, for both permit external assessment. In France, eighteenth-century melancholy—and we shall now turn our attention to its German "variant"—already meant a withdrawal into introversion. It had little in common with seventeenth-century resignation, which was closely allied with worldy affairs. The sentimental individual's desire to return to nature created the distance from society that allowed effective criticism of the system: Rousseau's successor was Robespierre.

4 On the Origins of Bourgeois Melancholy: Germany in the Eighteenth Century

> ... for things German and things bourgeois—are
> one and the same.
>
> Thomas Mann, *Observations of an Unpolitical Person*

Bourgeois Escapism

In this chapter we will focus exclusively on melancholy within the German bourgeoisie, in order to lend greater definition to a trend that was decisive for the development of Germany. Progressive approaches to this topic, such as those which Georg Lukács contrasts in *Goethe and His Age* and *The Destruction of Reason,* will not be treated in detail. We shall emphasize that aspect of the wretched state of Germany which resulted from the permanent belatedness of the German bourgeoisie: having at long last made up its mind to do progressive battle with the feudal aristocracy, in a process of vigorous economic emancipation, it found itself confronted by an up-and-coming proletariat at a stage when it itself was only just forming. Marx and Engels described the genesis of bourgeois melancholy, the latter when he claimed that the Schillerian flight into Kantian ideals merely entailed the replacement of a blatant form of misery by a rapturous one ("German Socialism in Verse and Prose"); and both of them when they denounced the "ideational raising of things to a status above the earth" for being a mystification of real impotence. In *The German Ideology,* Marx and Engels condemn Max Stirner for something that could be traced back to the eighteenth century: "The unity of sentimentality and bragging is *rebellion.* Directed outwards, against others, it is bragging; directed inwards, like grumbling-in-oneself, it is sentimentality. It is the specific expression of the impotent dissatisfaction of the philistine."[1] In this chapter we shall concentrate more on

sentimentality (or, in terms of its being a supposed fact of anthropology, melancholy) and less on ostentation, and even less on attempts to oppose something to the philistine mixture of the two. Only Kant's work contains a hint at a possible alternative, which we shall examine briefly. To return to the polemic against Stirner: the "critical hurrah" resounds perhaps more weakly than it once did, yet the "uncritical miserable state" is all the more vociferous.[2]

To characterize the eighteenth century, Norbert Elias speaks of the difference between the francophile, French-speaking upper stratum of German society and

> a German-speaking, middle-class stratum of intelligentsia, recruited chiefly from the bourgeois "servers of princes" or officials in the broadest sense, and occasionally also from the landed nobility. This latter is a stratum *far removed from political activity*, scarcely thinking in political terms and only tentatively in national ones, whose legitimation consists primarily in its intellectual, scientific or artistic *accomplishments*. Counterposed to it is an upper class which "accomplishes" nothing in the sense in which others do, but for which the shaping of its distinguished and distinctive *behavior* is central to its self-image and self-justification.[3]

Elias acknowledges that there are thoughts and feelings in this bourgeois middle-class stratum of the intelligentsia, but "nothing which was able in any sense to lead to concrete political action. The structure of this absolutist society of petty states offered no opening for it. Bourgeois elements gained self-assurance, but the framework of the absolute states was completely unshaken. The bourgeois elements were excluded from any political activity. At most, they could 'think and write' independently; they could not act independently. In this situation, writing becomes the most important outlet." And (following the thought through to its end) these people "driven" to writing often lived "in isolation or solitude; an elite in relation to the people, persons of the second rank in the eyes of the courtly aristocracy. Again and again one can see in these works the connection between this social situation and the ideals of which they speak: the love of nature and freedom, the solitary exaltation, the surrender to the excitement of one's own heart, unhindered by 'cold reason.'"[4]

In the context of our study, great importance must be attached to studying the behavior of a stratum of society—the bourgeoisie—who, having been elbowed out of political action, are forced among other things to retreat into literature. Elements of this flight (which will be of significance later) are outlined by Elias: the concept of the ideal, the opposition between "accomplishment" (by the bourgeoisie) on the one hand, and "behavior" (of the aristocracy) on the other, a rapturous enthusiasm for nature, a yearning for solitude, and above all "the emotions of one's own heart"—a phrase laden with feeling, yet so empty of meaning. All of these elements express the *form assumed by* bourgeois escapism at this time. Here we shall examine the connection between enforced political abstinence and the rearrangement of "the structure of affects" among precisely these inhibited strata; a link emerges with exceptional clarity in the literature of the day. In his essay "Towards a Sociology of the Mind," Karl Mannheim uses a form of argument similar to that adopted by Elias; both works were conceived at the same time.[5] Our method thus far can be classified as employing a sociology of knowledge—part of a discipline of which more is expected and demanded than some banal and comical "reflections on the hunter in the green coat or the diplomat in the black tails."[6]

Mannheim's overall conception cannot be presented here in detail. To prove that his hypotheses can be applied to the time span studied here, let us recall the praise that Mannheim gives to Hegel's phenomenology in "Towards a Sociology of the Mind": "Hegel's system was not mere philosophy, but a climactic expression of the insights of preceding epochs."[7] Of these past epochs, the one primarily of concern is that which, with the appearance of an educated middle class, first made possible philosophies such as Hegel's.

Mannheim's attack was leveled initially against an immanentist history of ideas that suppressed any link between ideational and real factors, granting illicit primacy to the former. Adherents of such a conception, he claims, are found in the "teaching profession"; they have "mostly been philologists, historians and philosophers." Mannheim believes this leads to the following conclusion: "an existence which is some steps removed from the theatre of events tends to be contemplative and therefore subject to certain delusions about the nature of reality." He goes on to speak of the "intramural illusion" of such theoreticians of "self-begotten intellect" and considers their false generalizations and one-sidedness to be caused by their abstaining from action, for "action exposes an illusion quicker than contemplation." Mannheim attributes the flight from reality and the suppression of a social "third dimension" to the "over-sublimation of the spirit" that began with Luther and to the conception—also originating with Luther—that spiritual freedom is independent from the social structure, a view which culminated in Fichte's work. Particularly marked is a syndrome characterized by an actual inhibited state of action, the inclination toward contemplation, and the preference for absolute conceptions of what constituted "spirit" in eighteenth- and nineteenth-century Germany: "This process was motivated by the thwarted aspirations of the German peasantry and the middle classes in the eighteenth and nineteenth centuries." The affinity between Elias and Mannheim is especially clear when the latter continues: "Lacking a concrete socio-political focus for their thought and actions, the educated German middle classes made their accommodation to the bureaucratic state and spiritualized the idea of freedom to mean intellectual indeterminism. This introverted concept of freedom has become the keystone of the immanence theory and one of the main academic barriers to a sociological approach to history, thought, and politics."[8]

Mannheim's train of thought corresponds to some of the arguments Elias puts forward. However, the former perhaps overly suppresses the compulsive character of this development: "contemplative aloofness" is a concept that contains an excessively strong active component and hides the fact that the bourgeois flight into introversion was forced upon it by the prevailing relations of power. Ultimately, we are dealing with the admissible suspicion as to whether this is an ideological affair; yet, such a suspicion is grounded not in the situation itself but rather in the false consciousness that justifies such an adverse situation.[9] This problematic question need not, however, detain us here.

Before concluding our survey of the power relations predominant in Germany in the eighteenth century, we must note the high degree of abstraction and the level of generalization inherent in the statements adopted by Mannheim and Elias. In a comprehensive study of the "*embourgeoisement* of German art, literature, and music in the eighteenth century," Leo Balet further differentiated the middle bourgeois stratum, discerning a group that aspired to rise into the ranks of the grand bourgeoisie in order to participate in economic expansion, and another group that was reactionary and "resigned and . . . [harked] back to the good old days with their fixed guild-like obligations and associations . . . The ruling prince skillfully played off the bourgeois against the aristocracy and the aristocracy against the burgher class, thus keeping both more comfortably in check and preserving his absolute powers."[10]

Retreat from the World

The following is not intended to provide what would in any case necessarily be a fragmentary cultural history of the nineteenth century. The time span involved demarcates only roughly the bounds of the present investigation: our topic will be social constellations of dominance and affective trends, and we shall explore how the bourgeoisie, striving for power but still excluded from it, dealt with this exclusion.

In his diary, Wilhelm Dilthey attempted to analyze eighteenth- and early nineteenth-century *Weltschmerz*. After assuring the reader that the cause and nature of such *Weltschmerz* had seldom been determined accurately, Dilthey continued: "It was clear that the eighteenth and early nineteenth centuries, being the age of individualism, would bring forth a thoroughly pathological literature in which the individual's endeavors to engender the overall life of humankind, of the ideal, became a painful, fatal (!) disease, for the time was not ripe for the ideal to be grasped within life." If we bear Mannheim's and Elias's statements in mind, quite apart from Marx's concrete, economic analysis of "German wretchedness," we notice how Dilthey inappropriately gives an "adequate" treatment of his subject—that is, one lacking in distance. He excludes the social context from his analysis in a manner quite in keeping with an immanentist theory of the Spirit, and he posits the age of individualism without inquiring as to its cause. The Fichtean system, he says, looks down "from the clear heights of the ideal into the common activities of reality"—yet he does not become suspicious and inquire how it arrived at those heights in the first place and what right it had to be there. Philosophy, he claims, turned its back painfully on common life and transported itself to "the silent, holy, pure heart of Nature. It is this that is the source from which the fatal (sic) pain of Werther and Hyperion flows."[11]

Dilthey's mention of Werther and Hyperion shows both how he attempts to derive literature from Idealist premises, and the extent to which in so doing he neglects society as a mediating agency. Bourgeois melancholy, and particularly the bourgeois literature of the eighteenth century, is, however, an expression of a particular social situation. This melancholy describes a trend of the times that can be clearly recognized if one takes the existing *power relations* and the *atmosphere* typical of the day as one's point of reference. If, by contrast, one takes rationalist philosophy as a yardstick (as does Rudolf Unger, for example), then one can emphasize the self-assurance and joyfulness of the age.[12] In this case it must be pietism that causes the turn toward "introversion and the personal" and away from "untenable enthusing, world-escaping asceticism, empty subjectivism, or the frivolous ranking of emotions." However, such an argument fails to recognize the specific character of German rationalism, which is a typical "school," not a world philosophy, and never became a doctrine that determined the shape of society. At best it found a form in personalities such as Lessing, who, however, remained isolated cases.

If, when analyzing eighteeneth-century melancholy, we search back in time for the historical boundary involved, we again encounter the problem of order which figured so prominently in our observations on utopias and the prohibition of melancholy, and which also appeared in our investigation of French society, ossified in its order at the high point of absolutism. Compared with the seventeenth century, the hundred years that followed showed a certain loss of order. The stability of absolutism, under the pressure of economic developments, began to give way. The balance of economic power shifted to such an extent that by the middle of the eighteenth century, merchant capital already exerted more power than did the imitative absolutist rulers of Germany's petty princedoms. This economic dominance did not, however, extend to the arena of politics: only the monied bourgeois was in a position to place stock in the immediate future, whereas the great majority of the petit bourgeois continued to be excluded from participating in economic expansion and real political power. Resignation, the thorn in the side of the petit bourgeoisie, became a greater affliction than ever.

The order that had originally entered into flux with the rise of a monied bourgeoisie and aristocracy found renewed stability through a bureaucratic apparatus strengthened by (in Hauser's words) "bureaucratization of government, the transfer of functions erstwhile exercised by autonomous bodies to state offices, the preference for decrees and regulations and the general tendency to regiment public and private life." [13] Whereas in France an aristocratic bureaucracy took its place alongside the court nobles, the aristocracy, and the landed gentry, in Germany the aristocracy itself became an aristocratic officialdom, and the bourgeoisie had to be satisfied with subaltern positions. Its passivity stemmed from this state of affairs; and because the intelligentsia was composed of members of a middle class that was economically weak, this passivity seized the whole of cultural life and led to a fatal division between the private and the political spheres. At this time, what Flaubert would later describe as the "dogma in the life of the artist" (namely, "to live like a bourgeois and think like a demi-god") [14] and what Gottfried Benn termed a "double life" already held true as a syndrome in bourgeois aesthetics.

Wilhelm von Humboldt, in his essay on the eighteenth century,

expressed something similar when he stated that "the external activities of Man can never be sufficiently reclaimed for the realm of Necessity, his Spirit never sufficiently reinstated in the sphere of the Infinite."
Humboldt, however, perceived the extent to which this maxim had
already been prescribed by an age in which "one encounters more
frequently than elsewhere passivity and laxness hand in hand with
education and intellectual ability," and to which he later ascribed a
"sickly mental disposition" that "made a person more thoughtfully
contemplative and sensitive than active and productive." [15]

Weltschmerz, melancholy, and hypochondria resulted from the
enforced hypertrophy of the realm of reflection, from imposed loss
of the ability to exercise real power, and from the consequent pressure
to justify one's situation. The three concepts cannot be separated,
because at the time they were all used as synonyms; and not least for
this reason, each had a characteristic hue of its own. This situation is
not peculiar to eighteenth-century Germany, but it takes on such a
pronounced form there that we need not look at conditions elsewhere. (Here we have a good vantage point from which to outline
the relationship between political behavior and a melancholic attitude
that was so fatal specifically for German history: from the melancholy
of the German bourgeoisie when embarking on an economic emancipation that could never be followed by political freedom, to the
"inability to mourn"—Alexander Mitscherlich's phrase, describing
the psychological situation in post–World War II Germany—which
prevented an appropriate reaction to the political and moral collapse
of fascism. In the former case, melancholy took the place of progressive political activity; in the latter, it was an absence of mourning in
the face of criminal behavior. The German economic miracle served
as, and remained, compensation for this.)

What is of sociological relevance here is that the early form of personal *Weltschmerz* was expanded to become general or cosmological,[16]
an overall "imbalance between a feeling for life" and "a view of the
world" (Max Wieser).[17] For "*this is what was strange with regard to
eighteenth-century sentimentality—namely, that the individual's sentimental
affliction was also the sentimental affliction of most people of the time* . . . The
sentimentality of the age could be described as a disease, for people
felt themselves to be sick with it, even if they heightened this feeling
of sickness to the point of an imaginary sense of well-being."[18] (The
culmination of this line of argument needs to be amended. The
feeling of sickness did not turn into a sense of well-being; but the
consciousness that people created the disease *themselves*—whether
they admitted this or not—itself engendered a sense of satisfaction.)

In eighteenth-century German society the phenomenon of bourgeois melancholy assumed a glittering variety of forms; only a rough outline, a mere selection, will be provided here. This "splintering" or differentiation of the phenomenon is most certainly of a secondary nature and stems from the fact that eighteenth-century sources are available and have been sifted through and studied by scholars in numerous disciplines, including sociology. Nevertheless, what may strike the eye most is the manner in which melancholy spread within one particular social class, one that took literature as its refuge in its flight from society. The resignative phenomena of the age thus lost their collective character as a result of individual artistic creations, which, although they could not escape the overall affective state of the day, nevertheless managed to process and reflect this in an original fashion.

It becomes clear that the bourgeoisie was attempting to deny that the socially caused resignation was indeed thus caused—for resignation, because it was transformed into melancholy in the above manner, was supposedly engendered solely in the individual's psyche. Melancholy and the search for originality must be viewed as part and parcel of the same thing.

The eighteenth century's affinity to the Renaissance resides more in its craving for originality than in its forms of resignation. A "socially withdrawn" type of literature (as Hans Norbert Fügen calls it) can evolve only when bourgeois society has attained its goals. The "genius" movement of the late eighteenth century—a trend in German literature that is commonly associated with Lessing, the young Herder, and Goethe, and that emphasized the unique and transcendent power of creative "original genius" *(Originalgenie)*—took the Renaissance as its reference point in its craving for originality; yet it was unable to lessen the pressure for enforcing resignation.

Society and Solitude

Solitude is *the* topic of our age. And hardly anyone today can reflect on solitude without referring to Johann Georg Zimmermann's book, which we shall discuss below. Until well into the sixteenth century, the meaning of the word "solitude" *(Einsamkeit)* was not far from that of "unity," "harmony," "community" *(Einheit, Eintracht, Gemeinsamkeit,* each of which contains the word *ein,* meaning "one").[19] And this is no coincidence, if an immanentist theory of Spirit and the notion of an inner freedom independent of external circumstance can both be traced back to Luther, as Mannheim believed. Let us therefore keep in mind that when solitude and society became separate terms, the differentiation constituted, historically speaking, a special case of its own. The picture Karl Vossler draws of Spanish recluses (or rather "incluses" in the true plural form) is foreign to current thinking, bound up as it is in a wealth of what were then self-evident thoughts: recluses "are not to be confused with the hermits [who had] themselves walled up near monasteries or even on very busy streets or public squares—a chilling sight, a wonder, and a solace for the passer-by."[20] Here, solitude and society are not separate terms but interwoven. This again shows the capacity of stable traditional cultures to integrate a certain degree of deviance, to "absorb" it and "insert" it into the overall design of things. In France, the salon fulfilled a similar function. In his family chronicle, W. H. Riehl termed the salon "a foreign offshoot grafted onto the German house" and described the building alterations that were aimed at promoting not a sociable atmosphere but solitude: members of a family began, as a habit, to isolate themselves *within* the house.

The love of solitude in the eighteenth century also sprang from aesthetic motives: the dictum *solitudo musis amica* holds true not only for Tibur, Tusculum, and Sils Maria[21] but also for the bourgeois poets of the eighteenth century. However, the penchant for solitude has the same source as the ornamental version of it presented in poetry: isolation from power, and despair in the face of a social order that cannot be dismantled. Johann Georg Zimmermann most clearly expressed this proclivity (especially in his four-volume work *Solitude Considered*), without himself falling prey to it. His views, like those of Freiherr von Knigge, occasionally approximated presociological insights, such as when he described as solitary "a Lady brought up with all the prejudices of an inhabitant of an ancient German castle," and "in a society where no one other than she has sixteen rooms to themselves" (1796 translation).[22] Yet such starting points were rarely expanded upon subsequently.

Zimmermann clearly recognized that the bourgeoisie's inclination to at least imitate an aristocracy it could not actually aspire to become was a proclivity specific to that class: "Germany . . . was perhaps never as sociable as now. All the distractions of the world of the great are parroted by the lower strata. Time is in general wasted. A person who is nothing by his own efforts occasionally hangs on to other people in order not to have to do anything of his own volition. To stand on one's own two feet is, as is living alone, considered a disgrace in Germany today" (I, p. 26). However: "Everything that we conduct or do, be it sitting or walking, effecting something or transacting, often all this is driven on by only one motive: the fear of boredom!" (I, p. 30). Furthermore, boredom appears to have been caused by doing the rounds of visits," a practice likewise copied from the aristocracy; solitude remained an aid against this boredom. Typically, the motif of genius that had been resorted to at least since Petrarch was then applied, for the "common man" knew neither boredom nor solitude. Leopardi, Schopenhauer, and Nietzsche were to take up this quasi-aristocratic conception.[23] And just as in Petrarch's work, where the *miser occupatus* was juxtaposed with the *felix solitarius*, this solitude was conceived not in religious but in secular terms. The site of solitude was no longer the monastery but the small town: "Small towns have an undeniable advantage over large cities with reference to one's dealings with oneself. How one profits from the time and leisure available, freedom and tranquility; and how such happiness flees from large cities, in which our every thought suffocates under the verbage heeped upon us from all sides" (III, p. 228). Admittedly, the small town was an advantage only if one could save oneself from the "boredom of the high aristocracy." The inconsistency in Zimmermann's thought can be easily explained: his polemic, aimed at Jacob Hermann Obereit,[24] was intended to contest the latter's view that the true "vanquishers of worldliness" were to be found in monasteries. Zimmermann countered this by arguing that "fearful boredom and muiltifarious illnesses of the body and the soul are an undeniable effect of solitude on monks and hermits" (II, p. 111); by contrast, the "striving for solitude" was "the most general sympton of melancholy" (II, p. 159).

This link between boredom, solitude, and melancholy, which Zimmermann criticized, disappeared—or rather completely changed in nature—as soon as the solitude in question became secular as opposed to religious. In the latter context, Zimmermann says suddenly that "all time lost by an earthling is time won for the solitary person" (III, p. 295) and advises the writer to "segregate himself off from people, to seek out the woods and forests, to withdraw completely into himself. In other words, everything he does, everything he achieves, is an affect of solitude" (III, p. 353).[25] Ultimately, melancholy is rehabilitated: "A sort of sweet melancholy overcomes us . . . from time to time, in the lap of rural tranquility, when viewing all Nature's beauty," and "solitude on occasion, but of course not always, transforms deep despondency into sweet melancholy" (IV, pp. 38, 196).

Zimmermann's virtually concealed conception of solitude is particularly well suited to demonstrate the affinity such concepts had to melancholic thought of the time. Those parts of his notion which seem to have risen above the bounds laid down by his age prove to be polemical elements directed against a religious understanding of solitude; in contrast to the latter, the secular approach ventured to play the world off against an "overcoming of the world." Viewed thus, Zimmerman's polemic yields insights, as it were, by chance—for instance, when he derides the "troublesome pestilence of the genius in Germany," which would perhaps have been less virulent "had it not circulated most amongst raw young people who lived cut off from all dealings with the world [and who] were subject to wild attacks of self-importance in their bacchantic solitude and to pathetic dreams of their powers" (II, p. 9). When he turns once more to his own conception, his view of the solitude of his age is immediately perceivable and his preference for a "great society" is, like that of the clergy with whom he feuded, merely the wish "to be allowed to have a say in an area where no inhibiting barriers originating in society, the estates, or tradition block the 'genius' from taking his place as a full-fledged member among other full-fledged members in the field of art."[26]

The noted translator Johann Nicolaus Meinhard (1727–1767) seems to have been less affected by the ambiguity necessitated by the polemic against rivals in literary matters. Meinhard was a "down-to-earth person of the age who led an imaginary life in novels, dramas, letters, and weekly periodicals and yet took on historical reality in such personalities as Haller, Gellert, Lichtenberg, Hamman, and even Frederick the Great—as a hypochondriac."[27] At the time, hypochondria and melancholy were synonyms, and so the reference to melancholy is naturally included in Helmut Rehder's description of how Meinhard chose "tranquil and idyllic Erfurt" (a perfect phrase for this small town!) as his place of work, "purportedly because this town was most conducive to his health, but in reality because he could live out his work here undisturbed in melancholic solitude. Thus, he spent almost two years living incognito in an inn . . . In this manner, his scholarly existence was pursued within the narrow confines of contemplative monotony."[28]

In Christian Garve's reflections in his book *On Society and Solitude*, which appeared at the turn of the nineteenth century, the battle lines had already shifted. The image of cozy escapism still existed: "According to everything that can contribute to Tranquillity, Leisure, and Tenacity when one concerns oneself with the Culture of the Mind—in all this, Philosophy with its lonely lamp has an advantage over the Rich and the Great, when they are assembled in their sumptuous illuminated ballrooms, and even over the rulers of the earth, when they stand at the head of their armies or ponder in their Council Chambers the fate of a people." Nevertheless, the disadvantages of such seclusion do not elude Garve: "But because of this the person in question must fear a different abyss, which holds as much danger for true instruction and especially for the exaltation of the spirit as do distraction and irritated sensuousness; I refer to sluggishness, torpidity, and a certain depression of the spirit."[29] Throughout his work, Garve adopts a critical, enlightened stance with respect to solitude, and in statements such as the following, the eighteenth-century conception of solitude has already receded far into the background: "In general, a strain of melancholy always goes hand in hand with solitude, whereas society is linked with cheerfulness." And he says: "Overall, and in the nature of things, society seems to be made for times of health, vivacity, and amusement; solitude, by contrast, seems to be the natural haven of the infirm, the grieved, and the stricken."[30]

The eighteenth-century bourgeoisie, in its yearning for solitude, created the preconditions for an appreciation of melancholy. Impotent in the face of rule by the aristocracy, the bourgeoisie preferred nature to society, and the small town idyll is then juxtaposed with the residential palace, which was often enough a small town in itself. This conception of solitude contained, however, additional components of the affinity for melancholy: a cult of friendship and of letter writing, and above all a turn back to the self and a privileging of the emotions.[31] It is here that practical psychology created a safety valve for itself so that it could find a source of intrinsic value within enforced inactivity and powerlessness. The introversion espoused by a large portion of German bourgeois literature in the eighteenth century first became possible when solitude was played off against society, genius against worldliness, leisure against (aristocratic) boredom, country against city, small town against residential palace, nature against community, and inner freedom against external compulsion.

On the Court Jester

Bourgeois melancholy assumed forms unlike those of the melancholy displayed by a nobility disempowered through an unsuccessful revolt. Indeed, the phenomenon of solitude helps us describe this difference: the category of the individual was bourgeois in nature, whereas the courtier, who was also a man of the world, remained the aristocratic ideal, since for the aristocrat the court signified the world. It was necessary to continue to ban melancholy from the court; sover-

eignty could countenance no mournfulness. At most, it was accorded
to the ruler himself, as a privilege. That melancholy was out of place
at court had already been shown by medieval knighthood, where joy
appeared as the expression of an "incontestable demand made by
social life" and where the term *werelt* ("a worldly person," "the world
of the court") was used to describe the "sociable person in a joyful,
festive society." Karl Korn added that "one instinctively thinks of the
French equivalent, *monde*." Hartmann von Aue, a medieval German
epic poet, laid out the rules of behavior when he wrote, "Swer ze
hove wesen sol, dem zimet freude wol" ("It behooves him who wants
to aspire to court life to be joyful"). The *precept of joy* is an integral
part of the court: "*Trûren*—being sad—is possible only insofar as the
individual segregates himself from his community of feudal peers."[32]

This double prescription of a *ban on melancholy* and a simultaneous
turning toward the world appears to have been typical for utopian
conceptions of society. The idea that was to be made reality—namely,
the totality of a planned life that was seamlessly absorbed into
society—allowed for no mournfulness, for its ultimate goal was to
engender happiness. The court likewise had to ban mournfulness,
for in the court—that is, "in the world"—even the emotions were
regulated. Courtly mournfulness was therefore the result of an order,
an emotional state prescribed by etiquette. Here, we once again see
the link between the reality of rulership and the modeling of affects.

In his heyday, the court jester became an institution: *le fou du Roi*
("the king's fool") was a *titre d'office,* a title of office. It was not only
the "customs of rich Irishmen" that obliged court jesters to "dispel by
means of a multiplicity of stories and tales all boredom and melancholy from those in the family who could not sleep."[33] The court
jester functioned as a herald of relief whose task consisted of exor-
cising the ruler's melancholy and affirming the latter in his position
as the only person privileged to enjoy melancholy at court. At the
same time, the jester served as a substitute: he took upon himself
everything that, by distracting the emotions, could prevent the ruler
from ruling. As a consequence, clowns today are still "officially"
funny and let mournfulness show through their make-up only in private—a legacy of their original function as court jesters. Thus, some
nobles "also found amusement in simpleminded, silly, melancholic
people and real buffoons, and used them as court jesters."[34] The
"court thinker," the phrase that Brentano used to refer to this figure,
alludes to the way in which the jester provided relief from the reflection inspired by melancholy, a point to be discussed below. Pascal
frequently touches on the theme: "The king is surrounded by people

who think only of distracting him and preventing him from thinking about himself. For any king who thinks about himself is unhappy."[35]

The jester was accepted to the extent that he remained within the system, and even when he displayed a permissible, preordained, minimal deviance from it. If he caused "minor abuses and breaches of the given order to be discovered" (Leo Balet), then he ceased to be treated preferentially. At a later date, Louis XIV even permitted La Bruyère to attack the court, provided that the king himself was treated with suitable devotion. Nick was thus justified in arguing that the agony of the court jester began with the rule of Louis XIV. For by then, the literary scholar had replaced the jester and was in a position to distinguish between court and ruler when treating the former as an object worthy of criticism. The court jester finally died out in the eighteenth century, and thus serves as a sort of clamp binding together different parts of our investigation. Balet dates the jester's end to 1763, asserting that he disappeared because other concepts, such as human rights and human dignity, gradually came into vogue. These were not the only factors accelerating the jester's decline, though we must not forget that the jester, despite his preferential position and freedom within the system, remained deprived of all rights, despite his title.

Nick attempted to explain the court jester's gradual extinction in the eighteenth century by referring to the gradual reconciliation between aristocracy and bourgeoisie: "German literature suddenly rose to amazing prominence. There were now German nobles who surrounded themselves with German authors not for the purpose of some barren entertainment but with a view to serious intellectual enjoyment. Here and there an amusing councillor became aulic councillor, or even privy councillor."[36] The jester, however, found himself out of a job above all because bourgeois melancholy came into being. If people other than the ruler were allowed to be melancholic, then any institution that dispelled melancholy and at the same time attested to melancholy as a privilege was bound to become redundant. Baudelaire described the age following the July Monarchy as one of "eternal sadness." The eighteenth-century bourgeoisie began to lay claim to the attitude of resignation that had once been reserved for the ruler. Yet only briefly did "blinkered, resigned conformism" (Adorno) signify that people no longer aspired to power; the paradox of bourgeois melancholy resides in the fact that the individual had already usurped what had hitherto been a forbidden privilege. The charge of boredom—when, as in Zimmermann's work, it was manifested as a complaint on the part of the aristocracy—now reappeared: life à la Rousseau seemed "boring and unrefined" to the aristocracy.[37]

At this juncture, nature became an indicator of boredom, just as the aristocratic *intérieur* inhabited by the court jester had in earlier times appeared to the bourgeoisie as an intimation of boredom. Nature knows no jesters. By means of the jester, whose function was to transform boredom into entertainment, court boredom began to spread among the common people. It was no longer the principle of power but rather the spirit that served as a *passepartout* for boredom: animals cannot be bored as can, supposedly, the average person, and if they are indeed bored, then we have to do with only "the most refined and most active of animals," as Nietzsche put it. The jester's loss of function revealed that the bourgeois world was turning away from courtly melancholy and aristocratic ennui.

And what happened to the office of dispeller of melancholy now vacated by the court jester? The dandy, on the model of Beau Brummell, was one form of successor. His "rule," as Otto Mann wrote, commenced in 1794 and had an effect because "he satisfied the need for whim felt by a bored society confined within strict convention."[38] The dandy, who has been memorably described as an aristocrat without a birthright,[39] relieved the court jester of his duties: the new jester donned an aristocratic attitude. The *flâneur*, whom Walter Benjamin studied in Baudelaire's work, must also be counted among the jester's successors: "Boredom in the production process arises when the latter is speeded up [by the machine]. With his ostentatious casualness, the *flâneur* protests this production process."[40] Now the jester dispelled only his own boredom. The struggle with the machine gave him an air of Don Quixote tilting at windmills.

Benjamin drew a connection between the *flâneur* and the problematics of melancholy when he spoke of the former's "spleen, a dam holding back pessimism." The reproach that we are exploiting an ambiguity here can immediately be parried, for the word, which first appeared in the fourteenth century as "splen," refers anatomically speaking to the spleen, which characteristically is linked to melancholy and in a metaphorical sense is a source of mournfulness and joy. In Alexander Pope's time, spleen came to denote a "melancholic disposition of the spirit."[41] In Baudelaire's writing, spleen has detached itself from melancholy and has become a form of eccentricity that allows one to link the *flâneur* with the court jester. For the *flâneur*, the boulevard becomes an *intérieur*, and the world becomes a mirror before which he must live and die (Benjamin). The fact that the *flâneur* has a touch of the detective about him, as Edgar Allen Poe noted, also points to the jester's acumen in a regimented world that claims to be free of chance. The loneliness in the crowd, which determined the character of Baudelaire's poetry, also appeared as "strangely jesting"; Benjamin wrote of the monadological structure of the *Flowers of Evil.*[42]

In like manner, the dandy could be defined as the court jester stripped of an audience—except that he himself wishes to become the audience. Making such great demands on the ability to reflect, the dandy claims for himself the label "genius": "The man of genius wants to be *one,* and thus solitary," says Baudelaire. He adds a demand for eccentricity that is in itself satisfying to the genius' traditional claim to solitude: "Glory is to remain as *one,* and to prostitute the self in a particular manner."[43] From this point on, the court jester remained alone, unto himself: "Dandyism is a degraded form of asceticism," said Camus. Robbed of an audience, the dandy played to himself. It is obvious that in such a situation melancholy is replaced by spleen, which knows only eccentricity as its object. The court jester, who was employed to dispel melancholy—or, to put it in modern terms, was an "entertainer"[44]—made use of his own eccentricity, meaning his own position as an outsider, in order to stabilize the system's "interior," namely the court. The deviance allowed the jester reflected the total conformity within the court. The eccentric stance adopted by the *flâneur* and the dandy served to stabilize not a system but only themselves: the *flâneur* protested the production process, and the dandy everyday norms. The *flâneur* and the dandy adhered to a program that no longer served society, which enjoyed that program from a distance; it served only the person who produced it. The "emotionless isolation of each individual within his or her private interests" (Engels) that characterizes modern commodity production is also seen in the *flâneur.* Benjamin hinted at this with reference to Baudelaire when he spoke of the mime "who plays the role of the poet when playing before the stalls and society, a role the genuine poet no longer needs and which only allocates him a free space in which to move in the form of mimicry."[45]

It does not matter whether Benjamin is referring to a poet or a court jester; the fact remains that literature assumed the jester's function. The case of the mime, who was once a poet, and the dandy, who evolved out of the court jester, demonstrates the differentiation within a society that was already so splintered internally that it could no longer have its emotional resources put back into order by employees hired specially for this purpose. The problem of how to dispel one's ennui arose only during people's organized leisure time, the obverse of which was the unchanging monotony of the world of work. Thus, the comic opera—"a mutual insurance company for the struggle against boredom," as Jacques Offenbach termed it—came into being during an age in which capitalism was prospering. The institutions that dispelled melancholy continued to do so in the interests of the rulers; but they became progressively more ineffective with the increasing diffuseness of the emotions they were intended to regulate. There was no longer a closed and dominant culture with defined centers (such as the absolutist court) from which ennui could be held at bay, at least superficially. With the dissolution of such "melancholic centers," melancholy proceeded to infuse those people who were meant to banish it: the nineteenth century was the age of the great melancholic lone wolves. Yet this does not mean that the old theme of the sad joker had died away. For the first time, the jester had won the legitimation and the ability that permitted him to question the state of his emotions. A court jester who laid claim to melancholy would have posed a threat to the court system; the dandy portrayed himself as the counterimage of a society that stared at him either with amazed indifference or with inconsequential amazement.

Even the "free-floating intelligentsia" (Alfred Weber) took on part of the orphaned role of the court jester. Karl Mannheim wrote that "a sudden change in mood if things went wrong or did not proceed according to some abstract conception" was the "sure sign of what is initially a free-floating interest."[46] In other words, this tends to be a condition that triggers melancholy. Adorno's critique of this position, which strongly rebukes the sociology of knowledge for "setting up indoctrination camps for the homeless intelligentsia, where it is supposed to learn to forget itself,"[47] describes in its metaphor a sanatorium for distraction in which jesters are prepared for their future profession. We cannot devote more space here to this presumed evolution of the court jester from king's fool into the bourgeois era's privileged intellectual, trained to kill time. All the various scientific disciplines have an element of the jester's function about them, and they are all in danger of being unable to apply their knowledge-constitutive interests freely, being forced to place them at the disposal of the ruling powers. Sociology puts up with this role as a bourgeois science that wishes to be nothing more than sociology—just as the jester was in former times permitted to be only a jester and nothing more, in order to be appreciated by the ruler. And before deciding whether Dahrendorf is right in contending that no tyrant ever kept a "court sociologist," we should first determine who is to be regarded as a tyrant. The "court sociologist"[48] has become the descendant of the court jester.

Flight into Nature and Introversion

Having failed in the Fronde, La Rochefoucauld fled to the salon, but his melancholy remained almost worldly. The bourgeois citizen of eighteenth-century Germany, who had never held power but had striven for it—not least because of his growing economic importance—fell addictively prey to a melancholy that turned its face away from the world, since this world "belonged" to the aristocracy. Havens of bourgeois melancholy could be found outside society. The appreciation of solitude was a precondition for the flight out of society. As Michael Landmann writes, "The individual is . . . indirectly beholden to society for his very being. For precisely this reason, however, the animosity he shows society goes far beyond mere ethical animosity. Regardless of how much he may be indebted to it, or perhaps precisely because of this, beginning at a certain stage in the development of individualization and reflexivity he bears a grudge against it."[49]

This stage of reflexivity existed for the bourgeoisie from the moment it desired power but could not yet attain that power. The disjunction generated extreme reflection in the form of wishful thinking; melancholy and the flight from society grew out of the failure of the bourgeoisie when confronted with reality. Goethe's Werther is someone "who flees the world."[50] Leibniz's monadology, the conception of reality as composed of simple, discrete substances ("monads"), turns out to be a "metaphysics of solitude" and represents the German petty principality.[51]

In this context, Helmuth Plessner has spoken of an escape route available to a body of thought which surrounded an abandoned humankind dwelling "within the empty cavities of introversion or in revolutionary action."[52] This was not a sharp dichotomy, because it juxtaposed haven and action. If the course of action was blocked, nature still remained as an alternative to introversion. Nature and introversion began to complement each other with the discovery of nature as a principle of melancholic flight that could be diametrically opposed to society: solitude as a behavioral form of introversion could henceforth be achieved only in nature.

Introversion, the individual's withdrawal from society and into the self, was a consequence of the bourgeois' flight from the world. This flight received support from philosophy, which had a penchant for solitude and which furthermore became an anthropological, empirical psychology in the eighteenth century, thus making it possible for the first time to nurture what is authentically human.[53] In contrast to the Renaissance doctrine of emotions and indeed to the anthropology of the sixteenth and seventeenth centuries in general, "mournfulness and all related emotions" were now no longer understood in Descartes' terms, as "a contraction of the spirit . . . a weakening and degrading of the spirit." [54] Rather, the new meaning, because it was supported by an anthropologically oriented philosophy, which for the first time contained a notion of *what is human* (an antihistorical and to a lesser extent an antisocial category), led the bourgeois citizen to become "more intimately occupied with his own humanness. Of natural necessity, such reflection led to a subjectivist intellectual stance. This subjectivity permeated the whole of bourgeois life." [55] A subjectivity saturated in feeling was very clearly a response to an unattainable position of power, in that "even the most powerful on earth, even the people experiencing the emotions, were powerless" in the face of it.

The effectivity that cannot be achieved through action was transposed onto self-created emotions: "What was most enjoyable was, as a consequence, precisely what involved the most suffering, for suffering is understandably able to bring forth the deepest emotions and upset." Balet provides what are today merely amusing examples of this attitude—for instance, Darmstadt Lily (Louise Ziegler), "who had a grave dug for herself under the rose bushes in her garden and often lay down in it in order to savor to her heart's content the feelings of someone dying or already deceased, and to weep"; or the case of the poet Klopstock, who in his "Ode to Ebert" imagines his friend, who was alive at the time, to be lying dead in a grave, and uses this image only to conjure up a feeling of "melancholey" within himself; or the letter in which Matthias Claudius beseeches his fellow poet Heinrich Gerstenberg to "give us a tragedy or a tragic piece, so that one really must weep." [56] Martin Greiner took the trouble to count the references to weeping in Johann Martin Miller's novel *Siegwart: A Monastic Story*, which appeared in 1776. According to his findings, the three volumes taken together, totaling 1,179 pages, include 555 instances of a character weeping; Greiner consequently spoke of "chain weepers." [57] Even Adam Bernd, whose own "description of his life" otherwise keeps an astonishing distance from emotional issues, says: "Nostalgia welled up increasingly within me. I found it impossible to remain with the company, but stole away from the wedding guests and out into the open fields, where I gave full vent to my tears, and they were so plentiful that I could have bathed in them." [58]

At the risk of overinterpreting matters, a danger to which all extrapolations of anthropological theorems are exposed, one could at this juncture employ Plessner's maxim that laughter and weeping accompany loss of control over a situation.[59] The enjoyment of weeping was thus both a concomitant of lost power (or power that one had never actually gained) and documentation of an emotion that pressed upon the individual from within and that no one could ward off—and this latter point is decisive. What is of greater significance is that we are dealing here with a mechanism that grew ever stronger: isolation from power bred a form of melancholy that reverted to introversion, yet this retreat widened the distance between the individual and society. "The end of this deep inner shift in the sentimental person's . . . feeling for life is found in the *psychological dissolution of this feeling in self-elected pain* [whereby] the sentimental person *isolates himself from society* to an increasing degree in the 'peace' and 'tranquility' of self-chosen solitude."[60] Among other things, nature became the site of such isolation. If people wished to leave a society that no longer meant anything to them, then introversion and flight into nature were possible ways out. Both variants of escapist behavior were without risk, for they did not attack the prevailing order and they also had every chance of remaining unimpeded by negative sanctions. The fact that one's thoughts were free did not become sacrilegious until the age of brainwashing, and the flight into nature has still not lost its attractive, alternative character even today. It is not easy to pinpoint the location of such nature. Wieser called the "sentimental person" a "transitional human," and to his mind this human dwelled "between town and country." On the other hand, the growing eighteenth-century literature on country life (a literature that, according to Balet, reached its peak in 1780) allows us to plot the exact location of a melancholy flight from the world.

If one draws instead on more abstract points of reference and analytically juxtaposes entities that have long since been differentiated in reality, then we can state the following: nature was the opposite of courtly society and above all the antipode of the courtly residence. If the latter was small, as it typically was in the petty princedoms, then the distant city could appear just as much a haven as the landscape outside the gates. Whatever the case, the landscape was the symbol for a unity that the bourgeoisie was unable to find elsewhere in a world (still) governed by the aristocracy: "The landscape became a comprehensive symbol of a unified whole, within which the *individual* turned his attention to the infinite and saw himself both fulfilled by it and led out of and beyond his empirical existence. In the eighteenth century, a person still experienced this as an individual who had separated himself from society. Landscape could offer him only what he had renounced in society—namely, an opposite that satisfied his personal existence."[61]

Withdrawing from society led to a strange shift in social relations: these came to center on the cult of friendship and of letter writing. In letter writing, one's distance from the world was projected into one's personal relationships; the cult of friendship served less as a form of contact than as a means of increasing one's rapturous feelings of melancholia. The aversion to society allowed at most for the existence of the "other" as a reflection of oneself; nowhere do we get a sense of the "generalized other."

It is astonishing in this context that Friedrich Tenbruck, in one of the less sociologically oriented studies of friendship, could conceive of this complex phenomenon above all in terms of stabilization: "By entering into a personal relationship, an individual avoids the disorganization with which the heterogeneity of the world otherwise threatens him."[62] This interpretation ignores the fact that in the eighteenth century, attaching great esteem to personal friendships was a *bourgeois* characteristic, resulting from a resigned renunciation of power. Tenbruck goes on to speak of "an 'intensity' of personal relations (in both the good and bad meanings of the word) that was to have many consequences"—indeed of "relations that have persisted into our own century as a topic in the German experience of the world."[63] Here again Tenbruck makes too little of the fact that this was an experience of the German bourgeoisie, which came to understand itself not least through the pointed difference between courtly and bourgeois morals: in the latter, ethical convictions were fused with a sentimental stance.

Boredom and Melancholy in Philosophy

In Hegel's words, "History is not the soil in which happiness grows. The periods of happiness in it are the blank pages of history. There are certain moments of satisfaction in the history of the world, but this satisfaction is not to be equated with happiness."[64] Seen in this light, the pages of German philosophy at the end of the eighteenth century are not blank but are inscribed with a closely written and important text: they reflect—if we follow Hegel's argument—"unhappiness," that is, the era's conflicts and antagonisms.

This does not mean we should try to view German idealism simply as a mirror of its time and consider it only in terms of a one-sided conception. Such an attempt (like those undertaken by Karl Mannheim and Georg Lukács, for example) presupposes a critical debate in which the participants have thoroughly discussed the relation between sociology, history, and philosophy, or else it is secure in the knowledge that it has opted for the predominance of one of the three. We cannot make such an attempt here: its success would be problematic, given the complexity and importance of the project. It would also suppress the fact that the tension between, on the one hand a philosophy that has become a science and, on the other, a sociology that believes it has emancipated itself from science and now regards the latter critically carries within it a moment of fruitful conflict and interdisciplinary reflection on science which should be preserved rather than conjured away.

The debate between the aristocracy and the bourgeoisie is found again in eighteenth-century philosophy, along with the problematics of melancholy, boredom, and flight from the world. Our passing reference to this complex is not meant to suggest that a causal relationship exists, but rather to demonstrate that the problem takes similar forms at different levels. The arguments reproduced here serve, among other things, to discredit any attempts to provide a global assessment which subsumes eighteenth-century philosophy under the heading of introversion and thus prepares the way for a verdict to be passed on that basis—a notable case of assuming that something is ideological because it is ideologically founded. To counter this, we must remember that Kantian philosophy in particular—with reference to the aspects touched on here—retains a proximity to the "world," which forbids any recourse to introversion.

In *The Holy Family*, Marx viewed Kant's transferral of the realization of good will into the Beyond as an expression of "the German bourgeoisie's impotence, depression and misery"—a judgment that Engels endorsed in his essay "Feuerbach and the Decline of Classical German Philosophy." The progressive strands within Kantian philosophy recede into the background in these quite justified assessments. Even the division between active and passive citizens made in Section 46 on jurisprudence in *Foundation of the Metaphysics of Morals* is a proof of this. In 1793 the distinction between active and passive citizens was abolished in France, but women and those within the *état de la domesticité* ("state of the home") were still barred from enfranchisement. Schelling also regarded as positive what Marx described as the "theory" of the French Revolution in Kant's work, and did not charge Kant with something for which "the differences of nations and conditions" [65] were responsible. However, as Horkheimer emphasized, Kant believed that the mediation of the transcendental and inner worlds occurred not in faith alone or in introversion but in "life."

This would make Kant the exact opposite of the regressive bourgeois trends of his time. For recognizing the nature of this mediation does not lead to "resignation" in Kant's writings.[66] On this point, his philosophy culminated in a progressive alternative to an important trend of his epoch, but one that had disastrous consequences.

In his *Observations on the Feeling of the Beautiful and Sublime,* Kant described abstinence from the world in ethical terms: "Melancholy separation from the bustle of the world due to a legitimate weariness is noble," he states, asserting that "genuine virtue based on principles" has something about it "which seems to harmonize most with the *melancholy* frame of mind in the moderated understanding."[67] The same work also contains a passage that reflects the bourgeoisie's aversion to aristocratic boredom: "He whose words or deeds neither entertain us nor move us is *boring.* The bore, if he is nevertheless zealous to do both, is *insipid.* The insipid person, if he is conceited, is a fool" (XIII, pp. 56–57). This definition of boredom, which denies it any amusing or touching qualities, is leveled both at the *honnête homme* and the "gentleman"—aristocratic modes of behavior[68] that are based on maximum control of the emotions and that require the immediate transformation of inner excitement, if present, into a carefully crafted *bon mot* or a rebuff, acceptable because it is stylized. When Kant goes on to talk of melancholy or, as he puts it, "the man of melancholy frame of mind," he characterizes him as follows: "All chains, from the gilded ones worn at court to the heavy irons of galley slaves, are abominable to him" (XIII, p. 66). The implied rebuke is aimed at the court and opposes the sublimeness of the "natural" melancholy person to the system of enforced conformity.

Admittedly, Kant cannot be construed as an advocate of a bourgeois philosophy that was able to find affirmation only in self-created emotions and, through these, compensation for the "loss of world" which had resulted from its exclusion from power. As we have seen, Kant even referred to a "legitimate weariness," thus tying the evaluation of melancholy to an external cause—in other words, one that originates in the *world.* Bourgeois melancholy and sensibility (*Empfindsamkeit,* the sentimental current in German culture in the eighteenth century) should not be seen as causes of such feelings. Rather, the sentimental person insisted on generating emotions "within himself," on fabricating his own suffering. Only in this manner could he preserve the principle of his autonomy—so that he could freely decide to do harm to himself. Bourgeois melancholy tending toward sentimentality was the paradoxical attempt to generate endogenous melancholy. In "The Analytic of the Sublime" in his *Critique of Judgment*, Kant showed how the "sublime" could be fabricated, and emphasized through contrast: "But although the judgment upon the sublime in nature needs culture (more than the judgment upon the beautiful), it is not therefore primarily produced by culture and introduced in a more conveniental way into society. Rather has it its root in human nature, even in that which, alike with common understanding, we can impute to and expect of everyone, viz. in the tendency to the feeling for (practical) ideas, i.e. to what is moral." Whereas this clearly contains—in the polemic against "convention"—a rebuke of the court, Kant specifically criticizes a sentimentality that has become a business. He opposes a sublimeness produced by conventions to one directly provided by nature, not in order to give bourgeois sublimeness a firm philosophical grounding but to oppose its overexaggeration, as emerges in the following catalogue of bourgeois ideas of sublimeness: "We have both *spirited* and *tender* emotions. The latter, if they rise to (strong) affections, are worthless; the propensity to them is called sentimentalizing . . . Romances [novels], lachrymose plays, shallow moral precepts . . . these are not compatible with any frame of mind that can be counted beautiful, still less one which is to be counted sublime" (*Critique of Judgment*, pp. 113–114). Here Kant is clearly directing his polemic against a bourgeois variant of fabricated melancholy, and he speaks even more strongly in the passage in which he turns the accusation of boredom—traditionally raised by the bourgeoisie against the aristocracy— against the bourgeois citizen: "The pleasant exhaustion, consequent upon such disturbance produced by the play of the affections, is an enjoyment of our well-being arising from the restored equilibrium of the various vital forces . . . Many a man believes himself to be edified by a sermon when indeed there is no edification at all (no system of good maxims), or to be improved by a tragedy when he is only glad at his ennui being happily dispelled" (pp. 114–115).

At another point, Kant discusses the syndrome whereby the sublime is positively assessed by taking nature as the standard of reference (a standard characteristic for his thought) and links this with the rejection of fabricated sublimeness in the bourgeois world. In his "General Remark upon the Exposition of the Aesthetical Reflective Judgment" in the *Critique of Judgment*, Kant suggests:

> Now the satisfaction in the beautiful, like that in the sublime, is not alone distinguishable from other aesthetical judgments by its universal *communicability*, but also because it acquires an interest through this very property in reference to society (in which this communication is possible). We must, however, remark that separation from all

society is regarded as sublime if it rests upon ideas that overlook all sensible interest. To be sufficient for oneself, and consequently to have no need of society, without at the same time being unsociable, i.e. without flying from it, is something bordering on the sublime. (p. 116)

This excerpt clearly shows the pragmatic nature of Kant's thought. The insight contained in the closing sentence is based on an anthropologically founded principle of social antagonism—which has implications for the philosophy of history. In his *"Idea for a General History from the Viewpoint of a Citizen of the World,"* Kant calls this "unsociable sociability" the motive force behind social development. Even in the passages concerning bourgeois withdrawal from society—which Kant considers sublime if it "rests on ideas"—his description is not without irony: "Evidence of this is afforded by the propensity to solitude, the fantastic wish for a secluded country seat, or (in the case of young persons) by the dream of the happiness of passing one's life with a little family upon some island unknown to the rest of the world, a dream of which storytellers or writers of Robinsonades know how to make good use" (*Critique of Judgment*, p. 117).

Kant is criticizing not melancholic seclusion—whether this takes the form of a utopia or a mere wishful dream—but the flight from society that goes hand in hand with the denunciation of society. At no point in the passages quoted from the *Critique of Judgment* does the notion of solitude appear—a concept that, in the typical discussions of Kant's day, served as a value-laden counterpart to society, a society characterized by vigorous activity, licentiousness, and the boredom of courtly society. Kant endeavored to bring this idea of "proximity to the world" into harmony with both his aesthetic and his ethical convictions, as Friedrich Kaulbach has shown: "Good character ensures that an individual will not separate himself, even in the language he uses, from the ethical community, the realm of the intellectuals, and steal away into a 'private' life of action, thought, and speech . . . As an author, Kant saw himself as having been transposed into the field of tension between the ethics of communication on the one hand and the responsibility for the complex matters of philosophy on the other."[69]

The salience of the concept of world prevents an individual from following a one-way path to introversion, for "the world is a stage upon which the 'game of our dexterity is played.' On this stage we must acquire experience and then apply it. We take the world as our point of departure as observers, and turn back to it in activity; this means, however, that we must understand our potential and limitations as well as our position vis-à-vis the world." [70] As Jürgen Habermas has emphasized in a different context, "World in the transcendental sense, as the embodiment of all appearances, is the totality of the syntheses thereof and to this extent one with 'nature.'" [71] Here, the concept of world is more pragmatic, arising from a form of thought, which, to quote Kaulbach again, "even set human experience in motion, and consequently led to the development of anthropological theory." [72]

As Habermas points out, world is related to "humankind as a species, but only in terms of the public expression of that species: the world of that reasoning, reading public which was developing precisely at that time in the broad strata of the bourgeoisie." [73] This brings us to a sort of endpoint in our consideration of the Kantian concept of melancholy: melancholy is contained in such dignity as is concealed in sublimeness, but this quality is lost as soon as it becomes the consequence of a sought-after emotion or some "sentimentality." By not relating melancholy to a form of nature that is regarded as true nature and that facilitates the formation of ties to society or indeed makes this an obligation, and by instead assuming the point of reference to exist in both the world and society, Kant opposes the trend toward introversion that shaped his age.

Kant's argument in his psychiatric deliberations is likewise "close to society." In his "Essay on the Illnesses of the Mind" (1764), he expresses mild objections to a concept already overstrained by sentimentality when he defines a "melancholic" as "a dreamer with a view to the evils of life" (II, p. 266), and similar reservations are apparent when he comments on "anthropology's" fine distinction between a melancholic and someone melancholically inclined. This is especially true if we bear in mind that Kant's "psychiatric systematics" projected proximity to the world (already outlined in his aesthetics and ethics) into an area in which it was perhaps most difficult to gain such an insight. In his "systematics," Kant includes the following definition: "The only general characteristic of madness is the loss of "common sense" *(sensus communis)* and, in contrast, the manifestation of a "logical wilfullness" of one's own *(Eigensinn, sensus privatus)."* [74] Kant's dietetics—"the power of the sentiments through the simple will to master one's own feelings," which he claims exists and which he postulates in opposition to a tendency toward hypochondria (see "The Debate between the Faculties of Philosophy and Medicine," VII, pp. 95ff.)—separates itself completely from the bourgeois propensity for melancholia.

The increasing social importance of the relation to nature—

devised by the bourgeoisie as an antipode to the "unnature" of the aristocracy—was evident in the philosophy of the time. People's faulty affinity to their fellow social beings seems to have been projected onto an inanimate nature, and was also recognized as being insignificant there. Nature, by means of the concept of infinity traditionally accorded to it, was seen as promoting individuals who were able to live their lives to the full, and as encouraging an exaggeration of the emotions. In turn, such exaggeration—owing to the many opportunities to legitimate it that were given at the time (bursting into tears and so on)—led people to think that they could get by without personal contact. In addition, we must in this context not forget that although social contact offered opportunities to release emotions along prescribed avenues, it always entailed the risk that an individual might misunderstand another person's readiness to reciprocate in the "exchange of emotions" and thus be frustrated. Such contact was therefore usually restricted to only one person who, as a "supplementary" partner, facilitated the emergence of a cult of letter writing or friendship; alternatively, it was confined to a group that was from the very outset conditioned in a similar "emotional direction." Nature and the "things" that comprised it, however, offered themselves as "partners" guaranteeing that frustration could be avoided in all instances: they were mute recipients that "listened to" the purported venting of emotions, absorbed it, and thus satisfied it—even if they could not respond.

Helmuth Plessner, for example, emphasized Schelling's "compatriotism with the world." What he meant by this and what it has in common with the concept of world used here will become clear from the following passage:

> In *Elective Affinities* we read: "With every tree around us that blossoms, . . . with every shrub we pass, with every blade of grass upon which we tread, we have a true relationship; they are our true compatriots." This expresses not only a Franciscan feeling but also a form of cognition, whose influence continues today.
>
> Schelling tried his luck with it. Even if he can no longer guide us, he can still admonish us to take compatriotism with the world seriously, especially in those areas where it is no longer compatriotism, and to conquer in the elements of our thoughts the truth it contains.[75]

The symptom we have described, namely the flight from "society" into nature, is evident in Plessner's assertion: it is what remains of the world when one ascertains that it is no longer the world. Com-

patriotism means more contact with nature and less with the world—
in other words, with a nature that is understood to be the world.
Goethe again comes to mind here. Like *Elective Affinities*, his *Sufferings
of Young Werther* provides an instructive example:

> Incidentally, I am quite happy here, solitude is a precious balsam
> for my heart in this paradisiacal region, and this, the season of
> youth, deeply warms my oft shuddering heart. Every tree, every
> shrub is a bush of blossoms, and one wishes only that one could
> become a June beetle so that one could waft around in the sea of
> pleasant scents and find therein all the sustenance one needs.
>
> The town itself is unpleasant, by contrast in a circle round about
> it the inexpressible beauty of nature.[76]

The notion of melancholy that Goethe describes in *Werther* is similar to that seen in the case of Schelling and his "compatriotism" with
nature. "Even the most profound nature is dejection," Schelling says.
"It, too, mourns a lost possession, and all life is imbued with a touch
of indestructible melancholy, because it has something independent
of itself below and within it (the *Above* oneself raises one up, the
Below oneself drags one down)."[77] Karl Jaspers insists that Schelling's
despair "was either a depression unrelated to philosophy or the high
tone of the unrealness of his own reflected experience."[78] The word
"unrealness" conceals the distance from the world and its "bustle,"
which is checked by nature and "calmness." The neglect shown to
one's *socius*, one's companions, stems from this movement out of
society into nature.

Hermann Zeltner stresses that Schelling attempted to "see humankind in terms of its ties with the different areas of existence, in its
relation above all to nature, history, God."[79] Typically, one can glean
nothing about one's fellow humans at this point. Zeltner's deliberations subsequently investigate the fact that Schelling's philosophy
considers the role of fellow human beings: "The initial starting point
for an understanding of the 'individual in the role of fellow human'
is . . . given in Schelling's early work, but it is not developed further
at a later date."[80] And it is hardly possible that Schelling could have
derived such a development from the assertion that mankind is the
compatriot of things in a world conceived of as nature.

As we inquire more closely into both German philosophy in the
eighteenth century (especially idealism) and how the syndrome of a
flight from the world, melancholy, introversion, and a longing for
nature was reproduced in it, we must accord decisive significance to
the distinction arrived at using the concept of labor. It would appear

to be coincidence that Schelling's conception of an "indestructible melancholy," which tarnishes all life, is connected to the fact that thinkers have in vain searched for a concept of labor in that notion of melancholy.[81]

In this manner, Fichte, who in *The Characteristics of the Present Age* passes judgment on the boredom of an era that "was without the idea,"[82] clearly conforms to the psychology of the emotions that was characteristic of the eighteenth century: "I wish to love, I wish to lose myself, be happy and be depressed in commiseration. I myself am the highest object of such commiseration."[83] He does not, however, go on to develop the usual theme of affinity to nature: "I wish to be the master of nature, and it shall serve me, I wish to influence it to an extent commensurate with my powers, but it shall have no influence over me."[84] Fichte opposes a "philosophy of nature" that arises from rapturous enthusiasm, and instead devises a realistic picture of societal progress via increasing specialization and the division of labor:

> The powers of Man, again, shall be multiplied by a legitimate distribution of the necessary branches of labour among many members, each of whom shall acquire only one branch, but acquire that one well; these powers shall be armed with the knowledge of Nature and of Art, and with convenient implements and machinery, and then be raised superior to every power of Nature; so that all the more earthly purposes of man shall be attained without much expenditure of time or labour, and sufficient opportunity be left remaining for him to turn his attention upon inward and celestial things. This is the purpose of the Human Race, as such.[85]

Thus, Fichte insists on the boredom of the age, and his description of it could also be interpreted as characterizing melancholy. The passage in question shows, however, how far Fichte's critique is at this point from being "fundamental" and profound: "An Age without the idea must therefore be a weak and powerless Age, and all it does, all wherein it shows any sign of life, is accomplished in a languid and sickly manner and without any visible manifestation of energy."[86] This is biting criticism, but Fichte aims it only at the third of his historical epochs. Such historical relativization coupled with the use of a concept of labor that approaches that of real life (we can appraise this "forward distinction" if we think of Hegel's description of the relation between master and servant in the *Phenomenology*) renders any flight into nature and neglect of fellow humans unnecessary. This, needless to say, involves not a comment about Fichte's work in

general but rather a statement about one particular position cham-
pioned by him, in the *Characteristics*. We shall see later that in relation
to the problems that are of particular interest here, his *Closed Mercantile State* exhibits a much greater measure of intellectual rigor.

At this point I wish merely to suggest that it may be possible to
determine a particular writer's historico-philosophical position by
noting his stance on flight from the world, introversion, melancholy,
and predilection for nature.

The difficulty of any attempt to "locate" bourgeois melancholy
becomes clear when we realize that such a bourgeois concept of
nature—one that incorporates solitude, introversion, a melancholic
flight from the world, and an aversion to an inauthentic, courtly,
notorious boredom—is opposed in formal terms by a concept of history and society. Zimmermann, for instance, who speaks of Rousseau
as his "favorite scribe," and who knew the latter's work sufficiently
well "to equate the best form of state with the shortest distance
between mankind and nature,"[87] presents an example of the way in
which Rousseau's aversion to history and his concept of a Golden
Age of Nature affected sentimentality as a movement. Rousseau
labeled himself "a painter of nature and a historian of the human
heart." A self-confident subjectivity whose only compelling standard
is its own introversion lies concealed as a counterbalance within these
words, words that are paradigmatic not only for the flight into nature
but for bourgeois melancholy in general.

The need to think of the bourgeois concept of nature in formal
terms becomes apparent if we remember that in his discourse on the
arts and sciences, Rousseau himself says that his aim is "to know well
a state that no longer exists, and perhaps barely existed, and probably
never will exist, and yet of which it is necessary to have just concepts
so that we can appropriately judge our present state."[88] The ahistor-
ical nature of this statement is astounding, allowing the metaphor of
a natural state to appear only as a principle of methodology, as a
point de vue philosophique, from which to reflect on the current state of
humankind and society. In his commentary, however, Kurt Weigand
rejects such a surmise: "This passage speaks in favor of a Kantian
explication of the *Discours,* in keeping with which Rousseau saw
natural man as merely a yardstick for humankind that could be used
as an a priori condition of history. The standpoint Rousseau takes in
his foreword is simply not that of the *Discours*."[89]

Kant and Rousseau can both be viewed as representatives of a
bourgeois-oriented philosophy. Their differences, which must be
stressed despite the fact that Kant held Rousseau in high esteem,

delineate two variants of bourgeois melancholy. Rousseau's detaches itself from the static view fixated on a long-past Golden Age by rigorously devising the utopia of the *Social Contract,* in which the notion of the highest well-being for all reincorporates the ban on melancholy. Kant seems to carry resignation to an extreme when he speaks of humankind's being unable to attain satisfaction *(aquiescentia).* In fact, the latter observation actually makes a case against resignation. What is decisive is the standpoint from which one makes the reproach that someone is resigned. If one staunchly defends the possibility of a planned but thoroughly miscalculated utopia, then the assertion that a state of happiness cannot be reached implies the end of utopia. The chances of a utopia's being realized or even attempted are entailed in such an assertion only if it requests support for the promise of happiness for all. Such soliciting is foreign to Kant's argument. It renounces utopian happiness and thus precludes a resigned condemnation of the present. Rousseau's position, in contrast, does promise happiness: it not only permits but demands that it be complemented by a distance from the present. Rousseau's first and second discourses thus belong together.

In Section 61 of his *Anthropology* (VII, p. 233), Kant speaks of "boredom and amusement." This opposition to the "extravagant person," who can bore himself without any help from others ("As one said of Lord Mordaunt in Paris, 'The English hang themselves to pass the time'"), displays the somewhat malicious glee of a bourgeois aversion to the aristocracy and to aristocratic boredom as a symbol of rule. In addition to this aversion, which strengthened the resentment in bourgeois thought at that time, a reconciliation of nature and society lay in a conception of nature that "lodged pain in [man] like a thorn prompting him to action, a thorn he cannot escape" (VII, p. 235). The compulsion to act required the presence of a society in which one could act; this, too, was included in the "idea of a world history that, to a certain extent, contains a priori a practical manual" (VIII, p. 30).

Kant and Rousseau also represented, not least in their writings on the philosophy of history, two approaches to *overcoming* bourgeois melancholy. For the latter, the ban on melancholy became almost superfluous once the *Contract* had been concluded; for the former, the thorn of discord continued to inhere in a bourgeois society that was supposed to develop according to "cosmopolitan intentions." Whereas Rousseau's social contract promises happiness for all—which, as is always the case with such empty phrases, means the happiness of those who conform—Kant's scheme does not go so far: the view of human beings as "bent wood," from which nothing straight can ever be made, forbids deferring euphoria until the future. Yet Kantian bourgeois society seems free of boredom; its members are spurred on to activity, which, in the specific conception dominant in the eighteenth century, dispelled boredom. This state of prompted activity has a dialectical character. For with the hope that at some point "a state will be reached which, like a [common] bourgeois polity, can preserve itself like an *automaton*" (VIII, p. 25),[90] the compulsion to activity disappears in the ensuing automatism. In its place, boredom returns, because humankind has been completely released from any burden of labor. Kant accordingly ends with the prospect of a bourgeois society that will have lost both the thorn that prompts activity and the basis for melancholy—perhaps at the price of acquiring something that the bourgeoisie found despicable when it was a feature of the aristocracy, namely boredom.

Schopenhauer sensed this unwanted consequence when he emphasized in volume four of *The World as Will and Representation* that if the state should at some point perfectly fulfill its purpose, then people would henceforth live in a land of milk and honey in which boredom would occupy the place vacated by the other evils even if all the evils were removed.[91] The process of releasing people from burden cannot be prolonged *ad infinitum;* ultimately it changes back into a burden—one that is hardest of all to obviate, for there is literally nothing one can do to prevent it.

5   Spaces of Boredom and Melancholy

Melancholy and boredom belong together, even etymologically; "ennui" is not the only term to cover both. Ludwig Marcuse's observation that in the seventeenth century melancholy was as famous as boredom would be two hundred years later underscores the degree to which the two go hand in hand. One need only think of how often boredom which is forced upon a person gives rise to melancholy; and the melancholic, in the midst of his everyday boredom, has no choice but to get caught up in himself. Walter Benjamin, who described the seventeenth century in much the same terms as Marcuse, more aptly ascribed a specific form of melancholy to the nineteenth century—that era which has been regarded by Marcuse and others as the supreme period of boredom.[1]

The word "boredom" (in German *Lange-Weile,* meaning literally "a long whiling away of time") in itself establishes the temporal context. It was not until the eighteenth century that the two parts of the word were joined together to make one, and the link has barely been disguised since.[2] When we are bored, time grows long—it cannot be filled or used up; and finally, time is "killed" when we notice that it seems endless. Consequently, boredom appears to be eternal monotony, always the same, a gaping void.[3] And the reference to space is readily apparent in these metaphors; it is a necessary precondition for recognizing boredom: sameness can be determined only if there is a lack of sameness to which it can be compared; its identity can be proven only if the nonidentical is at hand. Thus, space forms the background for language and the fixed point on which boredom is focused before it can be noticed in the first place.

The insights into the nature of time which are important for both science and literature, particularly at the turn of the twentieth century, are based to some extent on the oldest conceptions of boredom. Subjectively experienced moods of boredom are oriented to an objective parameter, namely that of *regular mechanical* time, embodied in the image of the clock. The experience of boredom, which contradicts a concept of time based on precisely equal units, forces one to reflect on a new concept of time which could be called *irregular natural time* and can be determined by the ratio of the frequency of events to mechanical time. The common concept of boredom is characterized by this orientation. Its bourgeois characteristics are unmistakable in light of what has been said thus far. According to this view, one can break free from mechanical time only if the volume of events and experiences makes time shorter. These events may very well occur in the individual himself, for whom time threatens to grow too long: the prerequisite for this is naturally, as in the case of "outwardly directed action," a certain measure of independence which permits one to make things happen when nothing happens on its own. To the bourgeois way of thinking, something of this nature is impossible according to etiquette; the tendency is, therefore, to attribute boredom to the nobility. Thomas Mann's view of boredom as portrayed in *The Magic Mountain* ("Excursus on the Meaning of Time") is, by contrast, aristocratic in nature because it sees boredom as being dispelled by similitude and not by change: "Emptiness and monotony may stretch the moment and the hour and make for 'boredom,' but they shorten and dissolve the larger and largest masses of time to the point of nullifying them." However, it is of special interest here that this view of boredom, which, formally speaking, is antibourgeois in nature, is also geared to a particular location: reflection on boredom is set into motion by "a peculiar affinity to this settling into a strange place."

Kierkegaard, who insisted on the special temporal reference of boredom and drew the connection between the concept of melancholy and his category of repetition, ultimately provided a surprisingly spatially related conclusion to his views on boredom—one that took the existential-philosophical theory linked to the category of the "individual" and expanded it to include the sociological aspect. Kierkegaard's "Essay on the Theory of Social Prudence," called "The Rotation Method," already ends in "Either/Or," in a spatial symbol:

> The gods were bored, and so they created man. Adam was bored because he was alone, and so Eve was created. Thus boredom entered the world, and increased in proportion to the increase of population. Adam was bored alone; then Adam and Eve were bored together; then the population of the world increased, and the peoples were bored en masse. To divert themselves they conceived the idea of constructing a tower high enough to reach the heavens.

This idea is itself as boring as the tower was high, and constitutes a terrible proof of how boredom gained the upper hand.[4]

In his diary, Kierkegaard muses that time (which he calls "this succession") "is, or at least can be, man's worst enemy."[5] In contrast to his view of memory, however, Kierkegaard's view of repetition is similar to Proust's—namely, that it bears a positive principle: "Indeed, what would life be if there were no repetition? . . . If God himself had not willed repetition, the world would not have come into existence."[6] Whereas boredom's reference to time wavers in this manner, in Kierkegaard's *Point of View for My Work as an Author* (which he described as a "direct communication" and a "message to history," and which appeared sixteen years after *Repetition*), he provides a sociological resolution of the phenomenon of boredom that includes melancholy. On the one hand, he analyzes the disposition of someone who is bored, and who fears that "eternity could be boring," as part of the concept of genius—in other words, as part of an attribution that requires positive social sanctions, recognition, in order not to turn "inward" and thus into frustration. On the other hand, Kierkegaard reduces the fate of the bored and melancholy individual to a spatial phenomenon that contributes more to an understanding of melancholy and boredom than the merely fitting metaphor: "I have nothing further to say, but in conclusion I will let another speak, my poet, who when he comes will assign me a place among those who have suffered for the sake of an idea, and he will say: 'The martyrdom this author suffered may be briefly described thus: He suffered from *being a genius in a small town*.'"[7]

Thus, Kierkegaard's description draws together all that has been discussed into the syndrome of melancholy: the "suffering of introversion" is as much a part of it as the recognition that he is living in an "age of reflection."[8] This is where melancholy and boredom come together. The spatial fixation of the "place" of boredom and melancholy in the small town has more to do with what is urban than with what is provincial—the accumulation of a potential audience that fails to recognize the true nature of the "individual," who, after all, claims to be a "genius." The metaphor of the small town constitutes a polemic not against the world as such but against the state of being in which it finds itself, and is far from the mechanism of flight from the city so normal during the eighteenth century: "Often I tear myself away from the city and flee to a solitary area; then the beauty of nature purges my soul of all the disgust and all the odious impressions that have pursued me from the city."[9]

The concept that Kierkegaard opposes to the hated small town is not nature but the *intérieur*. The image of the small town represents less a reproach against "homely" bustling than the genius' hatred of mediocrity. This is also entailed in Kierkegaard's polemic against Copenhagen, which he criticizes for becoming a small town. As a result, his polemic becomes "economic," for in Danish "small town" means commercial center and market: both are contained in the term *Kjobstad*.[10] Thus, Kierkegaard's polemic takes on an additional air, namely that of the aristocrat. Kierkegaard desires the bustle and tumult of a large city, but away from work and without any duties—a fitting persuasion for a pensioner living on a strictly planned budget, who died at precisely the moment "when he had used up his fortune, which he had, in strict accordance with Christian belief, refused to invest with interest."[11] The criticism of the small town implies the search for an aristocratic center. Kierkegaard knew that small-town inhabitants were of course not immune to boredom, but he also alluded to the consolation of knowing this: "All men are bores. The word itself suggests the possibility of a subdivision . . . Those who bore others are the mob, the crowd, the infinite multitude of men in general. Those who bore themselves are the elect, the aristocracy."[12] Reducing boredom to a general characteristic does not preclude its elitist nature. Today anyone who claims to be aware of his own misery can become a self-styled aristocrat.

The importance of Kierkegaard's argument, which ultimately summarizes boredom and melancholy in the formula-like metaphor of the "genius in the small town," becomes clear when one realizes that the spatial reference is more closely related to sociological interpretation than is the reference to time—the lack of affinity with the latter having resulted in the sociology's undesirable antipathy for history. Maurice Halbwachs referred to Comte's remark that "mental equilibrium results largely and primarily from the fact that the material objects with which we come into contact every day do not change or at least change very little and provide us with a picture of permanence and continuity. They are comparable to a silent and immobile society which is indifferent to our bustling and our changes in mood, lending us the impression of calm and order."[13] Thus, the unchanged, if not immutable, space which derives its structure and meaning from material objects and their composition is an essential element in a sociological way of looking at things that has to rely on the development of static and dynamic categories without being able to make use of both at the same time. Changes in the mood of society can be traced throughout the various periods; the respective ways of dealing with the changed moods and affective states are likewise revealed in the views of the spaces in which these are worked or lived out.

Utopian thought, with its brooding that gives rise to utopia as a system, does not—as a reaction to the misery of the moment—allow for melancholy or for boredom. Mournfulness as a response to that which was and still is engenders a critique of the existing system— and such mournfulness must therefore be banned from utopia. This is also the reason for rejecting boredom. It can hardly be planned, anyway; it may, at most, become an undesired by-product that is left over as waste when leisure time is to be calculated. If utopia remains close to Cockaigne, or the land of milk and honey, then popular imagination, still quite far from being reflection, is so amazed at what the future has to offer that no one ever thinks it through to its logical conclusion: people talk about eating without thinking about the fact that you cannot stuff more into your stomach than it can hold. Utopia at this stage—surely one of the earliest to be anchored in popular belief—knows no boredom because there is no end to its amazement. The land of milk and honey is wishful thinking, open to the future: the end does not exist as a category. It is no more a part of this early form of utopia than it would be in a fairy tale that used the stereotyped ending to detract from any thought of an end— which is to say, "they lived happily ever after." And "only the fairy tale, forever instructive, and the fairy tale of the state know how to tell the story of 'the fool's paradise' and the land of milk and honey."[14]

If the utopian system arises from wishful thinking, the rigor of the planning and the sharpness of the categories with which it is to be brought into being also grow in direct relation to the degree of abstraction.[15] "Proceed according to plan!" is the highest command- ment, and not "Do as you like!"—to cite the rule of the monastery of Theleme in Rabelais. Whereas in Cockaigne one can lie around lazily and wait for the broiled goose, which—with knife and fork already inserted in place—flies into one's open mouth, in utopia one has to work, more in order to sharpen one's appetite than to earn a living. Cabet's "Organiser la fortune" is *the* utopian motto par excellence. The manner in which organization allows happiness to wither is shown by the history of the realized utopia: its fascist perversion con- stitutes the "organization of optimism" which Goebbels had set as a goal. The utopian system is oriented to the concept of order: it divides time down to the last dot, since it would appear easiest to create new life in order to preserve utopia (Campanella). Free time does not exist in utopia, because there are no empty spaces to be excluded from the plan. Work as well as leisure time is regimented. Bloch's dictum with regard to Campanella's City of the Sun does not apply only to Campanella: "Despite an even shorter working time than is the case with More, namely only four hours, and a communistic distribution of the profit, the charitable burden of the rule lies on every hour and on every pleasure."[16] Rulership in utopia is intended to benefit all. In the days when eudaemonistic utopias were still conceivable, it could be portrayed as compatible with the concept of totality.

We will have difficulty, however, subsuming boredom under this concept; rather, it characterizes a residue of privacy in the plan, of spontaneity in doing nothing. Doing nothing is not identical with boredom, but eudaemonistic utopia did not envisage any form of labor that, owing to its stereotyped procedures, would enable people to be bored and work in spite of this. Whoever works in utopia has no time for boredom. And whoever is finished with his work is still accounted for by the plan—subject to the rule of efficiency in his leisure time as well. Time and space yield to the pressure of order imposed by utopia: the former, because utopia appears as the "sublation of social coincidence, isolated case, fortunate case . . . *Utopia of the lack of coincidence, of the lack of situation*";[17] the latter, because it "is celebrated everywhere," not only where Bloch emphasizes it: the celebrated space is space that has been thoroughly planned and measured out. Empty spaces are not available, nor is free time: thus, boredom is remote because, if all goes according to the planners' intentions, there will be no space or time available for it to come into being. Therefore, in the thoroughly planned world of utopia, not only are specific and singular manifestations of the psyche eliminated, but so is the very science that would be able to deal with them, namely psychology. Adorno states in this respect, "The prebourgeois world does not yet have a knowledge of psychology, and the world that is thoroughly socialized no longer has a knowledge of it."[18]

Utopia is the system of total institutions, and it is difficult to specify which is more total: the smooth functioning or the fact of its painstaking conformity to functional authority, which reduces friction and thus also the potential for conflict. In his polemic against structural-functional theory, Ralf Dahrendorf referred to the kind of boredom that a particular form of theoretical sociological discussion has in common with a platonic dialogue.[19] Dahrendorf's description of utopia focuses on a specific utopia, namely *1984*. This is one of those pessimistic utopias where we need not be concerned as to whether or not they result in fruitful, future-oriented utopian thought—an ideological support for a present that is nonetheless worthy of improvement.

The world of *1984*, however, can serve as the endpoint of the perspective if we wish to examine what happens to the inhabitants of utopia when they discover boredom. "Winston's greatest pleasure in life was his work. Most of it was a tedious routine, but included in it there were also jobs so difficult and intricate that you could lose yourself in them as in the depths of a mathematical problem."[20] Orwell's passage shows how boredom that has been overcome stipulates directly a consensus for the despised system. Thus, in the system of total surveillance, melancholy behavior is not possible or permissible—either objectively, because totally planned time leaves no empty space for melancholy to set in, or subjectively, because a dissatisfied look already amounts to deviation: "Winston turned round abruptly. He had set his features into the expression of quiet optimism which it was advisable to wear when facing the telescreen" (p. 8). The "look of grim enjoyment" (p. 29) and the tendency to tolerate a despised system when a minimum of spontaneity remains—in working for the system—are guarantees of conformity. Smith's break with the system is also a revolt against his growing boredom; typically, unleashed spontaneity escapes into private space (Mr. Charrington's room). Orwell's *1984* shows utopia as the vain attempt to save the *intérieur,* which means flight from the world: "The room was a world, a pocket of the past where extinct animals could walk" (p. 123). The *intérieur* offers freedom, or rather the futile suggestion of it: "the room itself was sanctuary" (p. 124). When at the end of his failed attempt to break out of utopia Smith has been brainwashed and reeducated, he also lacks that psychic state which drove him to deviation: "He was not bored, he had no desire for conversation or distraction" (p. 221). The utopia of *1984* is the system of institutions that are permanent because they are sufficiently flexible. Dahrendorf distorted the perspective somewhat in speaking of the fact that a "general consensus . . . implicitly means the lack of structurally generated conflicts."[21] In *1984* we see, rather, a system that consciously generates conflicts (one need only think of the marginal society of the "prols") in order to preserve a smoothly functioning and viable utopia through contrived transformation. If boredom appears in this system, the wish for a private pastime becomes irrepressible: since private boredom is not part of the plan, however, it cannot be officially eliminated. Thus, the individual rebels against the system out of individual boredom, but one that is induced by the apparatus—and is defeated.

The deficiencies in the planning of the eudaemonistic utopias reveal themselves precisely in what they cover up. They are based on the idea of a total order that is regarded as unsurpassed, on a list of stereotyped schedules and fixed preferences that has been accepted once and for all. Boredom has no place in this view of things, nor does melancholy, both being based on a subjective valuation of individual segments of time and the demand for individual spaces for private purposes: the order that is generally accepted is replaced by a new order based on "feeling." Whether or not this substitute consists of mourning or of becoming aware of the senseless passage of time is a question that is irrelevant for, and at the same time damaging to, the system. But the boredom of the totally regulated system and the expediently planned procedure which condemns spontaneity as being planless are both exposed in the injunction that serves to raise private boredom to the level of sacrilege. Only a utopia that is "noninstitutional" in nature, such as B. F. Skinner's *Walden Two,* permits the expression of boredom and refrains from optimism.[22]

Fichte's closed mercantile state forbids extraterritorial mobility: "Only the scholar, and the higher artist, are allowed to travel out of a closed mercantile state: leisurely curiosity and the desire for distraction shall no longer be permitted to carry their boredom to all other countries."[23] This aversion to demonstrative boredom contains the norm by which the citizen of the mercantile state is measured: if he wishes to belong to it, he is to work according to regulations, to obey the few laws (!) and to allow himself to be assured of its satisfaction: "The people's relationship to the government, and in a monarchical state, to the ruling family, is one of complete happiness."[24] This is no longer a stamp designed to show how the individual is doing but has become the proof for the planners and rulers of the system that "everything is in order," for "the ease of the state's administration, as of all work, depends on proceeding in an orderly fashion, with an overview of the whole, and according to a fixed plan."[25] The old utopian link between regulated work, protection against the outside world, rigorous internal laws, and the resulting ban on melancholy is also no longer present here. The idea of the plan forbids boredom because it exposes the "empty gaps" which the plan forgot to take into consideration. The idea of contented, peaceful happiness is initially deduced formally from the plan's desired "functioning." Melancholy in the form of mourning over what is past needlessly holds things up when, after all, everything is supposed to be moving forward; it denounces the totality of utopia because it withdraws into the private sphere. Total utopia characterizes one aspect of the

dialectics of private and public; the other aspect is manifested by introversion. The public domain is humane if one can elude it by entering
the private domain; and, by the same token, the private domain is
humane if it does not become introversion. Planned utopia demands
conformity, and from this it deduces the happiness of the individual;
it overlooks the fact that the rigorous order itself gives rise to boredom
and thus to the thorn of discontent. Because it dispels boredom, as in
Fichte's model, and seeks to overcome melancholy, the eudaemonistic
utopia that is fixed according to a plan has an affinity to both.

Utopias such as Orwell's direct their reproaches *against* utopia
because they have borrowed their criticism from reality. They play off
the partially realized utopia against the envisioned utopia. They overlook the fact that reality is hardly necessary in order to perceive the
utopian thrust involved, which comes to light in the prohibitive rules
to which the utopians must submit: the planners of utopia forbid them
to be bored, owing to an awareness that boredom is the result of the
total plan; the planners categorically demand demonstrative happiness
because they know that the assertion of providing the highest good
for all can be proven only in formal terms—without preventing the
individual from trying to withdraw into private spaces in which he
can at least indulge in unplanned and unmeasured mourning.

According to the planned design, order and boredom are mutually
exclusive. In a totally planned system an empty space can be foreseen,
but this is not true of boredom: it cannot be planned, and what the
bored person does is not predictable. Thus, boredom can be neither
planned nor desired by the person who wishes to realize the plan.
Thought geared to order in the life of society distributes opportunities
for power. If ideas for order are to be realized, power must be
employed to achieve that end. Unlike the situation in utopia, there is
no prevailing consensus in reality as to the ways and means of distributing power or the mode by which it is already distributed. Power
is not the only means of upholding an existing system of order: there
is also dissimulation. One such method is etiquette, and the court is
the place where it is employed.

Etiquette has been described here as the "second-tier system of
order," a means of rendering the existence of the first system of order
acceptable, if not actually disguising it. Since the second-tier system
is oriented toward the first, its resemblance to the latter is more one
of form than one of real content; it is less "imbued with life," but
because of this it is all the stricter and more steeped in rules. Yet this
also poses a danger of boredom. Initially, it is counteracted by the
high degree of affect modeling, which is already present at the time

power is being concentrated and whose external features are represented by the court. Refinement of affects signifies the possibility for variance in a small space: a high number of operative behavioral alternatives with a constant space "for overspill"—this is where sublimation begins to appear.

The idea of "totality," already encountered in our examination of utopia, is alive and well at court: etiquette, the second-tier system of order, must be isomorphic with the first-tier system in order to function. Everyone has to submit to it, even the ruler, who can rely on subordination in reality only if he himself is able to subordinate in principle. There is no better way of demonstrating the conformity to the first system of order than by pointing to the alacrity with which the second is accepted. Only the good courtier is a good subject, even if rulers are soon inclined to suspect that the only reason someone can adapt well is to be able to conspire better—in other words, is also able to damage the existing order.

Since etiquette can be reduced to a concept of order in strict form, it creates boredom—as does any system of rigid behavioral procedure. Centralized power affords security, but at the seat of power this leads to the initially calming, then more unsettling and discouraging feeling of always having known beforehand what then actually happened. Chance, so abhorrent, is the order of the day in utopia; the mechanism of kingship excludes chance because it is liable to upset the delicate balance. In the nineteenth century, Stendhal criticized civilization, which had borrowed its order from utopia and taken its standards of measurement for bourgeois *contenance*[26] from courtly behavior: "Now that civilization has gotten rid of chance, there is nothing more that is unforeseen."[27] The world was thus no longer a "field for surprises," and thus in the actual sense had become inhuman. (Gehlen of course used the concept to mean precisely the opposite— denoting a state of the world which must be changed by taking action, which must be planned.) Lucien Leuwen does not realize that boredom is already threatening the society of the past, of which he expects the "pleasures bestowed by a former civilization," and Stendhal forgets that people were already exclaiming in bygone times what has in the meantime become a commonly heard lament in the salons of Nancy: "I am dying of boredom."[28]

Security toward the outside and boredom on the inside were characteristic of the seventeenth-century court; this theory is backed up by the games that were played to pass the time (such as the institutionalized alternation of going to war and life at the court), and also by the court jester's function. The salon became the place for those who had attempted to break through the first system of order and had failed. Their behavior engendered a significant change in the prevalence of melancholy and boredom. Whereas neither melancholy nor boredom was allowed to be displayed at court, since these would have amounted to a criticism of the system and robbed the ruler of a privilege, the salon enjoyed, on the periphery, a freedom that permitted people to be both bored and melancholic. At the same time, however, this freedom, which could not be "lived out" in the "world" signified by the court, was only tendentially present in the salon. It was not long before the universal ideal of behavior established itself, an ideal that insisted on affect modeling as embodied in the concept of the *honnête homme*. The freedom to be bored was tempting only if something could be done with it, if it could be used to hatch a plan. If such a possibility was not given—and none was given following the Fronde's failure—then the manifest boredom attested to the still prevailing primacy of the court, where boredom was dispelled. Killing it then became the maxim in the salon; but the battle against it assumed forms different from those at court. Literature was one such form, as was the increasing tendency to relax the rigid system of order to which the salon itself continued to cling. Eventually an open elite emerged which spawned those that would come to sweep aside the first-tier system of order. Whereas the boredom of the court became bearable owing to the illusion of power that took refuge in ceremonies, the boredom of the salon became bearable owing to the openness it permitted itself in the choice of its members and thus also in the forms of behavior they brought with them. *Eccentricity* was one of those categories that served to demonstrate that one belonged to a circle, without having succumbed to its maxims; it was a form of behavior more character-istic of the salon than of the court. Voiture, the wine dealer's son, is successful in the Hôtel de Rambouillet not least because of his "casual allure," which lends him an air of dandyism and belies his "inner sadness."[29]

The "reduction" of melancholy in the salons was clearly manifest. One need only compare the statements of Madame de Sévigné (cited above) with those made by Madame Geoffrin a century later, when she pretended to be reciting the fictitious first part of her memoirs: "The truthfulness of my character, the naturalness of my mind, the simplicity and flexibility of my taste have made me happy in all situa-tions of my life; thus I will take great pleasure in portraying myself."[30] This, of course, was also the specific difference between a noblewoman and a bourgeoise who was imbued with the spirit of the first salon of her time, but the contrast in the particular words chosen is a clear indication of the overall tendency. The Goncourt brothers expressed it this way:

> What the eighteenth century knows as the world does not exist yet in French society. The Versailles of Louis XIV still dominates everything; and it is not until the middle of his reign that social life breaks away from this focus and, falling back on itself, flows into Paris, branches and spreads, *throbs and flowers* in a thousand drawing-rooms. Only then do we see in its *full splendor and style,* at the apogee of its *power and charm, teeming and full-blown,* that great influence of the day, which was to end by annihilating Versailles—the *salon.*[31]

In the salons of the eighteenth century, sentimentality also replaced melancholy. When people wept together in seventeenth-century salons, it could be assumed, at least for the old Frondeurs and their entourage, that there was a "reason" for it; now weeping became a pleasure in itself: "and now the salons quake with gloomy little romances, lugubrious tales, and lachrymose recitations delivered by pretty young Muses—tears are so sweet, so sweet."[32] La Rochefoucauld's life showed us, in addition, how mourning in such a situation could appear appropriate and justifiable based on the circumstances of the time: melancholy was a way of mourning the loss of what could no longer be repeated. It was thus also the prestige-enhancing credential for those who had possessed something worth mourning. The salon of the failed Fronde found itself in the middle of "society," and cultivated the same ideal as the court. As the salons, by moving to Paris, became more distant from the court at Versailles, they also distanced themselves in the metaphorical sense. The courtly model of emotions, which demanded of La Rochefoucauld that he unveil the reasons for his melancholy, was now no longer valid. With the intrusion of the bourgeois into the salons, the ideal of inhibited emotions disappeared. What was henceforth lived out was no longer melancholy but sentimentality.

Whereas utopia recognized neither the individual nor the group but only the collective of all those who constituted the utopia, it became crucial that boredom as well as melancholy in the salon be contained in the group. The long-accomplished heights of affective discharge possible in the domain of society permitted the members of the group to find new and prestige-securing means of passing the time: it is astonishing how much satisfaction literary activity was able to offer that group, which had set out to overthrow the state.

In utopia, "never-never-land," boredom was never very far away. Even Marx seemed to harbor this insight when he dreamed of a future society whose members could change their profession any time they wished: another remedy for boredom![33] Under courtly absolutism, boredom and melancholy converged in two centers: the court and the salon. Initially, the only difference between the two types was that, in the first, one is bored but was not allowed to admit it; in the second, one was also bored, but the longer one was bored, the more and more openly one talked about it and did everything—in the group—to find new and effective means to combat this. With this concentration of boredom in two "places," ennui began to change into action. At the court, as the system of order geared to permanence, this connection was institutionalized in the alternation between life at the court and going to war. We need only refer to the writings of the Prince of Ligne—"a military and sentimental medley" (!). Hunting was the civilian counterpart of war, and was a privilege of the nobility probably also because it offered the opportunity to dispel boredom.

The Fronde represented the failed attempt to cope with boredom, from the vantage point of one center and then against it. Its failure led to the Frondeurs' expulsion from court. Not in the strict sense that they were no longer able to make an appearance there, but because they had forfeited the basis of trust they had copiously built up in order to acquire court offices, and had also lost the court's esteem. The melancholy of the salons did not develop in full force until the attempted conversion of boredom into action (which had already been considered under Louis XIII) ended in complete failure. Now mechanisms to eliminate boredom emerged which could rely on the salon as a group. Thus, on the one hand, the chances for achieving this goal were very good because the homogeneity of the members and their destinies stimulated similar means of approach; on the other hand, although an escape into brooding solipsism could not be prevented, it was inhibited. The method for coping with boredom in this way, via "proximity to the world," was literary behavior, a sphere in which the "other" was already included as potential critic, consumer, and coauthor. This "companion principle," which was always conducive to courtly literature because the writers were familiar with their audience and thus did not have to stylize their work in an exceptional way, created an enclave in the society, relying on the ideal of the *honnête homme*. If we consider La Rochefoucauld, we cannot but marvel at the speed with which he slipped out of the rugged warrior's role and into that of the "man of letters," although today this term has different connotations and is more or less intended to denote only the object of one's main preoccupation. La Rochefoucauld's flexibility was not only a personal trait but also a sign of the times. One of the peaks in civilization's development toward affect modeling clearly showed that it need not be considered only as a process of refinement in a certain "direction" but also as a high degree of readiness and a (trained) capability to redirect "inhibited" affects and use them in a different, more "appropriate" place. The fact that something of this nature remained possible although the same ideal of life was retained—a normative guiding criterion, in other words—was an indication of how minimal the space for such a refinement and redirection of the affects could be. It appears to have been, among other things, a means of combating the emergence of the resentment that "in terms of its terrain," as Max Scheler wrote, "is in particular limited to the respective *servants, the ruled,* to those who in vain lure against the thorn of an authority."[34] Scheler's further point, that the driving force behind criticism of resentment was less a will to power than an aversion to it, reveals that there was no place for resentment in the salon. There was something introverted about Scheler's archetypal resentful individual (he illustrated this, for example, by pointing to Tertullian, whom C. G. Jung used as the example par excellence of the introvert)—but in the salon there were no introverts. Rather, the salon was an attempt to block the trend toward introversion through group activity and thus to maintain proximity to society.

The Fronde had failed but "was defeated with honor," because "equals," noblemen, had fought against each other! Reference has already been made to this in connection with the rapidity with which social relations were again taken up, even between former enemies, during the period following the end of this conflict, or were even maintained in enmity (Louis XIV and La Rochefoucauld; Montmorency and Richelieu). The boredom of the salon was dispelled in the world, and the melancholy of those who frequented the salon remained surprisingly close to the lost spaces and relationships which themselves had become the impetus for adopting the melancholy stance in the first place. It would be interesting to examine the social dynamics of the salons, a force that began to build once the bourgeoisie felt at home in them, and that led to the Revolution. Thereafter, the movement appeared to wane; it was as taxing for Proust to make his way in life as it was for Swann in the *Remembrance* to gain entry to the salons of the Faubourg Saint-Germain. It was not until the bourgeoisie had already populated the salons that resentment began to grow there.

Our examination of boredom and melancholy in eighteenth-century Germany clearly reveals the link between the two phenomena and specific "spatial contexts." Unlike the unsuccessful Frondeurs, the class that made use of melancholy for self-affirmation and employed boredom to show disdain for the nobility was not an unsuccessful "clique" but only an ascendant class, in both the economic and social sense—namely, the bourgeoisie. The categories applied here are, of course, extremely blurred. In particular, we shall take the bourgeoisie to be a class that had not yet made its peace with the nobility but that did not yet possess enough power to openly oppose it. It included, in particular, the members of the bourgeoisie who knew how to express their emerging resentment in literary form or to take flight in the sciences. Groups delimited in these terms also appear in the works of Mannheim, Elias, and Balet.

Moreover, this is one of the approaches that all too easily serve as the basis for attributing melancholy to a specific *class*. Ever since Aristotle, the linking of melancholy to the question of genius has neglected the fact that someone who is able to articulate his feelings about melancholy is not necessarily the only type of person who suffers from it. Without much ado, scholars have assumed that the lower classes never felt boredom or melancholy; they have made this deficiency acceptable by ascribing both emotions to the upper classes as forms of supreme torture. This subject is far from exhausted; we allude to it here only to prevent the impression that the bourgeoisie of eighteenth-century Germany, for example, should be portrayed as being melancholic. Whether it was or not is irrelevant—regardless of the questionable validity of such a collective attribution. The crucial point is that in the process of its development and classification in society, a specific class (as yet still) excluded from power *described* its position as being melancholic. The general question then remaining is what functions such an attribution was intended to serve and, at this point, what spatial ideations might be linked to it.

The bourgeoisie of eighteenth-century Germany, which did not come to terms with the nobility or was unable to do so because it still did not have the requisite economic resources, discriminated against the latter for being "boring." Throughout the literature of the period the court is portrayed as a rigid system of useless rules, born of the princes' arbitrariness and serving no purpose other than to uphold artificial barriers between the false courtly life and the true human life. The reproach of boredom, which also gave rise to an addiction for what was new, was linked to a moral suspicion of everything: the nobility appeared not only corrupt but also morally inferior, at least in relation to the bourgeoisie. It is difficult, given the existence of petty princedoms, to determine the precise "place" that was the target of the bourgeoisie's suspicion of boredom; it varied from case to case and depended on the type of palace that was thought of as a formal principle (that is, as the ruler's seat of power), and appeared less as a uniform spatial image.

Scheler stated that the man of resentment "involuntarily slanders existence and the world in order to justify his inner sense of values."[35] This relationship also applies to the bourgeoisie's departure from the "world," the term in this case being a metaphor for society which in turn appears in a more subdued form in the concept of sociability. Scheler regards sociability as the place of semblance and disguise, as the compulsion "to pretend to be other than what one is," as the continous call for a positively sanctioned lie. Thus flawed, the bourgeois flight from society, or sociability, into the world of ideas (for it could not always be accomplished in reality) commences. Its counterpart is loneliness, which means nothing more than being alone, and thus takes on value, if only by virtue of its removal from the bustle of sociability. The term is sufficiently general to be applicable; it suggests the removal from what is spoiled as well as the return to what is original, and was explicitly conveyed in Rousseau's introductory remarks to *Emile:* "God makes all things good; man meddles with them and they become evil."[36] The everyday *bourgeois* psychology of the eighteenth century clearly recognized the degree to which society inhibited the display of affects; it was not prepared to acknowledge this inhibition and reservation as a value, which was, after all, originally *aristocratic.* This is also why nature became the bourgeois location for melancholy: it permitted affects to be lived out, since it was not subject to any inhibitions imposed by human beings. But bourgeois psychology demanded even more: the duplication of this feeling. The other person served as a means toward intensifying one's own emotions and not so much as a companion with whom one had to communicate in a world (= society = sociability). This gave rise to the cults of letter writing and friendship; these were indicative less of a rudiment of social relations than of an exaggeration of one's own mania for feeling, which served as a mark of affirmation for a powerless class.

Nature as the site of bourgeois melancholy contained the notion of the stance of the bourgeoisie in all of its variants and nuances: it heralded a class that did not think much of society because it did not have a say in society; it permitted distancing from the world of bustle while justifying this escapism; it permitted introversion to be lived out boundlessly because it was not subject to limits; it was designed as a refuge against the nobleman's palace and was thus characterized in turn ("tit for tat") by the aristocracy as being boring, and was used against the bourgeoisie as something that made them suspicious. (On the other hand, bourgeois and aristocratic tendencies overlapped in garden design. When the nobility began to lose its taste for French, artificial gardens in the style of André Le Nôtre and discovered its preference for English, "natural" gardens, it was adopting a bourgeois principle. This, as well, attested to the gradual blending of aristocracy and bourgeoisie.)

If we again bear in mind what has been said, the close ties between boredom, melancholy, and the spaces in which they "unfolded" become clear. It has always been a question of groups—of planners and inhabitants of "utopia," of courtiers and those living in the salon, of the nobility and the bourgeoisie; and there did exist "in that period a close relationship between the habits, the mental attitude of a group, and the appearance of the space in which it lived," as Maurice Halbwachs noted.[37] A juxtaposition of the German and French bourgeoisie reveals the degree to which attitudes changed, depending on whether we compare the same classes in different countries or different classes in the same country. The German *Bürgerlichkeit* of the eighteenth century combined flight from the cities, the yearning for nature, and introversion. The movement to the city began at an earlier stage in the French bourgeoisie because that is where "the offices, genteel life, everything that could tempt the most highly instructed" were located (Aynard).[38] Consequently, we cannot apply the notion of the resigned posture, which at least in the first half of the eighteenth century was crucial for the bourgeoisie's image of itself in Germany; it was already absent in the seventeenth century, where "costume, etiquette, language, and entertainment, all that is social, took on great importance among the bourgeoisie, as happens to the classes in a state of evolution, where everything is being debated."[39] Urbanity and the drive for society were linked in France, just as the yearning for nature and introversion were bound together in Germany. The phrases "inner domain" and "bourgeoisification of the poet," coined by Robert Minder, not only document the difference between French and German literature but also characterize the differences in the historical development of two bourgeoisies, one of which succeeded with 1789 and the other of which "saved" its introversion from the continually dashed attempts at revolution.[40]

The Intérieur

Adorno postulated a "need for a sociology of introversion in order to explicate the image of the *intériur* in historical terms. This idea only appears paradoxical. As a restriction of human existence, introversion enters a private domain which is supposed to be free of the power of reification. However, as a private domain it itself belongs, if only polemically, to the social order."[41] The *intérieur* of the nineteenth-century bourgeoisie takes us one step further in our discussion of the relationship between melancholy, boredom, and the spaces in which they "prevail." Adorno describes this connection more or less explicitly. An indirect link is established between *intérieur* and boredom, more characteristically accomplished in the well-known description of an undertaking that is intended to dispel the boredom lurking in the *intérieur*:

> Geismar quotes from one of the young Kierkegaard's writings the description of one of those "armchair outings" which strangely illuminate production by the isolated individual. He reports there of one "Johannes Climacus"—the pseudonym which later covers Kierkegaard's own standpoint—that "whenever Johannes occasionally asked for permission to go out, this was usually denied him; his father occasionally suggested that, as a substitute, he take him by the hand and that they go for a walk up and down the room. At first glance this was a pitiful substitute and yet . . . it concealed something altogether different. The suggestion was accepted, and it was left entirely up to Johannes to decide where they would go. Then they went out the driveway, to a nearby summer residence, or out to the beach, or back and forth in the streets, wherever Johannes wanted; for his father was able to do everything. While they were walking up and down the floor, his father told him all about what they were seeing: they greeted passersby, wagons rumbled past them, drowning out his father's voice, the wares of the pastry vendor were more inviting than ever . . ." This is how the flâneur goes for a walk without ever leaving the room; reality appears to him only as reflected by sheer introversion.[42]

Although the connection between boredom and the *intérieur* is thus established—with the *intérieur* appearing to be the place in which boredom occurs and must be dispelled in order to secure dominion (the father securing his over Johannes in Kierkegaard's case)—the link to gloom is not far off. Adorno sees this connection as being produced via the mirror of reflection, whose function consists of projecting the endless string of such apartment buildings into the closed bourgeois living room; at the same time subordinating it to the apartment and limiting the apartment with it . . . He who looks into the mirror of reflection, however, is the idle, private person who has quit the economy's production process. The mirror of reflection testifies to the lack of objects—it only brings the appearance of things into the apartment—and private reclusiveness. Mirror and mourning therefore belong together . . .

[Gloom] is part of the *intérieur* to which "mood"—the constellation of the material contents—binds it. Just as the historical image presents itself in mythical form, as bald nature—the melancholy temperament presents itself here as being historical. But in so doing as dialectical and as a "possibility" for reconciliation. Kierkegaard posits the indifference of the internal history of melancholy, just as that of subjectivity as a whole, to external history.[43]

Mirror and mourning belong together: this sentence contains the link between the melancholic situation of the *intérieur* and the recognition of a loss of world and a growing yearning for reflection. The mirror offers the external world as sheer appearance: as reality it has long been lost to anyone who uses the mirror. At the same time, however, the metaphor of the mirror manifests the chance of being able to watch oneself and at least duplicate the *intérieur*—to see it as reality and, at the same time, as appearance. In this way, loss of world, recourse to the mirrored subject of the *intérieur*—in other words, reflection—combines with the mourning at having lost the world. Adorno's apodictic formulation, however, overlooks the conditionality of the specific situation, or at least does not make it sufficiently clear. The mirror does not always have to document loss of world and compensate for it by flashing the very appearance of the lost world into the *intérieur: intérieur*, mirror, and melancholy are not necessarily interrelated. The dandy, who—as described by Baudelaire and expanded upon by Camus—dies in front of the mirror (like Wilde's Dorian Gray) after living in front of it, must also be placed in this context. Eccentricity and mirror fit together, just as the latter goes with introversion. The connection between introversion and the yearning for nature, on the other hand, remained a characteristic of bourgeois society. The utopia of Paul Scheerbart's *Glasarchitektur* (1914) is evidence of that continuity.[44] Designed as a protest against the "*boring* frontal architecture of the brick buildings" (p. 75) disturbing to utopia, glass architecture draws nature into the *intérieur*, which "lets sunlight and the light of the moon and stars into the rooms not only through a few windows but through as many walls as possible, made entirely of glass, of colored glass" (p. 11). That which preserves introversion in the dawning age of technology becomes "paradise on earth": "When I am in my room of glass, I want no part of the outside world . . . If I long for sky, clouds, trees, and pastures, I can always go outside or seek out a special veranda with 'transparent' panes of glass" (p. 47). In the course of its development, the bourgeoisie, which becomes economically emancipated, does not retain nature as a refuge but pockets it as its property, surrounded by glass walls designed to lend a possessed nature the illusion of being free, unpossessed. This is the illusion of bourgeois capitalism: "Given *modest* demands, every *houseowner* can draw on glass architecture" (p. 12). Being open to nature is the counterpart to the ruling class's awareness of having to maintain distance in social situations.

In an essay on loneliness, Alexander Rüstow quotes Flaubert, who in connection with *Madame Bovary* spoke of the many mediocre people, each of whom has his "own windowless world of mediocre, foolish stupidity." Rüstow later took up this metaphor, reminiscent of Leibniz; his descriptions of loneliness and the mirror that plays a central role in it nearly always imply the notion of the windowless monad.[45] But few people ever ask whether this Leibnizian metaphor may simply be transposed into the context of the nineteenth century. For the changes in social conditions, which also change the view of the *intérieur* and of the mirror that retrieves the world as appearance, would appear to affect the changes in the image. In his essay "Subjectivity, the Foundation of Knowledge, and Living Mirror in Leibniz,"[46] Friedrich Kaulbach explicitly calls attention to a connection that seems to be contrary to the thrust of Adorno's interpretation of Kierkegaard. Kaulbach makes it clear that the discussion of the mirror was originally an attempt to recognize and make use of that form of human subjectivity which in Kierkegaard's case had already long taken flight from the world. With Leibniz the "mirror is . . . the Copernican standpoint which consciousness has attained by crossing the borders of the here and now . . . Thus, the talk of the mirror illustrates consciousness' crossing over to the perspective of objectivity and worldliness."[47] One need only juxtapose the concept of "worldliness" with that of "objectlessness" employed by Adorno, or the idea of objectivity with the category of the "individual," to see how the image has changed. To be sure, in Leibniz's case it is a question of "model steps"—that is, "philosophical prospects on the world and the objects in it, expressed in model systems, according to respectively specific standpoints."[48] In Kierkegaard's case it is a question of a real coming to terms with the world, which culminates in the flight into the *intérieur* and the unwavering stance of the "individual." Nevertheless, the stance toward the world has shifted fundamentally here, in that it may now be observed in the model or in experience close to the body. The soul as "a little world" (Leibniz) or the "familiarization of each and every thing with every other thing"[49] documents the link between the philosophical situation and a view of the world which has confidence in prestabilized harmony, and places the aspiration toward *harmonia mundi* in opposition to growing individualization. The nineteenth-century *intérieur* is dominated by melancholy, which compensates for its loss of world with the image of the world presented to it by the mirror.

This recourse to a metaphor which originates in Leibniz's work and is often used in connection with nineteenth-century loneliness and melancholy was necessary in order to show that a situation of reflection need not by any means lead to the negation of world, flight from the mirror, and the melancholy of introversion. Rather, it was possible for a system to arise out of a subjectivity which could still be sure of itself; and this system was more geared to mastering the world and was optimistic in nature. The transformation of the metaphor from Leibniz to Kierkegaard documents the rise and fall of the Enlightenment.

Although Adorno links the mirror motif too exclusively to the individual living in the nineteenth-century *intérieur,* one must not downplay the importance of his indicating the degree to which nineteenth-century melancholy is an emotion of the individual as well as the degree to which boredom was to be found everywhere, far from the court and palace. Rüstow refers to this in the above-mentioned essay, highlighting the difficulty of delineating the sociological "current" in these "individualizations." The difficulty is in fact one of finding a common denominator for the various types of personalities. There are many from which to choose, and it is quite a task to select those that could be considered typical. Another problem is posed by the danger of arriving at a simplistic statistical average drawn from the abundance of "case studies" which would, in turn, have to be considered representative of a tendency for the era. Nevertheless, we can conclude our investigation of the spaces of boredom and melancholy by mentioning three names: Maine de Biran, Proust, and Valéry. Here again, the emphasis on literature is intentional. The difficulty of making generalizations based on the boredom of, say, Benjamin Constant, Chateaubriand, and Senancour becomes more acute if one looks at the circumstances of the lives of those involved and attempts, with a micrological approach to the sociology of knowledge, to deduce their views from the conditions in which they lived. Such a biographical undertaking may be justified, but is for the most part lacking in sociological value. It therefore appears more important for a sociological approach to take literature as a *direct* source from time to time, focusing less on its material dependence on reality than on the compatibility of its structures with those of reality, as Lucien Goldmann suggests: "The relation between collective ideology and great individual literary, philosophical, theological, etc. creations resides not in an identity of content, but in a more advanced coherence and in a homology of structures, which can be expressed in imaginary contents very different from the real content of the collective consciousness."[50]

Maine de Biran: Homme Intérieur *and* Homme Extérieur

Maine de Biran's *Journals,* which begin in February 1814, clearly signal the turning point after which melancholy and boredom may be considered categories of the individual. It is not until this reduction takes place, which from a sociological-historical viewpoint is determined most of all by the dissolution of traditional cultures and fixed relations of power, that boredom and melancholy may be regarded as "existential qualities" which are inherent "in man" and supposedly cannot be bypassed by any merely "external" sociological inquiry. (So far as the sociology of literature is concerned, it would also be in order to examine the connections between the diary as a literary form, on the one hand, and melancholy and boredom, on the other. It seems that sociable forms of melancholy—as are found in La Rochefoucauld—likewise breed sociable literature—such as aphorisms and maxims—whereas a melancholy of introversion, by contrast, withdraws into the diary.)

In our investigation of the spaces where melancholy and boredom could be found, it was obvious that both were allocated certain places. This allocation varied, depending on whether the allocating class was able to admit its boredom (salon) or not (court), and on whether it used boredom as a reproach (bourgeoisie versus nobility in the courts of eighteenth-century Germany) and even associated it with ethical considerations or planned its system to exclude boredom and melancholy entirely (utopia). In the case of Maine de Biran, it is clear that neither melancholy nor boredom is bound to any fixed place:

Having left Paris . . . I arrived at Grateloup on the third of February . . . In Paris I complained of the bustle there; here I complain of the lack of it. In the capital the number of objects, the variety of occupations, and the motives for activity make me somewhat giddy and confused, a state incompatible with happiness . . . Here, on the contrary, the movements impressed on my sensibility by the habit of an active and thoroughly external life are much more rapid than those of the objects whose impression surrounds me and which, because they are unable to strike a balance with my moods, result in tedium and boredom. Where is the balance point and how to find it?[51]

Consequently, boredom—and, according to Maine de Biran, who is explicit on this point, also melancholy—are experienced both in solitude and in company. "I am enjoying my solitude and a few hours of absolute repose, everyone being at Mass. Lanquid and ailing state; went for a walk; *idleness* without enjoying it, dizziness." This is his entry for June 2, 1816, with regard to boredom in solitude. On January 1, 1817, boredom at the court is dispelled only by means of a preferential act on the king's part, but one that does not become the rule: "I am beginning the year with a sort of meditative disposition, which contrasts with the activity imposed on me by the circumstances. I felt bored and under the weather at the Tuileries: a kind word from the king made up for it." As a result, no form of solitude is left as a "refuge": "It is a question of finding a solitude within one's soul where *the world cannot enter;* if this solitude were established, I would be able to face the world and all of its ups and downs; but so long as the solitude of the soul depends on place, time, mood, etc., . . . peace cannot be assured" (December 6, 1823).[52]

For Maine de Biran, there is no longer any possibility of fleeing melancholy and boredom or of playing off some boredom-free place against another where boredom prevails. For him, boredom is not socially determined; he finds its determining cause within himself, providing a portrait of the *homme intérieur:* "I remain by virtue of my habits or my natural dispositions an *homme intérieur,* yet without being able to make use of my active faculties; from which it follows that I am nothing, either on the inside or on the outside" (November 1818). And he is very much aware of having created something new by drawing this clear-cut distinction between *homme extérieur* and *homme intérieur:* "The distinction between *interior* man and *exterior* man is of utmost importance and will be the foundation of all my subsequent research: it is a question of making a clear-cut division, which has not yet been undertaken by any philosophy, even by those that seem to have taken meditation the furthest" (October 28, 1819).

Maine de Biran's typology, which corresponds, even in some of its details, to the Jungian distinction between introversion and extroversion, is the result of an experience which is no longer able to fix with any precision its feelings of boredom and melancholy. This is clearly expressed when Maine de Biran says that he is nothing, "either on the inside or on the outside." Owing to the impossibility of localizing one's own state of affect, the only remaining way out is to ascribe it to a type. The *homme intérieur* reveals himself as such. He is characterized equally by his *"withdrawal of interest* in things on the outside" and his conviction that he was not born to act—thus reaffirming the aforementioned connection between *intérieur,* loss of world (a state of objectlessness), and the penchant for reflection. There is an important, albeit subtle, difference between the *homme intérieur* and the individual in the *intérieur,* though the two concepts are very closely related: Maine de Biran recognizes that the *homme intérieur* is a type to which another type can be juxtaposed. He describes one of the possible forms of human behavior as being exemplified in a specific manner by the phenomena of boredom and melancholy. In the case of Kierkegaard and a philosophy focused on the concept of existence, the individual who must endure his boredom and melancholy is not a type. Rather, the melancholic, bored individual recognizes something in himself that is part of the human condition per se: boredom and gloom. Although Maine de Biran's distinction is more exclusive (no one can become an introvert who is, in fact, extroverted), in the Kierkegaardian philosophy and the schools of philosophy that follow its example, the individual's process of (re)cognition possesses a higher dignity: here the human being *as such* is recognized, whereas in the former case it is only a type that is pinpointed. The two notions are similar in that they both come close to a theory of the elite that is, after all, always situated in the realm of speculation on boredom and melancholy. Maine de Biran's type ranks higher on the scale of exclusivity because it is not—even potentially—within reach of every human being; the recognition of boredom and melancholy as existential elements represents the most definitive statement that can be made about the human being *as such.* After all, the *intérieur* is still viewed as space by Kierkegaard, even if it remains closed to the world, whereas with Maine de Biran the inner world of the specific type is all that is left.

Marcel Proust

In addition to Balzac's *Human Comedy, Remembrance of Things Past* may be the most important modern novel that lends itself to sociological

analysis. The work as a whole should actually be the subject of investigation, but since this is not possible in the present context, we shall
have to restrict our analysis to fragmentary aperçus on the topic of
the link between melancholy and boredom in certain spaces.[53]
Proust's image is tied, more than that of virtually any other writer, to
the notion of a specific *intérieur*—namely, the room at 102 boulevard
Haussmann. When Proust inherited it from his uncle, he was disappointed: it had gilded decor on flesh-colored walls, it was incessantly
filled with the noise of the neighborhood, and the trees were growing
in through the windows. That was all to change. "Finally," André
Maurois wrote, "he discovered a remedy, which was to have his room
entirely lined with cork. Thus, it was between four walls padded with
this material, a proof against all noise from outside, that he wrote his
great work."[54] This image, which with a certain amount of justifica-
tion can be compared to the windowless monad (Proust speaks of it
at a similar point in *Remembrance*—II, p. 497), arises when we
examine the Proustian *intérieur*. The comments offered here are
intended to show that this *intérieur,* in turn, differs considerably from
the one described in connection with Kierkegaard.

Proust's reception has been based to a large extent on the concept
of time; readers have taken their cue from the author's own words.
Georges Poulet, however, emphatically countered this one-sided
approach in his book *Proustian Space,* pointing out that the concept
of time in *Remembrance* radically contradicts Bergson's concept.[55] He
focused instead on the significance of space: "Proust's time is spatially
transformed, adjacently transposed time."[56]

In Proust's work the *intérieur* becomes a site where "world" can be
recovered, both in life and in the novel. Proust's state of isolation was
ultimately conditioned by society, as Hannah Arendt emphasized in
her description of the Faubourg Saint-Germain: "The individual and
his reconsiderations belong to society, even when he retires into the
mute and incommunicative solitude in which Proust himself finally
disappeared when he decided to write his work. There his inner life,
which insisted on transforming all worldly happiness into inner
experience, became like a mirror in whose reflection truth might
appear."[57] The "notorious boredom" of the Faubourg Saint-Germain
also characterizes *Remembrance of Things Past.* Swann, who keeps a
similar distance from the Faubourg and is, in turn, viewed by it as
distantly as it views the narrator of *Remembrance* and Proust himself,
develops a veritable palliative against boredom by means of what
Proust calls "amusing sociological experiments" (I, p. 561); these
consist of cutting the corners of the unwritten laws of etiquette and

inviting the widest variety of different people all at once. In the Ver-
durins' salon, they "avoided the company" of everyone they regarded
as "bores" (II, p. 1078); Proust appears to be paraphrasing Saint-
Simon here. Madame Verdurin ultimately considers it an important
factor in her upbringing that she was taught at an early age how to
be bored (III, p. 284). And at the Faubourg itself, boredom prevails
because those who live there are usually, like the duchess, "too far
above the milieu of their origins not to be bored there" (II, p. 908).
Although Bergotte in *Remembrance* suggests to the narrator that
"perhaps some of the great masterpieces were written while their
authors yawned" (III, p. 284), it is safe to assume that Proust's work,
in any case, was influenced by the boredom of the Faubourg, and to
some extent also by the boredom of those who aspired to gain entry
to it.

In fact, one could say that Proust's accomplishment consists in
having provided a masterful portrayal of boredom—which in turn
has something to do with the fact that, as Benjamin wrote, "the problems of Proust's characters . . . are those of a satiated society."[58] This
society lives at a specific, fixed place, the Faubourg Saint-Germain,
which instills society with its elite quality. The public sphere of this
society is the salon, which develops a market atmosphere every bit
like that of a market itself. At the same time, the *intérieur* is not only
the focal point from which boredom is described but also the site of
melancholic sensibility. Even as a student, Proust wrote about the
"center of things, each of which gives me grandiose and melancholy
feelings and sensations, which I enjoy."[59] Enjoyable melancholy in
this case does not correspond to an adoption of the old theme of
"sweet melancholy" or to a mechanism of ideological mystification of
the state of affects that one cannot escape. Rather, melancholy and
the element inducing it appear to be welcome aids for recognizing
reality and subsequently being able to portray it in literature: "Well,
sir, infirmity alone makes us take notice and learn, and enables us to
analyse mechanisms of which otherwise we should know nothing"
(II, pp. 675–676). This is an eminently reflexive act, "because, true
reality being discoverable only by the mind, being the object of a
mental process, we acquire a true knowledge only of things that we
are obliged to recreate by thought, things that are hidden from us in
everyday life" (II, p. 797).

Thus, the *intérieur* in which the novel takes shape becomes the location where the world is recognized and described—an attitude that is
"social" in a manner similar to that occasionally taken by the narrator
in *Remembrance:* "Though conducted in silence, this exercise was

nonetheless a conversation and not a meditation, my solitude a mental social round in which it was not I myself but imaginary inter-locutors who controlled my choice of words, and in which, as I for-mulated, instead of the thoughts that I believed to be true, those that came easily to my mind and involved no retrogression from the out-ward inwards, I experienced the sort of pleasure, entirely passive, which sitting still affords to anyone who is burdened with a sluggish digestion" (I, p. 623).

In Proust's work, the *intérieur* becomes less a refuge from the world and more a place where the individual "copes with" the world—namely, in the novel. It seems to be of some significance that the novel assumes the form of a system whose parts are all interrelated and do not reveal their specific function until the end of the novel, when the reader has a knowledge of the whole system. As Proust put it in a letter to Jacques Rivière (February 7, 1914), "I have finally found a reader who *guessed* that my book is a dogmatic, systematically designed work!"[60] The "phenomenon of the *mémoire involontaire*," in which lost moments and lost places are retrieved, precludes a melan-cholic stance characterized by mourning for something which is lost and can no longer be found, and characterized by resignation to the fact that such is and probably must be the case. For Proust, the "power of evocation equal to that of former days but capable now of evoking only pain (III, p. 488) is just as much a characteristic of the person who lives in the *intérieur* as the ability to evoke the past or to be—involuntarily—surprised by it; however, this is "optimism . . . the philosophy of the past" (III, p. 676). The *intérieur,* in invoking the past, becomes the place where not melancholy but trust grows within the person who creates the world anew in designing the literary system. In this connection, we would do well to recall Leib-niz's metaphor of the mirror, as Poulet did:

And perhaps the clearest and most emphatic metaphoric symbol for this relationship between the variety and unity of the work is that of Marcel's bedroom in Balbec, the walls of which are covered by a glass bookcase, in whose panes the colors of the sky are reflected in a series of totally different images . . . The metaphor is thus one of absolute precision . . . When Proust's novel closes, and when the consciousness that unabatedly registered the events is in a position to cast a concluding clarifying glance back on it, what happens in the mind of the person who has an overview of the whole is that the discontinuous variety of the episodes, which until then resembled a series of isolated and adjacent pictures, gives way to a coherent plurality of images that are interrelated, illuminate one other and, to express it as a whole, form a *composition* . . . In other words, no other conclusion can be drawn than that Proust's novel ends with the proof of its inner coherence.[61]

The formal similarities of this procedure to that of utopian thought are obvious. The approaches converge in the concept of the system, which in this case—as with Poulet—coincides with that of composition.[62] Coherence—which can also be called "harmony"—is the overriding goal of both. But whereas utopia projects harmony into the future, Proust draws it from the past by means of *mémoire involontaire:* regained time corresponds to a realized, retrospective utopia. Melancholy is no longer to be found in this realized utopia, since the lost places and times have been recovered; boredom has likewise vanished, since the persistent process of involuntary remembrance (diametrically opposed to the "cruelty of memory" (III, p. 569) prevents the boredom caused by a static existence.

The conclusion that in the Proustian utopia the individual recovers the world by looking backward must, however, be modified. For the site of fulfillment (Proust speaks of the "disillusion of fulfillment"— II, p. 398) is a system that takes possession of past reality by means of memories, but in its satisfaction at having done so it can then exclude the reality of the present. The Proustian *intérieur*'s proximity to the world does not, unlike that of the salon, consist of *actual* proximity to the world, but is *fictitious:* it is the proximity of literature. The system that regains its shape in its proximity to the world and recovers the world provides legitimation for the person who creates that system. The conclusion begins to weaken as soon as one begins to question its legitimacy for the person who recreates the system—that is, who receives the work. Proust's "remembered time" appears optimistic in nature because it is not at all compelling. Although it does not declare a solipsistic introversion to be the only true form and does not defame the world, it points to a second reality that corresponds to the first—as its reflection. Thus, the mirror motif also appears, in that Proust's proximity to the world is alluded to by the mirror, is derived from the aesthetic design. It is sufficient for the writer as a type and is sufficient for literature as a referential category. In the case of Valéry, we shall see how this element of the constructive, of system building, derives its validity from aesthetics—a factor of appearance that tries to persuade itself that it has regained being.

* * *

Paul Valéry and Monsieur Teste

> The intellect remains private, and that is the melancholy secret of Monsieur Teste.
>
> Walter Benjamin, *On the Current Social Position of the French Writer*

The tendencies in the monumental work *Remembrance of Things Past* are even more apparent in the hundred or so pages of *Monsieur Teste.* Valéry's own interpretation of Monsieur Teste was that this man virtually never has a thought that is "not accompanied by the feeling that it is tentative . . . The short, intense life of this brain is spent in supervising the mechanism by which the relations of the known and the unknown are established and organized. It even uses its obscure and transcendental powers in the obstinate pretense that it is an *isolated system* in which the infinite has no part."[63] To an even greater extent than the general thrust of the interpretation, the concept of the "isolated system" is reminiscent of Proust, and the unambiguous mention of it shows that the tendency is similar. There is also a strong affinity with the concept of order: every system promises order, and the isolated system is a guarantee of this.

"Stupidity is not my strong point" (p. 9): thus begins *An Evening with M. Teste,* and the statement fits Monsieur Teste himself. "M. Teste was perhaps forty years old. His speech was extraordinarily rapid, and his voice quiet. Everything about him was fading, his eyes, his hands. His shoulders, however, were military, and his step had a regularity that was amazing. When he spoke he never raised an arm or finger: *he had killed his puppet.* He did not smile, and said neither hallo nor good-by. He seemed not to hear a 'How do you do?'" (p. 12). Permanence and time are of interest to Edmond Teste: "He watched for the repetition of certain ideas; he watered them down with numbers" (p. 13). Teste dreams of his "own malleability"; he is "a being absorbed in his own variation, one who becomes his own system" (p. 13). He has "no opinions. I believe he could become impassioned *at will,* and to attain a definite end. What had he done with his personality? How did he see himself? . . . He never laughed, never a look of unhappiness on his face. *He hated melancholy*" (p. 14, italics added). Boredom is also foreign to him, for when the narrator attempts to imagine how Teste would "normally" be, he says, "He loves, he suffers, he is bored" (p. 16). Finally, the narrator describes Teste's apartment:

> I *did not see a book.* Nothing indicated the traditional manner of work, at a table, under a lamp, in the midst of papers and pens.
>
> In the greenish bedroom, smelling of mint, there was only a candle

and, sitting around it, the dull abstract furniture—the bed, the clock, the wardrobe with a mirror, two armchairs—like rational beings. On the mantle, a few newspapers, a dozen visiting cards covered with figures, and a medicine bottle. I had never had a stronger impression of the ordinary. It was any lodging, like geometry's any point—and perhaps as useful. My host existed in the most general interior. I thought of the hours he had spent in that armchair. I was frightened at the infinite drabness possible in this pure and banal room. I have ... M. Teste talked of money ... I can still hear his voice, lowered and slow, making the flame dance above the single candle that burned between us, as he recited very large numbers, wearily. Eight hundred ten million seventy-five thousand five hundred fifty ... I listened to this unheard-of music without following the calculation. He conveyed to me the fever of the Bourse and these long series of names of numbers gripped me like poetry. He correlated news events, industrial phenomena, public taste and the passions, and still more figures, one with another. He was saying: "Gold is, as it were, the mind of society." (pp. 20–21)

Let us summarize what the above description tells us about Monsieur Teste: he conspicuously arranges his life (which consists largely of thought) in a mechanical way; he lives in arbitrariness, in the general *intérieur;* he characterizes society in terms of money; he is not melancholy or bored. This abbreviated description resembles Claessen's essay "Rationality Revised" and Niklas Luhmann's "Reflexive Mechanisms." Monsieur Teste is an expression of Luhmann's observation that "reflexivity is both a product and a condition of civilization."[64] And we get the equally strong impression that Teste has something to offer that Luhmann does not include: a "theory of the reduction of complexity." Like Luhmann, Teste would refuse to understand being relieved of any duties as the proclivity to lead a comfortable existence free of tension. "It is, totally to the contrary, a facility for the absorption and processing of ... complexity." The reduced *intérieur* ultimately documents (turned inside out) the "increase in the human capacity to absorb complexity in relation to the extremely complex world."[65]

Claessens describes, in the same vein as Norbert Elias, the evolution toward higher rationality through the pacification of spaces, the resulting possibility of conceptualizing long chains of action, and the refinement of mores. The phenomenon of money, which according to Georg Simmel can be viewed as the symbol for the proportions and form of exchangeability, is a big step in the direction of modern rationality. "Arbitrariness" would appear to be an "ingredient of rationality" beyond the stage of "distancing from the things of the world" and the intellect's assertion of itself against "the tradition-bound emotionality desiring a commitment to being."[66] This shows how close the two essays by Claessens and Luhmann come to the thoughts of Valéry. Monsieur Teste is a reflective type in a highly complex world where everything depends on being able to come to terms with this complexity. For Teste, one means of doing so is offered by the *intérieur*. However, it is important to bear in mind that here we are no longer dealing with the nineteenth-century *intérieur* (a form that we can almost still apply in the case of Proust), which involves devising a private sphere that can no longer be realized in the "world."[67] Teste's *intérieur* is arbitrary and interchangeable in nature. It is no longer private, for by virtue of its interchangeability, it acquires a public nature. Teste does not take flight from the complexity of the world; he reduces the complexity of "home" and allows only his thoughts a certain amount of independence. In a world where the private sphere is fashionable as a refuge, the private spaces resemble each other like the monotony of the world from which they are intended to serve as an escape in the first place. This is Teste's good fortune: his *intérieur* can be fixed and has a "strangeness" of its own precisely because it is distinct from the customary private sphere. Mobility is offered by the arbitrariness of the *intérieur,* which affords the opportunity of being at home "everywhere," while safety is afforded by the similarity that this room and its inhabitant bear to the world: Teste is the paradigm of the arbitrary world, and the figures that he mumbles speak of the exchangeable nature of the things outside of it.

Teste is no longer bound to the *intérieur* because he knows how to find the urgently needed distraction in reflection. This is why boredom is foreign to him; the narrator finally imagines how Teste is bored, in order to make Teste like himself. Valéry, who planned to write "The System,"[68] had long achieved this with "testism." Here, however, we are dealing not with the ordered fullness of regained times and places that appear as a system (as was the case in Proust) but with the thinking of the person who, in his arbitrariness, adapted to the world. External conformity permits Teste the mobility of his reflections. The question previously raised with regard to the distinction between world and introversion no longer presents a problem for Teste, is no longer "questionable." A private refuge is unnecessary if the mere functioning of the mind in its arbitrariness is preserved. Teste stabilizes himself through the external world: free-floating reflection compensates him for it. However, one element of dis-order remains: melancholy. Hatred of it is the only emotion that Teste allows himself; he reflects on the actual threat it poses. Teste the thinker has not yet gained control of his psyche: one could call him perfect only after he had dispelled it. Melancholy represents an element of dis-order in this respect as well, although it has been channeled into the individual. Control of boredom stands in complete opposition to this. At this point we must note something that we have already seen in the case of Proust: 'Teste,' like the system of *Remembrance*, is elitist in nature. The solutions found here are those of the aesthetically oriented loner. This is true of the narrator in Proust's work, whose *mémoire involontaire* recovers the world for him; and it is also true of Teste, who counteracts the growing complexity of the world by fixing an arbitrary, internal world.

The Transformation of Boredom: "Camp"

The connection between literary conceptions and the formulation of a way of dispelling boredom implies the need for a general aesthetic investigation. Yet we shall not undertake such a study, even though phenomena in painting (for example, Piet Mondrian and monochromatics), in literature (the French *nouveau roman*), and a certain tendency in modern music would lend themselves to such an investigation. Adorno states: "To the extent that music is pursued without reflection, to the extent that it does not itself recognize its problems as a precondition for its own existence and addresses them, it becomes a mere repetition of things that have already been said a hundred times, a kind of tautology of the world which, moreover, places an aura around these things. At most it confirms that that which is sad is immutable and possibly even 'as it should be.'" [69] In conclusion, we can only note the extent to which, in our own day, aesthetic forms and rules of the game catch hold of boredom in the belief that they have thereby escaped it.

In a polemic against Max Bense, Horst Enders emphasized the role played by boredom in a theory of texts proposed by Bense. Enders wrote: "Boredom forms the basis, so to speak, for communication, in an attempt (using the simple trick of 'reduction' renders the means to support it highly questionable) to sanction experimental poetry by means of historical determinacy." [70] We can easily see the paradox: boredom, once a sign that communication with the eternally unchanging world was no longer possible, now becomes the very means of communication. Reduction, which may justifiably be described as "questionable," reveals the proximity to the fundamental ontological intention: boredom as a basic state pertaining to all people should also be able to serve as a means of communication. Enders, however, pointed to a second effect of reduction which usually receives too little attention: "So long as textual literature understands, first of all, what it is expected to do by means of all kinds of theoretical distortions, and does not see itself as the provisional end of a clearly visible literary-historical process, it will continue to justify its boredom to itself in terms of a highly regarded spiritual background and the reduction of vital human existence—and theoretical decisions will not be made."[71] Enders used this as a polemical argument in the name of "vital human existence," and against boredom as a stylistic principle. Today Enders would not have to resort to such imprecise phrasing: the camp movement, as Susan Sontag describes it, has dealt a death blow to boredom as an aesthetic principle. Camp, which as Sontag herself says defies description, cannot be defined here, but certain aspects can nevertheless be outlined. Sontag writes: "Detachment is the prerogative of an elite; and as the dandy is the nineteenth century's surrogate for the aristocrat in matters of culture, so Camp is the modern dandyism. Camp is the answer to the problem: how to be a dandy in the age of mass culture." The answer is relatively simple: one partakes of mass culture according to a selective principle which is difficult to define. (Some examples of camp: "Tiffany lamps, . . . the Brown Derby restaurant on Sunset Boulevard in L.A., *The Enquirer*, . . . Aubrey Beardsley drawings, *Swan Lake*, Bellini's operas, . . . certain turn-of-the-century picture postcards, . . . the old Flash Gordon comics . . .") Whereas Sontag attributes a posture "of disdain, or else ennui" to the dandy (she wrongly mentions *Monsieur Teste* in this connection shortly thereafter), this is precisely where camp differs from dandyism:

> The old-style dandy hated vulgarity. The new-style dandy, the lover of Camp, appreciates vulgarity. Where the dandy would be continually offended or bored, the connoisseur of Camp is continually amused, delighted. The dandy held a perfumed handkerchief to his nostrils and was liable to swoon; the connoisseur of Camp sniffs the stink and prides himself on his strong nerves . . . It is a feat, of course. A feat goaded on, in the last analysis, by the threat of boredom. The relation between boredom and Camp taste cannot be overestimated. Camp taste is by its nature possible only in affluent societies, in societies or circles capable of experiencing the psychopathology of affluence.[72]

In short, camp is dandyism without elitism, if one disregards the question of whether the appreciation of mass culture might not harbor an elitist motivation—namely, the desire to enjoy something that the masses (of art consumers) do not want to acknowledge. The (suggested) absence of a claim to elitism is the reason for foregoing the appreciation of boredom, which appeared to be necessary for the dandy to identify himself as an elitist: Leopardi, Schopenhauer, and Nietzsche are thus all dandies. In this way the dandy amuses the aristocracy, which always appreciates the bohemian. The bourgeois is the opponent of the bohemian. The bohemian's eccentricity assures the aristocrat that his boredom will be dispelled and must therefore appear suspicious to someone who views peacefulness, and with it immobility, as the citizen's prime obligation. By dispensing with boredom as a standard of legitimation, there is no longer any reason for the melancholic attitude: the psyche of the person who advocates camp is vigorous and enthusiastic.

Camp is a further attempt to deal with boredom by means of an aesthetic approach. The replacement of being by appearance was already implied in Kierkegaard's works and pursued by Proust. In this respect, camp has its ancestors. Susan Sontag quotes Sartre's comment in *Saint-Genet:* "Elegance is the quality of conduct which transforms the greatest degree of being into appearing." [73] In this sense Proust had already spoken of society as the "realm of nullity" (3, 278). The transformation of being into appearing is the aesthetic response to the question of how to deal with the loss of the world. The appreciation of appearing is connected with the existence of the "affluent society": the legitimation for the concept of the mere appearance of the world is derived from the comforting feeling of possessing enough to have one hand free.

Whereas the utopia from which this view stems does not include boredom or melancholy because it designs a new world in which neither any longer has a place, camp eludes boredom because all things can become important to it and because their arbitrary interchangeability and replaceability offer the guarantee of constantly changing pleasure. This outlook also dispels the melancholic attitude. Utopian thought and camp coincide in this respect. Yet whereas utopia projects total political planning into the future, camp clings to the exchangeable things of the present. Whereas utopia had no more room for boredom because all that existed was the totally planned utopia, camp does not allow for boredom because the arbitrariness of the world's contents does not permit a specification of taste and the reduction of behavioral forms to aesthetic pleasure. Whereas utopian thought is forced, one-track politics, camp culminates in the nonpolitical stance: "It goes without saying that the Camp sensibility is disengaged, depoliticized—or at least apolitical."[74] Whereas boredom, according to the will of the seventeenth-century utopian thinker, was no longer possible for political reasons, it disappears in camp because the world's spaces have become as arbitrary as their contents, which can always be used in the aesthetic game.

The description of the "spaces" of boredom and melancholy yields yet another bridge linking reflection with the syndrome of action-inhibition. Once we have described this, we will be able to return to the theme of space: it seems logical to assume that reflection arising from the inhibition of action withdraws from the society in which action must occur. Boredom and melancholy would then have to be understood in terms of action-inhibition and reflection, and the liberation of reflection is the first opportunity to withdraw from certain spaces and to "take refuge" in others. This path does not lead straight from society to the ultimately windowless inner world; it may also lead to nature, where introversion can be felt freely, or to arbitrariness, which frees aesthetic action from any taint of boredom.

The Problem of Space in Psychiatric and Psychopathological Discussions of Melancholy

The phenomena of boredom and melancholy have up to this point been related to specific forms of "space" in which they are "played out." We took as a precondition for our discussion the idea that the spatial view is useful for a sociologically oriented analysis: in comparison to the concept of time, the concept of space appears to offer us more opportunity to discern social structures indirectly and analyze them in spatial metaphors. Maurice Halbwachs' assumption that "the dreamer [leaves] the time of wakefulness much more completely than the space of wakefulness" means that the category of space lies closer to reality for human behavior and thus is more difficult to separate from it.[75] There does appear to be a certain inner connection: Norbert Elias' theory, according to which the chance for refinement of mores and thus for increased rationality arises from the pacification of spaces through monopolized violence, is also of significance in the context of our analysis. Terms used by Simmel, such as the "intersection of social circles" and the "continuity of locality," are further examples of the many possible labels available. In his study of the "sociology of space," which was later incorporated into his longer work on sociology, Simmel formulated the following program:

Kant defines space, on the one hand, as the opportunity for being together; by means of the various forms of reciprocal effect among individuals, socialization brought forth other possibilities for being together, in the mental sense; some of them, however, materialize in such a way that the spatial form in which this ensues, as is the case for all others, deserves special emphasis for the purposes of our insight. *Thus, in the interest of establishing the forms of socialization, we seek the meaning that the spatial conditions of a socialization have for other sociological specifics of its determination and development* (italics added).[76]

Without wishing to conclude from this that the concept of space is necessarily preponderant, we must note that Simmel's comparison of sociology with geometry and microscopy is spatially oriented; the tension of his formal sociology also arises from the attempt to unite generalized, spatially related ideas with a historically derived example—that is, with the factor of time.[77] (Normally, concepts of time are applied spatially without any inhibitions: an hour then means no more than the turning of the hand on a clock during a segment of time selected by social agreement.) The spatial quality of language itself provides similar reinforcement for this statement: because we think in spatial terms, this reference is something we take for granted and no longer "question"; it possesses dignity in and of itself and requires no "external" legitimation. To put things more sociologically: structures without reference to the factor of time (that is, ultimately, functions) are conceivable, but functions require already existing structures if they are to be conceivable in the first place!

Thus the spatial reference, which appears to be anchored as a category in language, is also of significance in psychological, psychoanalytical, psychiatric, and psychopathological literature. In what follows, we shall disregard the psychological side of the issue and confine our discussion to the problem of melancholy. It is important to bear in mind that connecting sociological questions with the above-mentioned disciplines does not merely yield a beneficial side effect, in that it defines as a worthy object of scientific inquiry something that falls outside the bounds of the other sciences. Such an approach can probably be adequately judged only if we not merely discuss the actual issue, but also investigate what part of this side effect arises from the requirements and envious quarrels of a science organized according to the division of labor. We cannot accomplish this in the space available here. Nevertheless, if we are aware that a scientific "approach" can be determined not only by the matter of a discipline but also by its concern to establish itself in its own right, we can sharpen our critical sensitivity to subjects that are perpetually concerned with securing scientific territories. Kraepelin's animosity toward Kant and Hegel and their attempt to "have an opinion with regard to the classification and origin of mental illnesses"[78] shows how a scholar could make jealous efforts to protect his discipline against a philosophy which had already become a science. This rejection is nothing new to sociology and, on the contrary, is an integral part of it—at least with reference to the humanities.

At the same time, we should not forget that there are areas into which sociological inquiry should not venture, for we can see beforehand how minimal the results would be. This does not mean proscribing all inquiry, nor does it favor an extension of ideological suspicion. This "modesty" stems rather from the pragmatically oriented effort to allow ourselves time to formulate questions for which a meaningful answer may be found, to withhold other questions whose answers might have questionable effects, and finally to relinquish still other questions that can no longer be answered. Just as we might do well to follow Plessner's admonition that we refrain from metaphysics, so, too, we might be wise to avoid other fields of science, regardless of whether these insist on their respective autonomy or not. If, in what follows, we refer to observations in psychoanalysis, psychiatry, and psychopathology, we shall not be making a disguised attempt to draw the object of these disciplines into sociology; we shall, however, be pointing up similarities in the observations made and suggesting assumptions as to how questions with a sociological orientation might be answered in these areas in the first place.

The need to bear in mind if not a specific sociological approach then at least vaguely sociological notions becomes immediately clear when, for example, Hans Hoff in his article "The Changed Image of Melancholy" speaks of the expression of the "melancholy of *our* time in images of illness which, in comparison to classical types, are less clear and *apparently better adapted to life*" (italics added).[79] This interpretation may very well arouse sociological interest. The logical explanation, however, tends paradoxically in a direction that seems to preclude a sociological approach; for we should first ask whether in fact illness has become more differentiated and more adapted, and not whether the methods of science have become so refined that insight into a phenomenon which has not really changed has become "too deep" and can no longer recognize the phenomenon.

Also important is Hoff's comment that, despite the changed image of melancholy, the factor triggering it still poses "the danger of a threatening process of isolation."[80] The clinical perspective thus emphasizes, as well, that the retreat into the isolated ego is the essential element of the phenomenon of melancholy. When Hoff speaks further of the significance of "existential triggers" (among which he includes, for example, mothers' problems with breastfeeding)[81] and stresses the importance of the "mother-child relationship," these disturbances or the very lack of them corresponds to the disturbance of a "social formation which cannot be ignored in terms of a philosophical-anthropological viewpoint"[82] (Claessens), and thus defines a field which can be treated as a legitimate subject of sociology. In this light, melancholy is seen as hampered access to the world and impaired coping with the world, and represents humans being thrown back into a situation in which they are deprived of world. At this point, the question is not whether perhaps the sick (the melancholic) isolate themselves "of their own accord" and inflict their own loss of world, so to speak. This question is sociologically irrelevant with regard to the individual; yet we should not underestimate its significance when, in comparing several eras and cultures, we examine the structural conditions that favor or hinder isolation, a problem that Michel Foucault in particular addressed.[83] Loss of world by a particular sick person is usually not of interest in sociological terms; we are not talking of La Rochefoucauld's resigned attitude when we note how, in the salons of his day, a socially accepted form was created that made possible a form of melancholy suited to the particular social stratum.

Here, we can clearly see the relationship of the "loss of world" issue to the conception proposed by Freud, who considered regression of the libido to the ego, ambivalence, and object loss to be the three prerequisites for melancholy, particularly with respect to his concept of regression. Compared with mourning, "a normal affect," melancholy is similarly determined by "a deeply painful bad mood, a suspension of interest in the outside world"; yet is distinguished from mourning by the fact that in the latter case "the world has become poor and empty," whereas in the case of melancholy, world is "the ego itself."[84] We can see how in Freud's view, melancholy moves one space "farther," so to speak—becomes more removed from the possibility of a sociological approach. The issue of a void ego does not in general lend itself to sociological inquiry; it would be more feasible to investigate which structures condition the loss of world and thus indirectly favor ego impoverishment. The phenomenon of mourning in which the impoverishment of the world is revealed (to use Freud's terminology) would more easily lend itself to sociological analysis. In this context, we should recall that Ludwig Binswanger, who took exception to Freud's methods, promulgated a view precluding sociologically oriented analysis, because its aim, phrased very much in Heidegger's vein, was "to describe mental illnesses based on their state of being"; in this respect, Husserl's science "does for psychiatry what biology does for physical medicine."[85]

Hubert Tellenbach, who dealt explicitly with this issue in his essay "The Spatial Quality of the Melancholic,"[86] linked the question of order to that of space in a particularly interesting way by referring to Henry of Ghent, who referred to mathematically imaginative types as "melancholics who can become outstanding mathematicians but only the worst metaphysicians; for they are unable to apply their mind to places and quantities, in which all that is mathematical is grounded."[87] Subsequent to this historical excursus (and a great advantage of Tellenbach's publications on the problem of melancholy actually lies in his use of research in the fields of history, classical studies, mythology, iconography, and literature), the author emphasizes the predominance of housewives and "precision professions" among melancholics.[88] He then stresses the importance of a number of factors in the melancholic's life: order in the working world, a "measure of accuracy that is out of the ordinary" (p. 55), the experience of the day as a "unit of work and order," the "pernicious cycle of the extent and precision of achieving" (p. 57), "structural sensibility for order" (p. 66), and the "limitedness of his order" (p. 104).

The link between space and the concept of order is not new; Aristotle, in his essay on categories, emphasized the possibility of expressing continuums such as space in numbers and thereby substituting discreet quanta for them. However, these are abstract quantities and of a more general nature. The reduction of the idea of space to a numerical concept as a concept of order thus means a higher degree of abstraction, as well as greater removal from reality. All that finally remains is inner space: "My view is always directed toward the inside,"[89] a patient of Tellenbach's says. Tellenbach then arrives at an observation that fits into the complex of interrelations detailed thus far—namely, that the spatial in melancholic experience is *arbitrary:* "In melancholy being-in-the-world, that which is being-in-the-inner-world reveals itself in a spatiality characterized by pure presence, directionless and nontopographical remoteness, finally in spatiality characterized by the arbitrariness of the punctual."[90] Tellenbach consequently sees in the "constellation of *includence*" the depressive type's "being-locked-in or locking-himself-in within bounds which he finally can no longer take beyond the regular completion of his orders" (p. 113). Werther is an example of such includence, which is distinguished from "remanence" by Kierkegaard, among others. When Tellenbach speaks of the family framework, marriage, being alone, depression resulting from moving, and one's apartment as further phenomena of includence, he is alluding to that which we have called melancholy of the inner world. In this case the inner world has been further reduced—to the ego itself. There thus seem to be greater possibilities for differentiation, such as those types of remanent[91] and includent melancholy that we see in Kierkegaard and Werther. These distinctions can hardly be dealt with in sociological terms. On the other hand, Tellenbach does not mention the differentiation, which in our framework warrants considerable importance, that arises from the fact that Kierkegaard no longer has the possibility of taking refuge in nature, a possibility that was still open to Werther.

Tellenbach considers "practicing the transcendental"[92] to be the principle of a "psychotherapeutic prophylaxis for melancholy." For one thing, this means transcending the fixed space. For another, it is linked to the issue of order:

> The type of individual whose structural potential allows for future melancholy gravitates with the constancy of the typical toward the unambiguity of what is established, regulated, secured—in short, toward a form of order in all aspects of existence, which is characterized by a progressive elimination of that which is *only possible,* of the possible above all as possible dis-order . . . The essence of the melancholic type is marked by a tendency to dwell exclusively in the finite and to neglect the practice of transcendence of finiteness, without which no metamorphosis can exist.[93]

Finally, the concept of "includent melancholy" (which in this respect is very similar to that of the "remanent" type) means spatial fixation and the resulting impossibility of spatial change. Here we see the hypertrophy of order against which Tellenbach expressly juxtaposes, as a prophylaxis, a tendency toward dis-order—a concept that is close to "possibility." Whereas the relationship of the issue of space to that which has been described thus far is obvious, the dichotomy between order and dis-order requires further examination.

Georges Dumas ascribes an accordingly higher degree of "coenesthesis" to melancholics, because they are "withdrawn from the world"; they are filled with a "feeling of weakness and boredom."

The description of this melancholy "retreatist behavior" clearly incor-porates a reflexive moment, for Dumas speaks of the subject as being "separated from the external world by illness, folded in upon him-self."[94] Norman Cameron's study is even more significant in this respect;[95] it is open to sociological inquiry even in terms of the pre-suppositions on which it rests. On the basis of empirical studies con-ducted by Rennie, he reports, in opposition to Kahlbaum and Kraepelin, "This finding contrasts strikingly with the old contention that manic and depressive disorders are unrelated to personal and situational factors" (p. 498). It seems significant to me that Cameron states that "the patient in a retarded depression is characteristically involved in delusional convictions, in a pseudocommunity which is relatively well-organized and centers about his actual or imagined shortcomings" (p. 508). Cameron's view with regard to the formation of "pseudocommunities" is not confined to manic-depressive psy-choses. Nor is the link to melancholy alone so very crucial. More important is the link to a state of isolated solipsism which, according to Cameron, tends to recreate the lost society "conceptually" or to reconstruct the lost world in one's imagination. Cameron's assump-tions cannot be examined here. They point to the importance of a dialogic model, present in the human being as (to use Claessens' words) a "formal instinctual principle"; it is so important that it is not only preserved in the "deviants" and sick but evolves, so to speak, and functions in a way which is formally similar to normal behavior "directed toward the world." With reference to the spatial side of melancholy, we should look again from this vantage point (now that we have examined it and subjected it to extensive criticism) at how melancholy remains in "proximity to the world," despite loss of world, if only in order for the individual to maintain the communica-tive principle, which the human psyche cannot easily be persuaded to relinquish.[96]

In this context it is only a question of suggestions as to how findings in psychology, psychopathology, psychoanalysis, and other fields might be applied in the framework of a sociologically oriented examination of melancholy. Our discussion here is limited to the problem of melancholy because it has already been dealt with exten-sively in the disciplines mentioned under that rubric and despite the generally conceded dilemmas involved in defining it. Links to the complex of boredom, and even to the theme of utopian thought, could easily be drawn: in his study *Melancholy and Mania,* for exam-ple, Binswanger takes up Husserl's *Phenomenology of the Inner Con-sciousness of Time* and traces the gravity of melancholy for this disturbed sense of time. The categories of "protentio," "retentio," and "presentatio" play a decisive role in this view. Although for the time being we should not unreservedly affirm the significance of phenomenology for the subject of our investigation, an analysis of a disturbed sense of time—which is, after all, also of crucial importance for boredom—can be linked to the sociological approach. For "when mental illnesses are the result of failure in interpersonal relationships, then the investigation of their motivations must show what our social relationships with one another are like in reality" (Mitscherlich).[97] From this we would have to conclude that a disturbed sense of time underlies melancholy as an illness, thus also curtailing utopian thought as a possibility. Even Tellenbach brought to light how melancholy corresponds to an impoverishment of the realm of possibility, until ultimately the lack of alternatives gives rise to an inhibition of behavior and an impoverishment of references to the world. This hindrance of utopian thought, again resulting from the disturbance of a sense of time, provides the link back to our examination of eudaemonistic utopian thought and its "prohibition of melancholy." But this connection is not characterized as if it exhibited direct influences—as if, for example, the inclination toward utopian thought arose from a surplus of a "forward-oriented" sense of time which then perhaps could be taken as a negative image of melancholy. We will therefore not undertake any analyses of this type, which ultimately would result only in a psychography of the utopians in the style of Lange-Eichbaum.

Rather, we would do better to emphasize the appearance of homologous structures, which have already come to light in the psychopathological investigation of spatial qualities in melancholic life and the description of the "social spaces" of melancholic behavior. We must, of course, take care to avoid drawing hasty conclusions from the recognition of homologous structures, a recognition that seems to mirror the limits of our own faculties for recognition rather than the alleged complexity of the world reduced to a simple formula. Structuralism is a systematic attempt to do justice to the complex correspondence between different phenomena by employing the concept of structure. But the analogies are not always so readily available as they are in Lucien Goldmann's comparisons of novel and society, although Michel Foucault also described insanity as a "total structure" within which a culture tries out its values, is open or unbending toward illness, behaves sensitively or dully ("Psychology and Mental Illness"). This does not yet specify the manner in which the structure of the private world may be related to the social structure. The search must go on, however, if we are not to declare something to be intrinsic and immutable when in fact it can be changed.

Psychology, psychopathology, and other similar fields, as well as the objects of their inquiries, can all be related to the realm of social structure. The relation between various scientific disciplines, which deserves special interest in terms of a sociology of knowledge, is of less significance here. It is much more important for us to consider how functions and structures of the "normal world" of society are reproduced in the contents and forms of pathological actions. The pathological would, from this viewpoint, serve as an image from which we could then extrapolate to the realm of the social. Cameron's discovery of the "pseudocommunity" that "retarded depressives" build for themselves can serve as an example of how contents and forms of pathological behavior are also socially communicated. There is no question that distinctions must be made according to the various mental illnesses. There seems to be considerable discrepancy between Cameron's "pragmatic approach" and a view that links mental illnesses to Heidegger's concept of being and that, in addition to viewing melancholy as a "clinical form of illness," also speaks of "so-called existential gloom as a special *form of existence*" (Binswanger).[98]

The homology between melancholy behavior "in the world" and melancholy behavior as an illness was described long ago by Paracelsus, when he emphasized that "the human being is a small world, which is why he has in his small world all that the big world understands and has in itself—both the healthy and the unhealthy."[99] Surely Paracelsus is referring here to the asserted connection between micro- and macrological structures, between cosmological speculation and individual viewpoint; nevertheless, this formal means of comparison could be established for the pathological and social domains. Sándor Radó implicitly expressed the idea of homology when he mentioned that the "melancholic process" "does not unfold at the correct place, in relation to the object world; given a narcissistic regression, it unfolds only between the individual mental instances of the afflicted person."[100] Nevertheless, it remains doubtful whether (to cite Albert Cohen) "the pathology of personality is not, as such, subject matter for the sociology of deviant behavior."[101] However, we would still do well to ask at this juncture whether a comparison of structures of action could not be sociologically relevant: "In general, a sociological field is concerned with the structure of interactional systems, not with personalities, and the distribution and articulation of events within those systems."[102] Thus defined, Cameron's pseudocommunity could also become the subject of sociological analysis—in connection with an observation of sociologically discernible structures. For Cohen's definition is purely formal and thus entirely applicable in the suggested sense if the related points are transferred accordingly.

These methodological comments are not oriented toward viewing the points of connection between sociology and psychopathology in the manner of, for example, August de Belmont Hollingshead and Frederick Redlich in their essay "Social Stratification and Psychiatric Disorders,"[103] or of Robert Kleiner and Seymour Parker in "Goal-Striving, Social Status, and Mental Disorder: A Research Review."[104] Toward the end of their survey, Kleiner and Parker do, however, remark that "the research cited in this section indicates that the stability of socio-economic position in predicting mental disorder is open to question."[105] Thus, attempts in this area do not appear to have progressed further than Ludwig Stern's position in 1913.[106] Moreover, investigations of this type are always to some extent affected by the "debate among the faculties," whose value is itself a matter of debate—totally aside from the massive ideological implications that occasionally manifest themselves in such investigations.[107]

It would be more appropriate to counter the "revisionists," as Herbert Marcuse does, by referring to the sociological character of psychoanalytic terminology.[108] Marcuse uses "psychological categories, since they have become political categories," emphasizing that "private disorder . . . reflects more directly than before the disorder of the whole, and the cure of personal disorder depends more directly than before on the cure of the general disorder."[109] This statement assumes—as is so often the case when the aim is to "enlighten"—the significance of the current era, but it does not hypostasize it as the only significant one. And rightly so, for as early as in Burton's plan to rid the country of melancholy as a means of combating the melancholy of the individual, we find a sense of the interlinking of sociological and psychological categories, of social and psychic structures. We must hope that the relationship between the categories will become clear in our time as well: there is nothing to justify limiting our approaches to an analysis of homologous structures in the present. Rather, the historically posited problem of melancholy provides insights into how a "formal coincidence" of this type can be highly fruitful.

6 Arbitrariness and Bindingness

In Merton's work, the principle of defining melancholy as dis-order has a formal character and is derived from the idea of a system of society geared toward ensuring the functionality of its parts. This formal orientation did indeed exist in the early seventeenth century. Burton's endless enumeration of melancholic cases and aberrations is so complex that it can be covered only by a concept such as "dis-order," with its high degree of generalness. This is inseparably bound up, however, with the unreflected opportunity (that is, one far from self-evident) for this to be "filled out" with substance by constructing a utopian counterproject free of melancholy. To paraphrase Merton, one could—depending on one's standpoint—say that Burton either made the mistake of developing, or had the ability to develop, a "theory of the widest range." But even in Merton's description of melancholy, which is clearly embedded in a middle-range frame of reference, general concepts lie concealed—concepts that cover a range every bit as broad as that of order and dis-order.

In our discussion of melancholy, we pursued this orientation toward a concept of order, citing examples of utopias and aesthetic programs that exhibited a utopian element (for example, Futurism). We arrived at the assumption that utopian thought (including its tendency to crystallize into a utopian "system"), the orientation toward action and planning that result from it, the ban on melancholy, and institutionalized repulse of boredom all combine into a single syndrome. In this context, the action orientation of utopian projects is closely linked to the endeavor in such systems to eliminate possible dis-order. A person who sulkily or resignedly withdraws is just as much a part of this complex as his or her opposite, who, despite being yoked to an apparatus of labor and dictated leisure, finds empty time and empty spaces in which to be bored. Georges Duveau strongly emphasizes the active character of utopia, particularly in Mannheim's work, when he says utopias "have a thrust, in the sense of an activity that endeavors to change reality to conform with the objectives pursued."[1] The stress here is on activity but also on the conformity that it aims to achieve. Someone who mourns, or who is mourned, deviates from this in two ways: he does not act (we shall return to this point in Chapter 7) and so is not conformist in his behavior. Thus, the completely planned society—and the totalitarian versions in both the West and the East offer the most realistic examples of this—tends to render the melancholy of the individual just as impossible as the reasons that could lead to his being bored. The notion of "brainwashing" is clear enough: it is effective because the brain is the object of a profane process. Yet it also designates total cleanliness, which has always figured as a counterconcept to melancholy: "What is black . . . other than, so to speak, the stylization of dirtiness? The Egyptians went even further when they covered their faces with excrement and rolled in ash; other peoples tore their clothing to rags. Priam rolled in a pile of dung to show his mourning for Hector."[2]

The inhabitants of utopia are usually so satisfied because they already have their brainwashing behind them; in *1984*, melancholy and boredom both disappear once the apparatus has taken effect. It would be wrong to equate this simply with enforcement: the individual's psyche is perfidiously molded until it internalizes the objectives of the whole and the latter have become identical with the person's own wishes. The pressure to remove dis-order is just as stringent: in utopia, each person is statistically scanned and everything listed so that no space remains in which private boredom might arise. In Bellamy's Boston, people take their main meals in eating houses and thus amid a public that has lost its most important characteristic—namely, the spontaneity of the person who enters it and who has the freedom to leave it at will. Often enough the compulsion to become part of the totality switches over into the laughter that is sustained by imperfection. But this discrepancy is no longer in evidence in utopia, because here the difference between plan and reality has disappeared: reality is the plan in the form in which it has become reality. In a style of fiction that remains close to reality, Jorge Luis Borges describes the compilation of a map that eventually covers the same area as the region it is intended to portray.[3] The striving for a perfect order, which—once it becomes reality—will no longer allow boredom or melancholy to arise, bears a strange dialectic within it. The higher the degree of order attained, the finer the harmonization within the system, the more exactly one action must fit in with others—the more susceptible the system is. The utopians of the Renaissance had a vague inkling that systems which can prevail are self-regulating, meaning able to tolerate deviance. They located this deviance, having recognized it as necessary, in the leisure time they allowed the inhabitants of utopia. But even this leisure time was calculatedly planned and robbed of all spontaneity; the mania for order in these utopias permitted no exceptions. This is the reason for their fragility. In Beaurieu's *L'Elève de la nature*, a child that could endanger a dynasty is kept imprisoned in a cage. He is always fed at the same times. Dulled, he vegetates. And one day suddenly "a mishap occurs . . . that caused me to give birth to ideas." The feeding has not been punctual: "Up until that accident, which gave a great jolt to my organs, I had done nothing but vegetate in my cage, more like a plant than an animal. I thus became a new being, I sensed my faculties spreading out."[4] The abilities that subsequently developed put an end to utopia: they arise from the breaching of an order that was too fragile, for it was too perfect.

It would seem an obvious step to look for a counterconcept to the notion of melancholy as dis-order found in utopian thought (or systems thinking). The concept of melancholy as dis-order implies that melancholy arises out of dis-order, or is dis-order, or gives rise to it and can therefore be described as "deviant behavior" (Merton) and then put back "into order"—for example, by propagating a utopia (Burton). The essay "Rationality Revised," by Claessens, offers an analytic starting point.[5] What is initially of decisive importance is the concept of arbitrariness, which in itself constitutes a type of world view in which "the contents of the world are indifferent; in other words, the contents are of *equal validity* in terms of their claim to being accorded a particular value. Since a claimed value is necessary, however, last but not least for purely pragmatic and in the deeper sense anthropological reasons, namely in order to make action possible in the first place, in order to set a goal or goals for humankind's *besoin de faire quelque chose* (need to do something), one can also say that this view of the world sees the world as being arbitrary."[6] Since we are concerned here above all with developing an analytic starting point, which at a later stage is to take on the function of a filter that will define a continuum with two adequately determined endpoints from among the wealth of possible descriptions of melancholy, we can forgo a closer investigation of the supplementary implications adumbrated in Claessens' essay. The proposition that arbitrariness designates a view of the world for which the contents of the world are indifferent (that is, are of equal value) lends itself to describing in anthropological terms the concept of world that arises: as the sum total of that which has an effect on people, as a comprehensive "counterstructure" (Thure von Uexküll) which opposes humankind.

The high degree of "extremeness" entailed in the concept of arbitrariness already prompts us to seek an opposite pole to this concept, which constitutes one end of the continuum we have assumed to exist. Let us call this counterconcept "bindingness." It is the diametrical opposite of arbitrariness and, by contrast, entails a world view in which the contents of the world are not all of equal validity but subject to one particular form of dominance. In the essay quoted above, Claessens mentions his initial attempts to trace a body of thought based on arbitrariness; he finds proponents of such thought in Democritus, in medieval nominalism, and in Montaigne. Suffice it to indicate here—and this has merely the status of an aperçu—that on a scale of possible views of melancholy, Democritus, as a representative of an early mode of thinking in terms of arbitrariness, appears on the side of the continuum that considers melancholy to arise from dis-order. This was also Robert Burton's opinion of him; as we have seen, Burton wrote his utopia using Democritus Junior as a pseudonym.[7]

Claessens answers the obvious question as to why arbitrariness, once constituted, could not assert itself further, by pointing out that thinking in terms of arbitrariness has to run on in place until the corresponding technical capabilities are developed. If we add to this argument the newly introduced concept of bindingness, then we may suppose that a certain connection obtains between arbitrariness, bindingness, and technical capabilities. Historically, there are many instances of bindingness in connection with a tendency toward rational arbitrariness—for example, the polis in classical antiquity, and the authority of the Church in Europe in both the Middle Ages and modern times. Socrates and Galileo were both exponents of those conflicts in which the polis or the Church (once again) managed to assert itself in the face of a trend toward arbitrariness. Spiritually, the fact that despite the Church's substantial loss of authority in post-Reformation times "an unchanged need for a unified world view and structuring of life" persisted (Georg Stieler thus explains the genesis of the "rational system" in the seventeenth and eighteenth centuries) bears out the proposition that arbitrariness could not prevail without the requisite technical capabilities. Incidentally, Stieler's attempt clearly shows the extent to which the concept of system is intertwined with the thesis of bindingness.[8] With the growing capabilities afforded by technical means,[9] the need to think in terms of arbitrariness was, as it were, thrust upon people by the normative power of technology; and, at the same time, the claims made by an agency that was, irrespective of its form, geared toward achieving bindingness were reduced. We must not understand this agency only as a phenomenon of domination identified with a particular apparatus of power, for it was also evidenced in the internalized rules that controlled the determination of behavior and that determined the active person much more strongly than any external pressure.

At a particular point, arbitrariness and technical capabilities become so closely interlocked that no space remains for bindingness; we can see this point as one end of the continuum of possible world views. At the other end, hand in hand with the technical capabilities, arbitrariness has disappeared: all that remains is bindingness, the inflexible normative standardization of world views. This latter state characterizes the "primitive mentality" described by Arnold Gehlen in *Primeval Man and Late Culture:* an object in the world is not simply something that can be manipulated but signifies something, has a fixed determination. This view of the world is dismantled in equal part by monotheism and scientific civilization. Arbitrary and binding world views consider objects in the world from different perspectives: whereas according to arbitrariness all things in the world appear to be of equal value, in the realm of bindingness they are all determined—that is, ordered and subjected to one aspect of dominance. What now becomes decisive is the fact that in each of these two domains difficulties arise for human action in quite similar "categories." In Gehlen's words, a person must differentiate before being able to decide and thus to act. This is linked to the cognition of "a system of world orientation and action": "That cognition and action are at bottom inseparable, that world orientation and action are one process, is of great philosophical significance and must be borne in mind even when at a later stage both sides slowly grow farther apart."[10] Since human beings are dependent on action and must make themselves into that which they become, decision making and action constitute a life-sustaining process.

If we relate this state of affairs to the problematics of order contained in the concepts of arbitrariness and bindingness, then we see that both "extreme" world views impede the human urge to act. In the state of arbitrariness, all things appear to have the same value and thus to be interchangeable: their equivalence means a complete loss of preference. It is only preferences, however, that permit decisions to be made.[11] In their absence, chaos reigns in a world of "gray on gray," and human beings become unsure of themselves. When they are subjected to too much pressure to make decisions, they feel "too much discriminative strain." In a state of bindingness, everything that people are not directly "involved in" fades out of view. The remaining world view is thoroughly predetermined in terms of preferences. In such a prestructured world, human action runs smoothly on a single track; it is mechanical and monodirectional. Or, to use Gehlen's terms, the world is no longer a "field of surprises" for human beings. Whereas the state of arbitrariness, the chaos of indifference, is characterized by demands for stabilization and fixation of flexibility,[12] in the state of bindingness the hypertrophy of absolute order prevails. Whereas in the former state people are disconcerted by extreme pressure to make decisions, in the latter there is a deficit of such pressure—there is "too little discriminative strain." Action in the sense of differentiation (that is, the determination of "world" and the making of decisions within it) becomes impossible; for humankind has already been "relieved" of the whole process of differentiation and decision making, in the form indicated in the linguistic description of this iridescent process, where "relieving" means "taking away." Claessens describes the same dialectic with respect to the principle of openness, which demands as many different degrees of freedom as possible, and the principle of order, which limits freedom.[13] The concept of order brings us to the issue of melancholy. Our digression here is intended to provide analytic support for the distinction between a melancholy of dis-order and a melancholy of order. Melancholy that is designated as dis-order must be referred to as such from a point of view that takes the concept of order as the yardstick for its evaluation. Merton makes this judgment; and it becomes characteristic for utopias that are described in terms of systems of normed world views in which melancholy is taken to mean both deviance and the usurpation of various degrees of freedom, neither of which can be allowed by the system.

Our portrayal of La Rochefoucauld's melancholy demonstrated clearly that he could attain such a "structure of affects" (Elias) because his world was too much "in order," too little a "field of surprise," and because its power relations were predetermined. The Frondeur's melancholy arose from the abortive endeavor to set a rigid system in motion. The sanctions imposed brought about enforced quiet, and relieved people of the burden of order. This itself clearly bore the features of a sanction. La Rochefoucauld's turning toward literature resulted naturally from the reservoir of leisure that was available to aristocrats at that time: it was à la mode. But there was more to this than just the flight into an equally preprepared "interior" of aristocratic pastimes. The form taken by this literature—namely, the maxim—would suggest this. Here again we can adopt Lucien Goldmann's line of argument and inquire whether the form of the aphorism or the maxim—although in itself fixed and firmly imprinted, iridescent and "flexible," when viewed as a genre—can be considered a counterbalance to the imposed order of the unemployed Frondeur. This is a question, however, that can be decided only by thorough literary-sociological field research, as it were. The category of boredom, which is so closely linked to that of melancholy, would appear to be of greater importance with regard to La Rochefoucauld. It can be defined as a state in which the things of the world are similar to one another and gain no character or variety by virtue of the temporal dimension. We can again speak of arbitrariness, but are dealing here with an arbitrariness that renders everything similar to the extent that a person not only cannot but also is forbidden from getting involved with something. The resulting state of boredom creates a melancholic ambience: arbitrariness without availability. It is difficult to separate the concepts of rulership and melancholy at this juncture: obviously, La Rochefoucauld's mournfulness reflected his diminished chances for power.

The significance of the link between rulership and melancholy becomes particularly clear if we consider the situation of the German bourgeoisie in the eighteenth century. Here again we can speak to a certain extent of a process of disburdening. The realm of rulership was closed to bourgeois citizens; to be ruled meant, however, the chance of being relieved, a chance which the German bourgeoisie never let pass. Yet ambition in economic terms, which (via detours) at a later date would bring power, most assuredly developed out of the fact that in the eighteenth century the doors to power remained closed to the bourgeoisie. In the age of the decline of absolutism, this class ascribed melancholy to itself: indeed, it was proud to do so. Unlike La Rochefoucauld's melancholy, this mournfulness was not a response to lost power; rather, it signified resignation in the face of those who ruled. A comparison of these two forms of melancholy demonstrates that we have to decide how far removed from the "world" a particular form of melancholy is—that is, how far removed from the "control rooms" where the ruling was done and where rulership rights were allocated. The system of the salons originally developed as a second-tier "world" alongside that of the court; the same behavioral ideals prevailed in it, and melancholy was an emotional state of a group, not of individuals. The greater the flight from the world, the greater the significance of the individual: bourgeois psychology emphasized the individual's emotions, which could at most be intensified via the agency of a friend, acting as a mirror for them. In the nineteenth century only melancholics remained; melancholy no longer existed, even if the *mal du siècle* was a common topic of concern, as was the "Werther sickness" at an earlier date. Labels of this sort are aids to legitimation which can be bought cheaply at any counter. Thus, in the course of history, an ever greater measure of personal boredom and eccentricity must be deployed to dispel boredom and melancholy, or even merely to flirt with them. Increasing flexibility goes hand in hand with increasing arbitrariness; aesthetic theories such as that of "campness" form the endpoint in a trend toward an arbitrariness which no longer knows any prejudgments, but which gives itself over to assessing on the spur of the moment. Anything can be an object for the "interior world of facts" (Gehlen), even one's own subjectivity—that popular object of reflection and melancholy.

The investigation of the spaces occupied by melancholy and boredom can also be linked to the issues of arbitrariness and bindingness. There is no "room" for maneuver in the totally planned utopia, where even free time is fixed in advance. The individual comes into conflict with the system when he or she attempts to engage in private behavior. Deviance is thus tangible here in spatial terms, and sanctions are immediately forthcoming. Utopia knows of no alternatives and therefore does not want to know melancholy. However, total bindingness creates boredom, which in turn engenders melancholy. People always intend to create Cockaigne, and wind up creating Sparta. Danton long ago rebuked Saint-Just in precisely these terms.

In the salon a mechanism evolved that intercepted the flexibility released in an aristocracy "relieved" of power, and kept it under control. Here, the need for an arbitrariness that one could live to the full—which always arises when a person is deprived of power— found realization in literature. In the salon, arbitrariness remained in close proximity to the world; deviance remained under control; melancholy was no reason to flee the world into solipsism, but constituted a threatening emotion which, because it was oriented toward the behavioral ideal of an *honnête homme* who regulated his own feelings, was worked out within the group.

Bourgeois melancholy was further distanced from the "world" in that it renounced something it did not know, namely power. As a consequence, the measure of arbitrariness that developed was greater: the concept of nature posited a dependence on society, just as the notion of the interior posited a flight from society. Nature and the interior were spaces in which introversion (and thus also arbitrariness) "lived life to the full," oriented not toward the world's usual prescriptions for behavior but toward laws that were highly abstract, generalized, and devised out of an opposition to the aristocracy. Bourgeois melancholy resisted the ruling aristocracy by conjuring away factual norms and appealing to a law that "was not of this world": imagination was a bourgeois category. It was easier to violate a law such as this rather than a law, whatever its shape, which was sanctioned by very real barriers in society. In this manner, the appeal to nature and introversion was the precondition for an eccentric stance. Such "marginal" activity was nevertheless related directly to the center of things, from which it had distanced itself and which provided the measure for the distance aspired to in the first place. An eccentric was just as dependent on the bourgeois citizen's shock—which provided him with his legitimation—as the melancholic was on the sympathy of the people from whom he wished to distance himself; eccentric melancholy was not a paradox but was often the rule. He who insisted on persevering in his introversion hardly achieved the greatest distance from society. Just as bourgeois-oriented melancholy took pleasure in a pose that sought admiration from a world it did not respect, so too the concept of individual arbitrariness began to tend toward rigidity and bindingness. This result of bourgeois melancholy assumed an unintentional appearance: it calls to mind Gehlen's category of "secondary objective purposefulness," for it created institutions without wishing to do so, indeed sometimes against its own expressed interests. However, the aesthetic stances that became fashionable—such as the "Werther sickness" or even the *mal du siècle*—also had a rigidifying effect and eventually destroyed the individual need that gave rise to them in the first place. Parallel to this result of the unintended swing away from arbitrariness toward renewed bindingness, there followed a deliberate attempt to intercept the flexibility that has been generated. Gehlen points with aristocratic emphasis to the destructive effect that occurred when individuals either were catapulted out of their institutions or created a distance between these institutions and themselves. Thus, we encounter a paradox—namely, that with an increase in eccentricity came a greater inclination toward rigidification. Literature itself became an administrative edifice and in its creations came to resemble a system. Name after name could be mentioned here: Proust and Joyce, Musil and Broch, Beckett and Heimito von Doderer. Musil's Man without Qualities behaves with the same claim to universal validity as do the Merowings, the family von Doderer describes; nothing less than the world itself—embodied in Dublin—is the subject of *Ulysses,* and this is likewise true for the Faubourg Saint-

Germain in *Remembrance of Things Past*. And Murphy and Godot do not dumbly represent themselves, but stand for a whole world that is supposed to have fallen dumb. This is what Voegelin intended when he said (as noted above) that today we must read literature if we wish to become acquainted with the major systems of order. The flexibility released by modern rationality—arbitrariness—is already intercepted at the point where it was originally freed from its chains: in the realm of the aesthetic.

The close links that obtain between the issues of utopian thought, melancholy, and boredom are the result not least of the common affinity these three areas have to the realm of aesthetics, especially literature. The concept of a relief from burdens takes on particular significance here: utopia disburdens its inhabitants to such an extent that the consequences are just as comprehensive in the eudaemonistic variant as they are in the pessimistic form. What remains is an individual who is so totally planned as to be deprived of all spontaneity. Boredom signifies a state of disburdening ordained from above against the person's will. Melancholy is a reaction to the disburdening without this entailing the opportunity to "do" something once the individual is thus disburdened: disburdening can have an effect as an aid only if the category of the future has been left open. In melancholy, however, this category remains blocked, just as it is (paradoxically) in utopia. The eudaemonistic state cannot be improved upon. Utopia as the wish—implanted in literature—for total planning and the highest measure of order evolves from the experience of reality as something recalcitrant; yet frequently it engenders aspects in the counterimages it devises (even if these are eudaemonistic in conception) which can be generated only by a longing for the reality that has been condemned in the first place. The tension between fiction and reality remains. Aristocratic boredom can already be seen as having been transformed into production by literary means; here, disburdening that is imposed externally creates a counterbalance for those who have lost their specific "world." The bourgeois literary scholar who strikes a pose and stigmatizes boredom as a cross the aristocracy has to bear forgets that it was boredom that engendered literature—the very thing he uses when playing literature off against the aristocracy. And the antibourgeois eccentric likewise forgets that his distance from the world is connected with the concept of flight from the world and of introversion common to the bourgeoisie— whom he opposes.[14] Eccentric melancholy, like bourgeois melancholy, emphasizes the purely fashionable character of its affected way of behavior—by forever insisting on its authenticity and profoundness. The question of the legitimation of melancholy becomes especially acute at this point. Bourgeois melancholy signifies a form of loss of world which is considerably different from that entailed in aristocratic melancholy. The latter resulted from a loss of world, the former from having relinquished a world that had never been possessed. What both forms have in common is that they are cut off from action in terms of acting in the world and influencing that world: utopian, aristocratic, bourgeois-introverted, and eccentric-aesthetic forms of melancholy are all to be found in this type of inhibited action.

7   Reflection and the Inhibition of Action

Having spent five years in the Inquisition's dungeons, the Spanish writer Fry Luis de León (1527–1591) returned to Salamanca to resume his university lectures there. Many people expected that his first address following his imprisonment would consist of a bitter reckoning with or at least a description of his sufferings. But Luis de León began, as Vossler reports, "with words that have become famous and symbolic throughout the Spanish world: 'Decíamos ayer' . . . (Dicebamus hesterna die)—and went on with his class at the point where he had left off five years before."[1] Luis de León provides a vivid example of a type of quiet composure that aroused attention as early as the sixteenth century and that seems to us as stylized as the actions of characters in Spanish and French classical dramas. Aside from its clearly religious nature, such behavior derives its effectiveness to a large extent from the fact that it represents a totally atypical and conspicuous combination of reflection and the inhibition of action. Incarceration as a way of "sentencing a person to boredom" (Hans Müller-Eckard) already aroused the interest of Schopenhauer, who pointed to the high suicide rate among prisoners. The idea of the small, bare, cramped cell provides the paradigmatic image of a state of inhibited action, in which the incarcerated can pull himself together for one final action: suicide. Luis de León offers an example of behavior that has overcome the dangers of inhibition in meditation and religious involvement and does not fall prey to self-destructive reflection.

Precisely because Luis de León is such an atypical example, we should remember that this manner of dealing with imposed reflection is a matter for someone who has experience in meditation, and a confirmation for someone who has chosen to abstain from the world as the goal of his action.[2] Gontcharov's novel *Oblomov*, which appeared in 1859, gives us a more familiar picture of what we should understand as reflection and inhibition of action. The novel gave a name to a whole class of specifically Russian behavior—namely, "oblomovitis." The character of Oblomov had predecessors in Russian literature—in the works of, among others, Pushkin and Gogol; but we cannot deal with them in any detail here. The point is, Oblomov became the decisive figure. In the novel, he lies lethargically on his sofa, has big plans, conjures up rosy images of the future, and does— nothing. Dobrolyubov spoke of Oblomov as a "type": "in all this oblomovitis . . . we see something more than a successful production by the head of a strong talent; we see a product of Russian life, a sign of the times."[3] According to Dobrolyubov, Oblomov was bored with everything he did—not least because he always wanted to know the meaning of things. He had "an all too sluggish temperament" and was inclined toward "utter inertness." Contrary to Walter Rehm's interpretation, which views oblomovitis purely in terms of intellectual history (he believes it was caused by the "English and German ideas" that penetrated Russia), Wilhelm Goerdt provides the following perceptive arguments:

> In 1762 Czar Peter III issued his decree "On the Freedom of the Nobility." This relieved the nobility of its service to the state; it no longer had to serve in the military or in the civil administration . . . The nobility . . . was not allowed to keep its property, and this meant that the peasant was still obliged to support the noble estateowner by his own labor and in many cases to provide him with an amusing and pleasurable life in the capitals of Russia and Europe . . . Social *nullity* in Russia made it virtually a duty of the nobility to practice the sophistication of doing and thinking in the "as-if" of illusionary planning and of behavior divorced from any form of reality. That was the *birth of oblomovitis.*[4]

Goerdt's interpretation lists a number of key elements: a class relieved of its duties, lack of action, behavior and thought based on illusion, loss of reality. In his study on Oblomov, Walter Hilsbecher comes closer to the topic under consideration, speaking of how Oblomov assuages his pain with boredom and of how his imagination, "precipitating every possible action, . . . [forces] him to do nothing."[5] Oblomov's behavior, or rather his abstinence from any and every action, resembles something that we should see as inhibition of action. The fact that no violence is used, and moreover that Oblomov appears as representative of a *class* (nobility relieved of its duties) yet can explain this away by referring to his *natural disposition*—Dobrolyubov's reference to his temperament already suggests this—naturally endows him with a certain poetic appeal, an appeal that is arbitrary and cannot be investigated, thus putting an end to sociologically oriented interest. After all, this immortal type of Russian "estate-owner literature" might be seen as the embodiment of a form of action inhibition that is unconstrained and that is expressed more in idle speculation, noncommittal daydreaming, and rampant imagination than in incisive reflection.

Regardless of whether the idea of action inhibition and its resulting initiation of reflection brings to mind Oblomov on his divan or Boethius in prison ("chained by the neck, a book in hand . . . actionless and without hope"),[6] we must remember that the recommended means of counteracting reflection were diverse in nature and revealed totally diverse effects. The comfort of religion, which helped Luis de León, and the *consolatio philosophiae*, which came to the aid of Boethius when he was condemned to death, would have evoked scarcely any interest from someone like Oblomov. In this case it is a question not of differences in individual personal experience or of individual receptivity, but of structural conditions and overall social states which themselves generate the variability of the human willingness to react. The conditions and states that prevailed in the sixth century B.C. were very different from those that prevailed in the Spain of the Inquisition, and these in turn were unlike those of prerevolutionary Russia.

However, recourse to action—simply doing something quite banal and baldly effective—develops progressively into a form of suggested therapy for reflection: "You must keep encouraging the artist's apprentice to produce! Even if nothing more than little balls of bread were to come out of it! Make sure that they are nice and round! Just don't brood, keep doing things!"[7] This advice from Feuchtersleben sets out a regime of simple activities, much like one that Valéry describes:

> The philosopher chews his fingernails. The general scratches his head. The mathematician pulls at his hair. Bonaparte takes heap after heap of snuff. Where do the *solutions* come from? But on the other hand, someone who is bored can't stop whistling, pierces numerous identical holes in his paper, sucks on his pipe, paces back and forth—and does what the pendulum on the grandfather clock does . . . The chin, the nose, the forehead, the finger, the legs, the hair: tools of meditation. Also the stovepipe over there, Kant's tree. These objects, this biting and chewing are signs of orientation.[8]

In his anthropology, Arnold Gehlen was later to draw a picture of the acting person who is oriented toward such minimal actions and who explicitly directs himself against a form of reflection that keeps the human being from doing what he is intended to do—namely, act.

Claudius Galenus of Pergamon (Galen) mentioned excessive thinking as one of the factors favoring melancholy, and Constantinus Africanus, who was of a similar opinion, recommended physical exercise as a remedy. "Multa cogitatio" was considered a cause of melancholy by Rufus of Ephesus, Rhazes, and Marsiglio Ficino. Thomas Aquinas spoke of the acedia which "non movet ad agendum, magis retrahit ab agendo." Diderot, describing the human being who is isolated from society and limited in action, referred to the "extravagant thoughts" that "sprout in his mind like brambles in the wild." John Donne pinpointed "thoughtfulness" as provoking melancholy. Schopenhauer found life to be an unfortunate matter and decided to "sit it out by thinking about it." Schäffle called the "melancholy temperament . . . very unsuitable for energetic action." One "consequence of Blücher's melancholy in old age" is supposed to have been the "historically serious failure of strategic activity in this man of action during the battles of Laon."[9] And Joachim Ritter mentions the view that even "thinking about laughter makes one melancholy."[10] Helvetius, however, found that the human being must keep a cool head in order not to become bored. Paul Radin, finally, tells a story about the Winnebago Indians that makes the connection between reflection, lack of action, and sad disposition understandable even for a radically different, extremely distant culture: "In the beginning, Earthmaker was sitting in the empty room. When he became aware of himself, nothing existed anywhere. He began to think about what he should do, and finally he began to cry." Radin cites this story in order to characterize the "thinker" as a type, an exceptional phenomenon: "as in our own culture, the man of action is also prevalent as an overriding majority among the primeval peoples."[11]

These examples, to which countless others from the widest variety of sources could be added, reveal the great significance that the phenomenon of reflection—combined with melancholy—has acquired. We have already mentioned some of its implications; indeed, we could say that without focusing on this connection, we can deal with neither utopian thought nor melancholy nor boredom. Let us look again, briefly, at the links between the three main historically oriented complexes and the phenomenon of reflection as an inhibitor of action. Then let us use Gehlen's anthropology as an analytical approach to explain the reflection provoked by inhibition of action, as well as the resulting melancholy. This approach will raise further crucial questions—but these will have to remain largely unanswered.

Inhibition of Action as the Cause of Utopian Thought

The close connection between utopian thought and an inhibition of action which provokes reflection first becomes manifest when someone designs a utopia. We think immediately of Campanella, who was incarcerated for twenty-seven years, was tortured repeatedly, and was permitted to "write down the overabundance of his thoughts."[12] His experience combines imagination and reflection, thus revealing basic traits of utopian thought. Precisely because it is documented in literature, utopian thought is a sign of inhibition of action. Robert Burton, who wrote in order to dispel his melancholy, who was well educated, and who documented the extent to which the causes of melancholy were already known in classical times, designed his utopia of England because as a poor intellectual he could never hope to put his ideas into practice. To assert that utopias arise from an inhibition of action means that utopians are taken seriously: they would not think and design in such a way if they were able to act. Thomas More, the Lord High Chancellor, appeared on the scene as a counterimage, but Duveau speaks of him precisely in this connection: "Plato was disappointed, like More; but he was disappointed because he was not able to act, whereas More was disappointed by the action."[13] This is also a form of action inhibition which naturally remains closer to reality and accordingly also shapes its ideal and distant image "more realistically." According to Duveau, however, utopia arises in principle from "nostalgic relaxation": it is the "*relaxation* of man, whereas myth is *tension*."[14]

Utopian thought is the preparation for presenting one's disappointment with the world; and according to Sorel, one of the traits of utopia is that "the present world may be considered with sadness."[15] This sadness of the world sets utopian thought in motion because action is impossible—or action which starts off under a utopian banner but necessarily fails because it forgets about the harshness and resistance of reality. The sadness of the world as experienced—which can be described as the loss of self-evident cultural truths, for the latter would give no cause for mourning—can also be found indirectly in utopia: in the prohibition of melancholy, which permeates utopia and is proclaimed in opposition to the reality experienced. Thus, the "melancholy" character of utopia can be delineated from two sides: from the emergence of utopian thought, which is derived from the inhibition of action in this world, and from the melancholy conjured away in the ultimate realization of utopia. With respect to this element of stabilization, utopia bears a resemblance to the sects that Mühlmann described as *"stabilization at a low level."* "Psychologically, it corresponds to the state of resignation, after all eschatological hopes have been dashed, so that one must now begin to get along with the givens on this earth; sociologically, we call this 'institutionalization.'"[16] Utopia is built of similar elements—albeit in reverse. In the beginning there is dissatisfaction with one's subservience to the criticized present; the hopes that have not been fulfilled here are transferred into the future. Resignation is left behind and remains in the world. Institutionalization, however, also takes place, in precisely that "overlap of future projections" (Mühlmann) which—prior to the resignative failure—was characteristic of the world of the imagination. In this manner, utopian thought becomes a "composite of imaginary institutions" (Sorel)[17] within the system of utopia.

If one takes institutions simply to be permanent sequences of actions in predictable series, then the projective institutionalization of utopia can also be understood to rest on the connection between reflection and the inhibition of action. Utopia arises from reflection about the inadequacies of this world; it ends with the image of a better world in which there is no longer any place for reflection, because everything is "in order." People act in utopia, and the abundance of totally planned institutions designed for utopia proves this. The less adequate the present appears to be, the more colorful utopia becomes and the more precise the promised ideal of happiness. The degree of reflection increases in proportion to the degree to which action is inhibited, and this in turn constitutes unmistakable proof of proximity or distance from the "world." Yet nearly everyone who sallies forth to design the system of a new and better world sees himself disappointed by the old, bad one. Consequently, all utopias lie far from the world. They are "fruits of more or less arbitrary meditation, of more or less boastful musings: exercises of pure thought without much connection to the real."[18]

The relation to space can also be associated with the problem of reflection and inhibition of action. Utopia takes shape as a compressed space: "Plans for the re-formation of social conditions, especially those which were thought out to the last detail and were aimed at a definitive order, are . . . invariably initially designed for a closed space" (Freyer).[19] This fits in with the fact that in utopia, history has "come to a standstill," that utopia appears as the first form "in which history is conceived of as completely thought through."[20] Constrained space and the ability to survey it provide the chance for utopian institutions to function smoothly. Time has been laid to rest and thus prevents reflection, which after all has proven to be the instrument of change; utopia is proof of this. Thus, utopia ends up as the perfected counterimage to reality: the old world is so changed that nothing is left in it that *can* change, because the space created is definitive. Utopia has dispelled time—and with it, of course, boredom, after it has itself been projected into time. Utopia emerges from melancholy with the world and from the world's inadequacy and ends with the impossibility of reflection, the prohibition of melancholy, and the redeeming promise of a stable happiness within a manageable space.

La Rochefoucauld: Man of Action and Man of Thought

Despite the great importance assigned by La Rochefoucauld (in keeping with his time) to the "natural disposition" of the human being, in his *Portrait* he described his own melancholy as acquired. It was the result of the Frondeurs' failed attempts, and marked the end of a life primed for action. La Rochefoucauld's reflection thrived in this melancholy climate; it was caused by the inhibition of action: "The lack of resolution joined with the melancholy mood—is this not the characteristic mark of a man whose analytically inclined mind kills voluntary spontaneity? An excess of reflection always saps the resources of action. Thus, the author of the *Maximes* often made me think of the unhappy Prince of Denmark," says Ivanoff.[21] Vinet similarly emphasizes the crucial role of "inaction." Bourdeau, who speaks of "second melancholy," calls attention to the connection between reflection and inhibition of action: "Man of reflection and analysis, of hesitation and perplexity, timid, thrown back upon himself; instead of energetically following a line of behavior, he watches himself, he questions himself, he tries to untangle the mobile secrets in himself and in others. We see emerging in him *the critical mind,* rare in the preceding period, which tends to sap the resources of the will, to paralyze action."[22] Reflection, which in the case of La Rochefoucauld could be considered a reaction to that form of inhibition of action which no longer permits a socially relevant form of action, must be seen in the same framework as melancholy. Assuming that melancholy means the psyche's reaction—or that which is alleged to be a reaction—to the withdrawal of relevant oppportunities for action, then reflection represents more the ersatz action that results— namely, literary activity. When Hess speaks of the Frondeurs' literary ambition, the word "ambition" is actually too saturated with action and too much oriented toward the world. For La Rochefoucauld, literature was a substitute—important, but not significant enough to spur his ambition. Literature, certainly the *Maximes,* was the expression of a resigned attitude that remained in surprising proximity to the world.

This proximity to the world, which prevented reflection from becoming loss of world, was decisive in this context. "But if the life of action eluded him, if the life of the court was closed to him, then he was left with the life of society, where the mind alone was the criterion of rank" (Hémon).[23] This statement makes it clear that the order of the power relations of the day allowed the individual to give in to resignation initially, yet remain close to the world. The "mechanism of kingship" served first and foremost to keep the monarch's rule in balance. It was absolute in its claim, but not total: spaces for freedom were excluded. One of these spaces was the salon, which not only offered a substitute for those who were no longer permitted to appear at court, but also allowed people, even in boredom, to think that things were still worse at court. "Before I came to the court, I had never known boredom; but I have had ample opportunity since then," wrote Madame de Maintenon when she had become familiar with the court. And further: "Festive days are the most boring."[24]

The court was of course the only place an individual could catch a glimpse of power, and also acquire it if he bowed to the first system of order (absolute subjugation to the ruler) and was familiar with the nuances of the second-tier order; if he knew, for example, that the royal *cravatier* was by no means allowed to set the king's tie straight if it was crooked, but had to wait until the *maître de la garde-robe* or at least an *officier supérieur* arrived on the scene. This etiquette, which evolved from the demonstration of power and the willingness to submit to it, was absent in the salon. Here, however, many other refinements appeared; "lyricism taken to the point of greediness" (Hémon), which is repeatedly displayed in La Rochefoucauld's letters to Madame de Sablé, is a charming example.

Reflection was engendered by the inhibition of action—which did not always have to be imposed by the power relations of the day. Such inhibition nevertheless also offered an opportunity to be relieved of one's duties, and this cannot be sufficiently underestimated. But an individual had to be able to take advantage of this, as was the case with La Rochefoucauld. Another who had failed, such as Montmorency, would have had to waste away, even while protecting his life in society, because he had already been expelled from

one salon. Reflection as an opportunity to be relieved of one's obligations was granted to the person who was also *able* to disburden himself. The mechanism of disburdening reduced the consequences of
possible actions; it reduced them to a minimum because reflection
prevented action anyway. Trifles could thus be treated as "negligible
qualities"; one could develop a "refined mind" and did not necessarily have to take care that one's *bon mot* also pleased the monarch.
In a limited space, people could attain higher levels of freedom
and—since they were relieved of ambition—could achieve a degree
of spontaneity that did not prevail at court. At court everything was
of importance, and the pressure of the royal absolute power was so
great that trifles could assume gigantic proportions and fatal consequences could mushroom out of an awkward circumstance. This happened, for example, to Vatel, the Prince de Condé's *maître d'hotel*,
who had the misfortune of watching his provisions run out during
an outing of the royal hunting party at Chantilly in 1671: "We dined;
on several tables the roast was missing because there were some
guests who had not been anticipated. This greatly affected Vatel. He
said several times: 'I have lost my honor; this is an affront that I will
not bear.'"[25] And he ran on his sword. Certainly part of this is
attributable to Vatel's character, and surely the code of honor at the
time was of a rigor that today is difficult to understand, much less
follow. The decisive point is that the rigorous attitude developed
because the king, the absolute ruler, was present. Vatel would hardly
have run on his sword if he had had insufficient roasts for a meal in
a salon in the city. (On the eve of the Revolution, Mercier called
Vatel's behavior "insane"!)

In the society shaped by the mechanism of kingship, the opportunity for reflection brought the certitude of "not being able to
become anything" any longer, but also the reassuring feeling that
nothing much could happen to a person, either. The person who
acted was in danger; in reflection a person could make mistakes only
in his thoughts. This form of disburdening through reflection, and
the definitiveness which established that one could no longer become
active in this world or give ambition free rein, characterized the
melancholy of people like La Rochefoucauld. It revealed itself particularly strongly in him; it became characteristic of the society of the
period. The salon of Madame de Sablé produced not only the
Maximes of La Rochefoucauld but also those of Madame de Sablé
herself, the *Pensées diverses* of the Abbé d'Ailly, the *Fausseté des vertus
humaines* of Jacques Esprit, and the *Maximes, sentences et réflexions
morales et politiques* of de Plassac de Méré. Thus, La Rochefoucauld's
stance appears to have been embedded in a cosmos of possible alter-

natives for action which were surely limited in effectiveness but, on the other hand, could be carried out relatively free of controls and with a large measure of freedom. The revenge of the failed individual was enacted in literature: La Rochefoucauld "wrote one of his books with the obstinate rancor which is the revenge of the vanquished. Revenge for the dashed hopes and hurt pride with one blow; the revenge of the man of action who always observed more than he acted, and who, more than ever, in the impotence in which he was to act, sought consolation in the delicate joy of observing, in the bitter pleasure of remembering." [26]

In support of Hémon's view, as opposed to Vinet's, we can probably safely assert that the *Maximes* form a "systematic book." They are just as much a system as was La Rochefoucauld's life, with its logical progression from "man of action" or "man of thought." His melancholy occurred in the half of his life in which he was cut off from actions of socially relevant consequence and was at the mercy of the threats and opportunities of reflection. As liberated reflection stabilized itself in literature, the melancholy of the failures established itself in the salon, in a "society" far from the court, excluded from the center of power. Melancholy's proximity to society and the stabilization of liberated reflection were attributable in part to the presence of a class relieved of its duties—nobles who were not only literary amateurs but who could create new spaces of action for themselves. They were, in addition, attributable to the perpetuation of a common ideal, the *honnête homme*, which the court and the salon favored; and last but not least to the phenomenon of rule that was balanced out in the "mechanism of kingship," which was absolute but not total and which tolerated spaces of freedom where the failures could resign themselves with dignity.

Melancholic Renunciation of Power: The German Bourgeoisie

Wilhelm von Humboldt characterized the eighteenth century in terms of the connections we have described thus far:

> In our day and age, . . . when one finds passivity and lethargy in combination with education and mental faculty more frequently than in former times, the value of a power that is productive beyond its own bounds has sunk extremely low, and has been repressed by exaggerated ideas about what the human being, independent of all external activity, can be . . . We do not consider that a life that leaves behind no great deed, no important work, not even the memory of a useful occupation among a larger number of our fellow citizens, is a life forlorn and lived in vain.

He spoke further of the "ailing mood" that "characterizes our age more than those preceding it, even our nation more than those abroad. It is this which . . . in itself makes us more considered and sensitive in life than acting and active."[27] Humboldt described the proclivity for reflection and the absence of action, but he did not consider the social causes of the situation, and he failed to take account of a specific situation in the German bourgeoisie—a class that was still kept at a distance from the centers of power, the courts and palaces, and that could perhaps acquire posts as comptrollers or subaltern chancellors but never any real positions of power. Humboldt's criticism was a reflection of the situation of the bourgeoisie because he largely disregarded the social conditions and still regarded the inhibition of action, rampant reasoning, and (over)sensitivity as self-produced and autonomously desired.

If we recall the value attached to the Werther syndrome, hypochondria, and melancholy in the eighteenth century, Kant departed emphatically from the bourgeois standpoint when he linked melancholy with inhibition of action. Indeed, he turned against the bourgeois psychology of sensibility: "Listening to oneself and incessantly focusing attention on the state of one's feelings deprives one's mood of activity when viewing other things and is harmful to the head . . . The inner sensibility, since one is affected by one's own reflections, is harmful . . . Analytic people are very susceptible to illness"; the melancholic feels "the hindrance of life."[28] These passing notes of Kant's clearly show how melancholy, in its penchant for reflection, distanced itself from the world and withdrew into itself. Bourgeois sentimentality signified the retreat from the bustle of the world into the inner realm of individual sensibility. Kant emphasized that this path did not necessarily correspond to enrichment but instead led to impoverishment, as it was prevented from having any external effect. He was of course inclined more to blame the wrong choice of therapy than to analyze the etiology in question.

The reason for this proclivity for reflection among the German bourgeoisie was precisely the imposed "disburdening" from power. All of the forms of sublimation developed by the bourgeoisie can be traced to this imposed stance of reflection: the value assigned to the inner world, the cults of friendship and of letter writing, flight from the world, solitude, and disdain for the nobility. Goethe often described this constellation, most clearly in the scene from *Werther* in which the young man inadvertently remains in noble company until he is finally asked to leave by the Count of C., who is actually favorably disposed to him: "The Count pressed my hands with a warmth of feeling that was unmistakable. I stole quietly out of the aristocratic gathering, went out, got into a cabriolet, and drove to M. to watch the sunset from the height there, reading at the same time in my Homer the five cantos in which Ulysses enjoys the hospitality of the excellent swineherd. All that was good."[29] This scene contains everything at once: the burgher's deprivation of power, humiliation by the nobility, flight into nature, and literature. The objective constraint, required by the prevailing norms, becomes apparent in the person of the count, who definitely likes Werther and who is even said to possess great sensitivity (high praise from the bourgeoisie!) but who cannot do as he would like and instead must conduct himself as a member of the nobility must. This is why Werther feels "justified in not doing anything," and this is also the reason for his melancholy and his flight into action, the mark of melancholy which results from inhibition of action: "I had something in mind of which I was going to tell you nothing until it should be carried out; now that nothing is to come of it, it's perhaps just as well. I wanted to volunteer for war service; I have had that at heart for a long time."[30]

Reflection means nothing more than the compulsion (and opportunity) for people to turn back on themselves when they are relieved of the pressure to act. This "relief" can be an undesired result, owing to the conditions of the ruling situation. This was the situation of the German bourgeoisie. Their reaction was diverted inward: "O, what I know, anyone can know—my heart is mine alone," as Werther writes. The communicative ties to society were thus largely dissolved, and substitute forms developed which afforded the individual a higher degree of emotional gratification. In *Wilhelm Meister* the situation changed somewhat, though not fundamentally. The burgher still had the theater if he wanted to become a "public figure." The individual was brought up to function in society, and this process ended with "the subject's rubbing off its own horns" (Hegel).

The element of reflection in bourgeois melancholy was not a phenomenon of rational thought; rather, it represented a return of disempowered subjectivity to itself and the attempt to make a means of self-confirmation out of the inhibition of action. This was particularly true since pietism, whose influence on bourgeois melancholy cannot be underestimated, incorporated this element of reflection: "The ways and designs of divine providence are calculated in such a clever, almost sly way that we could call this kind of paradoxical religiosity 'negative intellectualism.' We inadvertently think of Leibniz's God, the great calculator; but the pietistic god seems to arise in the world of petty-bourgeois worries." Reflection as such became a reason for legitimation and the foundation of a new ethics:

> The basic pietistic-sentimental feeling rests on a predominance of painful feelings, religiously speaking: anguishing feelings of sin that spring from an inner ambivalence. These original feelings of displeasure, however, are now reshaped into positive feelings, into "pleasures." In a second stage of consciousness the individual becomes aware of his state of suffering; he "reflects" on it and begins to *enjoy* it. He seeks not only to relieve himself in bitter complaints, but even basks with great pleasure in self-conceived martyrs and asceticism. Pietism created an ethics of self-enjoyment with negative indicators: the point is to enjoy the serenity of the unserene self.[31]

This ethics became, in a secularized form, that of the bourgeoisie as such: even if the construed enjoyment of the unsaintly self did not always exist, value was always assigned to one's own, disempowered position. Pietism provided a religious pattern for this. As was the case with reflection, inhibition of action, and melancholy, here, too, literature became the way out for socially blocked avenues of meaning; indeed, Elias referred to writing as a "discharge." Expressions of this discharge can be seen clearly in poetry and especially in the novel. Lukács, referring to the genre of the novel, said that having to reflect is the deepest form of melancholy of any genuine and great novel."[32] Formally, this corresponds precisely to the situation of the bourgeoisie, and to this extent Lukács' statement anticipated the theories of Lucien Goldmann. Thus, it comes as no surprise that Lukács later distanced himself from his theory, believing that his ideas had taken shape "in a mood of permanent despair over the state of the world."[33] The novel became the literary form of sublimation for bourgeois melancholy.

The Transformation of the Concept of Labor

Utopia originates in the inability to influence reality and society. This state of being cut off from action meets its counterpart in the utopia itself: as the formation of "imaginary institutions," it is intimately linked to the necessity of labor. Even the Marxist redeeming promise of a "labor-free" utopia can, formally speaking, be reduced to the same denominator because the creation of paradise depends on a violent upsurge of action—namely, revolution—without which paradise cannot be created. Revolution as cumulative action compensates the proletariat for the imposed, forced inhibition of action; at the same time, it allows work to be abolished or to be put at the disposal of the individual, who may be a hunter, fisherman, or critic, as Marx said. The approach is also similar in the case of all utopias of the genre resembling fairy-tale lands: people must first work in order to enjoy rest and laziness, and whoever shirks the effort to eat his way through the big porridge will never make it to the Land of Milk and Honey or to Cockaigne.

The eudaemonistic utopia, which is drawn in greater detail and is not content with the general description of a paradisiacal land, has an ambivalent approach to work. It wants to alleviate the pressure of compulsory labor, but does not by any means want to do away with work, because such eradication would provoke uncontrolled idleness. Therefore, a reasonable "measure" of work is planned, just enough to dispel melancholy and ensure the economic security of utopia. Full-fledged eudaemonistic utopias promise not so much blue skies as the right measure, which must suffice for people's satisfaction but also ensures that they will be satisfied. Since mandatory labor cannot be universal (if it were, utopian thought would be jeopardized), idleness is also subject to control: the view that freedom is, to use Habermas' words, the "perpetuation of labor by other means" is not an invention of scientific civilization or of the current age, but is utopian in nature.

For a class (such as the nobility) that had been relieved of its duties, the problem of work was posed in a special way. Here, the classical Greek ideal persisted. According to this ideal, work was inhuman; it was appropriate only for slaves and promoted the development of a counterconcept to contemplation. Although being relieved of work constitutes double gratification—directly, in that people are liberated from toil, and indirectly, in that they are able to display their status by not doing anything (Thorstein Veblen)—it is nevertheless a burden in the same way. As W. H. Bruford has written:

> Experience seems to teach that a society which does not need to work has to invent for itself artifical restraints to replace the pull of external necessity. The ceremonial, even of the imperial court, was probably not felt as a cramping influence but as a welcome support . . . Regulation and custom lightened the burden of the prince and court officials, but if they took their duties seriously many of them still had plenty to do. The greater number of the residents at court however had no serious functions. Their duty was pleasure, and their enemy ennui.[34]

This ennui, which appears to have been bearable only because it served the nobility as an external symbol of gratification, marked the difference which evolved between nobility and bourgeoisie. It was impossible for the nobility to "work off" its boredom because this would have meant voluntarily relinquishing its manifest privilege. At least, there could be no question of allowing any form of work that appeared to be worthwhile—that always raised the issue of whether it was meaningful and at the same time answered it. Work of this type would not have been compatible with the climate of taken-for-grantedness which was the only way in which privileges could be enjoyed. If someone is too happy to receive a medal, this already shows that he or she has not earned it. That which a person rightfully expects is enjoyed without any outward display.

At first, particularly at the absolutist court, where the nobility enjoyed its privileges in an environment that deprived it of power, institutionalized mechanisms evolved in order to alleviate boredom: war on the outside, hunting on the inside, and peacetime. The boredom at court remained the same. As a result, a form of meaning-less work emerged that served no other purpose than to kill time. The French court set an example for the fashion of handicrafts: since "1770 the ladies occupy themselves with 'parfilage,' untwining gold tresses." That the only "purpose" of these tasks consisted in driving away boredom was shown by Madame du Deffand's poem, which she sent to a friend: "Long live parfilage! / No more pleasure without it! / This important work / Chases away boredom everythere."[35] The "mechanisms of burden," which were intended to counteract being excessively relieved of duties and the resulting threat of boredom, took on similar forms in the ruler's case as well. Ernst August von Weimar received the "Reports of his Architects, Gardeners and Ministers" in 1729, and Bruford rightfully comments: "The order in which they are named is instructive!"[36] This proclivity for super-fluous and secondary work, for a preoccupation with things that were "marginal," was possible only because rule was guaranteed and secured in this case and because by this very fact it afforded the pos-sibility of pursuing useless endeavors in good conscience.

The disburdened nobility documented its boredom. But members of the bourgeoisie combated boredom, because it afforded an oppor-tunity to cover up their own inhibition of action and to find legitima-tion in reflection, to opt for the introspective gaze, which the nobility, since they ruled or at least participated in ruling, did not need to seek in the first place. Whereas the nobility turned simply to pas-times, which not only may have been meaningless but indeed had to be so in order for them not to be considered work, the bourgeoisie developed an ethics that was directed against the nobility and invoked "humankind." The question of meaning is posed here because it is intended less to justify its own position than to undermine one that is different.

Sentimentality and melancholic reflection on one's own ego and mood would certainly have had relatively few consequences if the economic importance of the bourgeoisie had not gradually increased. Henceforth the balance shifted: the bourgeoisie discovered another means of asserting itself against the nobility and at the same time of fleeing its own melancholy, which in its action-inhibiting form did not exactly provide a psychologically favorable support for economic aspirations. As Nietzsche says in aphorism 329 of *The Gay Science:* "Yes, it could soon go so far that people will yield to an inclination toward *vita contemplativa* . . . not without despising themselves and having a guilty conscience. Well! It was the other way around before: work was something that caused a guilty conscience." This transformation of the view of work was a bourgeois development. When the bourgeoisie recognized that power could be attained via the economic road, it also found a means to confront the nobility and at the same time pull free of its own, previously sought melancholy. We would have to undertake a separate investigation to ascertain how, with the growing economic power of the bourgeoisie, the concept of labor came to be regarded as significant and work viewed as a palliative for melancholy.

It was not until melancholy no longer appeared as the desired affective state of the bourgeoisie, because the latter had found work to be a better means of self-legitimation, that it became possible for the individual to claim melancholy for himself. The "Werther syndrome" of the eighteenth century marked the state of consciousness of an entire class; in contrast, the *mal du siècle* was a label that applied to only a few individual melancholics. This is where the development began, leading from melancholy to spleen and from the melancholic to the dandy—to bourgeois literature with aristocratic mannerisms.

Kierkegaard was an early representative of this; he saw boredom as being very much aristocratic, as a distinction for the few. On the one hand, boredom was something objective, and the principle from which Kierkegaard proceeded was that all people were boring. On the other hand, not all of them could recognize this boredom, "for idleness can certainly be annulled by work, since it is its opposite, but not boredom, and experience shows that the busiest workers, whose constant buzzing most resembles an insect's hum, are the most tiresome of creatures; if they do not bore themselves, it is because they have no true conception of what boredom is, but then it can scarcely be said that they have overcome boredom."[37] These are the words of someone who was independently wealthy, who was as economically secure as the nobility had been in its position as rulers: in both cases, boredom was seen as a privilege. The aristocratic element in this attitude continued up to the dandies, and up to modern writers such as Proust (who—totally aside from his state of health—developed a typically aristocratic phobia against the working world) and Musil, who wrote: "That which is noble is boring: it is immobile."[38]

In other words, in bourgeois literature two strands of tradition mingled in the attitude toward reflection. One stemmed from the aristocratic reverence for boredom which documented the state of being exceptional; this, of course, consisted of an act of recognition (as with Kierkegaard) and no longer of the privileged allocation of chances at power. The second derived from the originally bourgeois tendency toward reflection, which regarded the return to introversion as a legitimation of its status. Flowing from these two sources was a type of literary stance that presented itself in an unbourgeois manner and was despised especially by the bourgeoisie because it was based in part on aristocratic models of behavior and also clung to principles that the bourgeoisie had long since thrown overboard. While the "leisure class" was happy about its well-earned right to do nothing, the eccentric writer documented in his life and his work how much he needed to drive away the boredom that marked him as being exceptional. Melancholy was a bourgeois form of behavior which the bourgeoisie abandoned with the advent of capitalism. Boredom was never bourgeois: it belonged to the aristocracy and to outsiders, who were always more welcome in the salons of the nobility than they were in bourgeois living rooms.

Reflection and the Inhibition of Action in Psychology, Psychiatry, and Psychopathology

The connection between reflection and the inhibition of action also plays a large role in the psychological, psychopathological, and psychiatric literature on melancholy. Although sometimes different terms are used for the phenomena described, they can nevertheless be studied in relation to this duality. It does not seem significant for our discussion that this characteristic applies not only to melancholy but also to autism and paranoid behavior (among other phenomena). Our point here is not to prepare a developed complex of symptoms that applies only to melancholy and is thus constitutive of it, but rather to inquire how the signs of melancholy described thus far coincide with those transmitted in the cited literature. Pierre Janet spelled out the problem discussed here in the titles of two of his essays. In the first article, "The Fear of Action," the connection between reflection and the inhibition of action is traced only diffusely: "The patients who are ill-satisfied with their action watch themselves and by dint of observations, through anxiety about themselves, they fall into a sort of perpetual auto-analysis. They become psychologists; which is in its way a disease of the mind."[39] Janet goes on to describe how people transform and reverse their actions out of fear of very specific actions. The syndrome that appears to be crucial here is defined in connection with melancholy: "In all fear of action there is, first of all, a check on action . . . In the case of melancholia there occurred a check on action." And in indirect form, Janet presents the connection between the concept of melancholy and work as therapy: "The investigations of pathological psychology have shown us the evil of sadness, and, at the same time, have evidenced a very important thing: the value of work and joy."[40]

Freud likewise reflected on this connection between work as therapy and melancholy when he wrote to a friend: "Today you may miss the note of melancholy . . . The reason is . . . I am already in the midst of work and full of hope."[41] Freud highlighted the role of inhibition in "Mourning and Melancholia": "Melancholy is characterized in psychic terms by a deeply painful bad mood, by a suspension of interest in the outside world, by the loss of the ability to love, by the *inhibition of any accomplishment,* and by the denigration of the feeling of self, which is expressed in self-reproaches and self-insults and increases to delusional expectations of punishment."[42] And at a different point Freud told of "a highly respectable man, himself an academic teacher," who was overcome by a state of melancholy "which excluded him from any type of activity for the next few years."[43] Evident in these descriptions is the bourgeois view of melancholy, which always announces itself when work is conceived of as a palliative against melancholy; this takes on the proportions of caricature in Carlyle's dictum "Work and do not despair." Usually when melancholy is described, inhibition does not appear exclusively as inhibition of *action,* as we have portrayed it thus far. Hans Hoff, for example, describes this symptom in much more universal terms: "This [inhibition] has the psychic effect of slowing down all processes of experience, of thought (!), of paying attention, of affective participation (psychic anaesthesia). The inhibition may have the motoric effect of making it difficult to get up in the morning, and in some cases is manifest as the absence of all vocal expression and as stupor."[44] Ribot therefore speaks of "maladies of the will," and for Schultz-Henke every genuine inhibition is suffering.[45]

Yet the inhibition of melancholics can, in many cases, be seen as the inhibition of action. There may even be a parallel to this in animal behavior, as N. R. F. Maier has shown. After experimenting with rats, he came to the following conclusions:

> The state of resignation is unique in that it does not represent a condition of goal orientation and it does not describe a type of action that is an end in itself. Rather it represents a *state in which action is lacking*, but which was preceded by types of frustrated behavior. Perhaps it represents an escape from reality in which further frustrations cannot be aroused . . . Resignation implies a rather complete loss in motivation and no effort to alter the state. It differs from other frustration-investigated symptoms in that *behavior is lacking*. A depressed individual likewise seems unable to respond constructively and lacks interest in his surroundings.[46]

In this case, however, the connection between reflection and inhibition is not founded on a reductive approach; instead it is derived through "phenomenological" indications—in the descriptions of the patients themselves. Georges Dumas spoke of the "law of inhibition," which revealed itself in patients' statements: "The patients declare themselves incapable of action."[47] The fact that Dumas' casuistry appears to weaken this group of assertions cannot reduce the value of such generalizing statements.[48] Ultimately, reasoning is directed only toward "inaction," and the motif of loss of world appears in those who have "withdrawn from the world."[49] Boredom appears in contradictory form, first as the symptom of melancholy (Marie D., thirty-nine years old, senses "a feeling of weakness and boredom")[50] and second as the missing constituent of the "healthy" situation: "I cannot reflect any more . . . I am not bored, I don't know how to be bored any more."[51] Some of Völkel's patients explain that "they now have to *think* ten times about things that caused them virtually no problem before."[52] They describe themselves as being "dull and lacking in motivation" (p. 43), are "clearly slowed down . . . in their motoric functions" (p. 53), and suffer from a "quiet, *inhibited sadness*" (p. 97).

Kraepelin describes melancholy in terms of "inhibitions that counteract the development of clear decisions and their implementation."[53] Patient 1 declares that "he could not work any longer."[54] "I haven't been able to work that way for six weeks," says Patient 2 (p. 8). Another patient was "lost in brooding" (p. 249) and "lost the joy in his work," and still another "did nothing but brood" (p. 252). Krafft-Ebing points to the role of boredom in the complaints of melancholics.[55] The letters in the second case he describes deserve special attention: "My thoughts are whole squadrons, are my tyrants—I am constantly forced to think" (p. 16); "Even at the best of times, I am absorbed by the worst of thoughts" (p. 17); "I almost always feel driven to commit something, and don't know what I am supposed to commit" (p. 18). Another patient speaks of the "compulsion to think" (p. 51). Yet another "made her whole past life the subject of embarrassing reflection" (p. 53) and claimed that she "had looked too much in the mirror." The wife of a professor laments the "embarrassing, unavoidable hunt of ideas" (p. 61). Another melancholic "avoids work."[56] Another "began to brood" (p. 324), was overcome by "fits of depression" (p. 327), was "constantly . . . tormented by sad and painful thoughts" (p. 398), was "always forced to think" (p. 398), and "feels bored" (p. 458).

Georges Dreyfus emphasized that "the *action* of the melancholic is always significantly afflicted at the same time."[57] "I travel all around the world in my thoughts," says a fifty-year-old woman. Another patient did not have the "feeling of being unable to think," "but his thoughts always went around in circles so that he could come neither to an end nor to a decision" (p. 94). In another case, Dreyfus reported the following: "The illness . . . had begun very slowly with 'weakness and thoughts.' She had always had to think; the thoughts came thick and fast. She had not been able to work any longer; her arms and legs were as if paralyzed" (p. 101). And another patient stated, "I wanted to work and couldn't . . . I had more to think about—one thought followed another" (p. 106). At one point the diagnosis is: "Incapable of the simplest activity. Painfully experienced inhibition" (p. 139). Many other case descriptions contain relevant passages: "'I don't feel like working anymore' . . . The patient states further that she has not slept very much recently, and when awake 'always had to think'" (p. 143). "She remembers that at the onset of her illness it was very hard for her to work, despite the most intensive will to do so . . . 'I had to think a lot then, more than usual'" (p. 199). Dreyfus then provides the following summary: "Work disability is not a result of fear, restlessness, or being absorbed in particular ideas, but of a feeling of inner *paralysis* that clearly comes into consciousness, of an *inhibition*. The *ability to think* was not disturbed in the large majority of our cases, whereas complaints of this nature are very characteristic in classic cases of manic depression" (p. 303).

Tellenbach, too, provides important material on the connection between reflection and the inhibition of action. Patients report that they have been brooding day and night, that their gaze is always introverted[58]; at another point, there are references to "insecure reflection on the past" and to "sacrificing ability by inhibition."[59] Tellenbach says of melancholics in general that they are characterized by "the constant willingness to reflect on their guilt,"[60] and "above-average willingness to reflect on their own guilt," and "reflection about the past" (p. 26). In his major work on melancholy,[61] Tellenbach speaks of the depressive's "having to be inactive" (p. 27), adopts Kraepelin's description of "sadness with the feeling of inhibition" (p. 45), emphasizes how easily the melancholic begins to "brood" after failing to attain self-established goals that are too "high" (p. 57), and, in response to one patient's statement, clearly sets out the connection between work and brooding: "'During the day I would have time to brood, but then that only happened at night'—which was not entirely true, in that she was incessantly active during the day and surely had no time to brood" (p. 66). The melancholic's qualms of conscience stem from "constantly increasing reflection" (p. 74) and are also characterized by "severe inhibition syndrome" (p. 76). One patient said, "If I now go on reading these books, pursue these thoughts, then I know that I will start brooding and get depressed again" (p. 77). Caroline Th.'s thoughts continually focus on herself (p. 86); Maria K. says, "I have to keep busy. Sitting around this way, with nothing in hand—I simply can't do it" (p. 89). These statements, coincidental as they are, connot of course provide anything like a complete picture of the melancholy state. We must note distinctions among these views; Binswanger, for example, is less insistent on inhibition than on "changes in the structure of temporal objectivity."[62] Yet the connection between reflection and the inhibition of action remains demonstrable, even in remote phenomena of human behavior, such as the blasé manner,[63] autistic thinking, or quite generally the pain that can be understood as "a positive inhibition of action"—which, however, also "develops with the greater unfolding of intelligence and consciousness" (Bleuler).[64]

The mirror motif likewise appears significant. Viktor von Gebsattel wrote of occurrences "in which the doctor can 'cure' the depression only by encouraging the patient to accept it. It is nothing to talk the needy out of his need. Rather, one must do just the opposite: it must be set up all around him, like a mirror of his existence which has deviated into the insanity of the flight from life."[65] And Felix Schottlaender described a patient who built himself a mirrored cabinet: "He made his own drama."[66] The mirror in this case represented the reconstitution of the lost relationship to society; but it was the duplication of the ego, which was intended to feign sociability, that allowed the illness to be deduced.

Often, however, the symptom of inhibition in melancholics also takes the form of inhibition of thought. It is not easy to discern what this means precisely. Usually it refers to the inability to productively "prethink" in the direction of action which has yet to be taken. Thus, inhibition of thought can be linked to the inhibition of action. There is an element of free-floating reflection that is not goal-oriented but pulls things back and forth, revealing the connection between action inhibition and reflection. In reports by both patients and their doctors, this connection is manifested in a dichotomy: on the one hand, an addiction to brooding and, on the other, an aversion to work and/or an inability to work. In formal terms, we again reveal a connection that has proven crucial for the problem of melancholy. We cannot determine here whether specific forms of behavior "in" society are already pathologically afflicted and thus carry the seeds of illness within them "unnoticed," or whether the alternatives of a healthy existence are reflected in the patients themselves. What remains important is the formal consonance we have described, which verifies the importance of the relation between reflection and action inhibition for every field. It would be useful to formulate a program that went beyond such parallels. Their description naively presumes what cannot be comprehended as the result of a historically conditioned dissociation. Based on this interest in recognition, Michel Foucault attempted to reestablish the forgotten synthesis of insanity and reason (in his *Madness and Civilization*). Klaus Dörner took a similar approach in his unpublished manuscript "Citizens and the Insane: Investigations in the Sociology of Knowledge on the Emergence of Psychiatry in the Bourgeois Society of England, France, and Germany." Treatment of the problem of melancholy thus involves considering how society judges melancholic behavior in society (up to the honoring of genius) in connection with the denunciation of asocial behavior (illness, insanity), and in particular revealing the economic dependencies which, given an unchanging and constant affective state and an identical psychic state, permit the rulers integration as well as condemn the underprivileged for punishable deviance.

8   Melancholy and the Search for Legitimation

Melancholy is a state of the psyche. Either it forms itself, or a form of it is already given in advance once resignation takes on the character of being "finitely" valid; in this way, the question of legitimation has already been answered quite "finitely," from the point of view of the person who poses it or to whom it is addressed. Melancholy appears to be enduring and indissoluble. In the context that interests us here, the most significant form of melancholy is that form which is simultaneously a rigidified type of reaction to "something" that "happens to" the person. In terms of psychopathology, we could speak here of "exogenous" melancholy. The inhibition of action is either cause or effect, sometimes both at once, in the sense that the enforced inhibition of action extends into areas completely beyond the reach of "external" power. In this connection, the urge to reflect on things becomes excessive.

The individual feels a need for legitimation only if a state of apathy has not already been reached, for the latter no longer tolerates the slightest reaction. Prior to this, the individual flees the world, in the sense that he no longer undertakes any action directed toward it. However, this means he has reached a stage where everything he regarded as self-evident has been forfeited; this in turn directly causes him to question legitimation and thus to establish new self-evident truths. An important question (which unfortunately we cannot address here) is whether this can in fact succeed—whether new self-evident truths might not accumulate from outside, be incorporated subconsciously by the individual, and then lose their self-evident character when they are jarred into the realm of consciousness. This was one of the major topics Arnold Gehlen addressed. What is of interest here is more the individual's attempt to process this loss of such truths, and less the extent to which he might meet with success. Yet we must stress once again: at no time are we asking whether it is "really" melancholy with which we are concerned. We

⌐ do not dare decide what melancholy really is. Rather, we inquire why
└ someone refers to himself or herself as melancholic or is labeled as
such by others, and how he or she then reacts to this. What conditions prompt people to refer to themselves or others in such terms,
and what have they thereby gained—in terms of, for example, legitimation? Thus, whereas we may only perhaps be speaking of melancholics, we are most certainly discussing people who *label* themselves
melancholics; we are also examining the social situations that exercise
a decisive influence on such a designation, and the behavioral forms
that result from it. If we furthermore assume that humankind is
driven by the "besoin de faire quelque chose" (to use Pareto's words),
then the question of legitimation takes on special weight if we understand melancholy as a syndrome of both reflection and inhibition of
action.

Renaissance Melancholy: Ficino or Tradition as the Pressure to be Binding

Marsiglio Ficino is one of the most important figures in the history of
the problem of melancholy, and the few pages we will devote to him
here will not do him justice. This omission can be excused only if we
bear in mind that it is not our purpose in this book to treat historical
considerations of melancholy. The decisive complex of problems is
described in detail in the following passage by Erwin Panofsky and
Fritz Saxl:

> There is no doubt that fundamentally, despite all his familiarity with
> Dante and ancient Neoplatonism, he [Ficino] regarded Saturn as an
> essentially unlucky star, and melancholy as an essentially unhappy
> fate, so that he attempted to counter it in himself and others by all
> the means of the medical art which he had learnt from his father,
> perfected by his own training, and finally firmly based on Neo-
> platonic astral magic. We can actually determine the moment at
> which the views of Proclus and Aristotle began to prevail in his mind
> against the views of Cacco d'Ascoli and Constantinus Africanus.
> In a letter between 1470 and 1480 he wrote to his great friend
> Giovanni Cavalcanti as follows: "Nowadays, I do not know, so to
> say, what I want, or perhaps I do not want what I know, and want
> what I do not know. The safety ensured you by the benevolence of
> your Jupiter standing in the sign of the Fish is denied me by the
> malevolence of my Saturn retrogressing in the sign of the Lion."
> But he received an indignant reply. How could he, as a good
> Christian Platonist, attribute an evil influence to the stars—he

who had every cause to venerate "that highest star" as a good planet?

"Did he regard you, when . . . Therefore do not complain of him, seeing that he raised you above other men as he himself is above the other planets. There is urgent need, believe me, of a palinode, and if you are wise you will sing one as soon as possible."

Marsilio Ficino did sing a palinode. His answer was already a recantation: "Because of that excessive timidity which you occasionally charge me with, I complain of my melancholy temperament, for to me it seems a very bitter thing, and one that I can only ease and sweeten a little by much lute-playing . . . Saturn methinks gave it me from the beginning, when in my horoscope he stood in the ascendant in the sign of the Water-Bearer . . . But where have I landed myself? I can see already that you will once more, with some justice, oblige me to embark on a new palinode on Saturn. So what shall I do? I will try to find a way out, and either I will say that melancholy, if you must have it so, does not come from Saturn; or else, if it necessarily comes from him, then I will agree with Aristotle, who described it as a unique and divine gift."

A few years later there appeared the three books *De Vita Triplici*, on the therapy and symptoms of the Saturnine character.[1]

The correspondence between Ficino and Cavalcanti reveals a complex process of legitimation typical for the age. Ficino felt that his melancholy was fateful. In the Renaissance, such a feeling was not considered "natural": after all, Ficino knew his Dante and knew what the neo-Platonic conception was! He should really have "known" what he had to feel.[2] Ficino attempted to legitimate melancholy by resorting to its psychological state, in which the process of legitimation was underpinned by a macrological form of argument—namely, astrological interpretation. Ficino made no effort to play off micro- and macrological forms of legitimation against each other. Rather, his intention was to assert an astrological viewpoint, which was more closely related to the psyche and therefore seemed to be more "natural," in opposition to another viewpoint, which appeared to be more "artificial" but had the advantage of being supported by its historical ancestry, something considered of higher merit at the time. The attempt failed, and on the basis of the correspondence cited there can be no doubt that Ficino quickly allowed himself to be swayed. The pronouncement, "I will try to find a way out, and either I will say that melancholy, if you must have it so, does not come from Saturn . . ." was his final attempt to redeem the natural state of the psyche without affronting tradition—by simply denying the existence of a connection between the complex of problems surrounding melancholy and that surrounding Saturn. But tradition was not to be duped so easily, and Ficino resignedly forestalled the objection that was inevitably forthcoming by professing his allegiance to Aristotelian tradition. Following this approach, the early Florentine Renaissance effected the ennoblement of melancholy. In the twenty-first canto of the *Paradiso*, Dante described Saturn's sphere as the realm of contemplation, and as a consequence melancholy became "what it has remained almost until the present day, *the intellectual pattern of 'modern Genius.'*"[3]

Acceptance finally came for Ficino's legitimation of his melancholy, an argument that was, to use David Riesman's words, "tradition-directed": tradition asserted itself over the psyche at this juncture. This was particularly marked in the case of Ficino, who, owing to his melancholy, did not console himself with the fact that it had acquired noble status (for that would have been tantamount to legitimating "cognitive dissonance," a point to which we will return later) but was actually forced into such consolation. If we recall the problematics of bindingness versus arbitrariness, then we could describe the above as a means by which a tradition-oriented bindingness asserted itself over the individual's tendency toward arbitrariness: Marsiglio Ficino attempted to negate tradition's claim to being binding, in order to save the arbitrary character of the psyche. Yet the ennoblement of Saturnine melancholy could not be upheld. Since the stance of the genius was given a foundation here in a very effective manner, this pressure to be binding contained a paradox: because bindingness won the day, this created opportunities for greater arbitrariness. Following the Enlightenment and the revolution in the natural sciences, although nothing much was left of astrology, the type of the genius nevertheless persisted. The genius could now develop randomly, freed from the fetters of astrological bindingness and speculation: thought and action were tied (in terms of intentions) only to one's own person. Or rather, this stance had at least become possible: after the final disappearance of the original agency of bindingness, the very fact of independence became proof of genius-like behavior. That other agencies now lay claim to influencing such behavior and that the attitude of the outsider was in the final instance required by society implied that things had reverted to a bindingness that could disguise itself all the better, the more it concealed the extent to which the imposed arbitrariness had in fact been already planned and required. The genius, when tied to rules laid down by macrological, cosmological speculation, was far more independent of society than the outsider, whose deviance was functional in terms of the whole and was demanded by those who conformed in order to gain support for themselves. Thus, the issue of legitimation entered a new phase: only now could the "inner world" be played out to the end, as was attempted, for example, by the Storm and Stress movement. Such legitimation was already itself a retreat—a reflection of powerlessness, of an absence of control in the broadest sense. This withdrawal into a personal inner world served solely to stabilize impotence vis-à-vis existing social relations: the solipsistic legitimation was valid only for the individual. It fled such noncommitment for a new external base: nature now provided the property that astrology had given the Renaissance. Thus, only the realm of speculation—to which such legitimation clung—shifted in the course of increasing though powerless arbitrariness.

Melancholy and Mysticism: Sabbatai Zevi, Nathan of Ghaza, and the Reduction of Cognitive Dissonance

The "case" treated below provides food for thought as to how certain aspects of the phenomenon of melancholy could be conceptualized using Leon Festinger's theory of cognitive dissonance. Festinger's theory has already been examined in Peter Schönbach's essay "Dissonance and Sequences of Interaction."[4] There is thus no need to repeat the analysis here.

Schönbach focuses on the relationship between Sabbatai Zevi and Nathan of Ghaza, who became Sabbatai's prophet—a relationship whose significance Gershom Scholem first recognized. Here is the history of Sabbatai Zevi, according to Schönbach:

> Sabbatai Zevi was born in 1626, the son of a Jewish merchant in Smyrna. As a youth, he—like many of his contemporaries—was filled with mystical excitement and hopes of salvation, after the terrible massacre of Jews and Poles by the Chmelnitzsky Cossacks in 1648. This mysticism, inspired largely by a prophcey in the Book of Zohar that the year 1648 would be the beginning of an age of miracles, crystallized, within Sabbatai, into a belief that he himself had been called on to bring the Jews salvation. Sabbatai decided to give symbolic manifestation of his divine mission and spoke the full name of Yahweh in public, an act of sacrilege that caused him to be banned from his hometown of Smyrna.
>
> After many years of wandering, he arrived in Jerusalem in 1662. By this time, he had acquired a number of followers who believed in

his messianic mission; but it was not until the ensuing years, after his encounter with Nathan, that he publicly declared himself the Messiah; an enormous mass of people adopted his cause, so that in 1669 Smyrna threw open its gates to greet his majestic entry when he returned there with his numerous disciples. His presence in Smyrna intensified the masses' enthusiasm to the point of ecstatic obsession, since the people expected an imminent change in history. Everyday life lost its meaning, work was neglected, and children no older than nine or ten were joined in marriage, so as to beget more children—that is, to incarnate as many souls as possible prior to the conclusion of the *tikkun*, the Messiah's re-creation of a whole out of the broken pieces of existence. The excitement spread throughout Europe . . . At the end of 1666 Sabbatai set out with his friends by ship for Constantinople, in order, by his own declaration, to wrest the crown from the sultan. As soon as he arrived he was arrested on the orders of the grand vizier, and, after a brief imprisonment in Constantinople, was taken to the fortress at Gallipoli, where he was able to lead a relatively comfortable life and, because his followers had bribed the Turkish authorities, ultimately to hold court almost like a noble. The sultan, Mehmet IV, hesitated to have him executed, for he wanted to prevent a sect from forming around the figure of a martyr. Clearly, he could not ignore the growing number of Sabbatai's followers.

He therefore ordered Sabbatai to be brought before him in Adrianopolis. The sultan's counsellors advised that an attempt be made to convert Sabbatai—and the sultan's personal physician, a relapsed Jew, was instructed to make the attempt. Surprisingly, he succeeded with ease. Brought before the sultan, Sabbatai donned a turban on the threshold to the audience room, as a sign of his conversion to Islam. The sultan, well pleased at the smooth solution to the problem, bestowed on him the names Mehmet Effendi and Sabbatai and the court title of Doorkeeper. (pp. 259–260)

In Schönbach's opinion, the conversion does not become interesting until Nathan of Ghaza appears on the scene. Nathan became acquainted with Sabbatai when the latter came to him as a manic-depressive patient. Manic periods "and depressive ones, filled with heavy melancholy and a fear of demons, alternated with phases characterized by a relatively normal psychic condition in which he did not understand his antinomian acts and deeply regretted them. The basic cognitive components of extreme dissonance reveal themselves here, and Sabbatai Zevi, owing to his illness, was unable to reduce them in a rational manner; rather, the dissonance was repeatedly renewed by the cyclical periods of his psychosis and was strengthened by the reactions of his environment, which generated alternately consonant and dissonant elements" (p. 262). In Nathan of Ghaza's view, the most important dissonances arose from Sabbatai's vision of himself as the Savior, which he did not dare yield to for fear he was wrong; they also stemmed from Sabbatai's exaltations, which arose during his manic-depressive periods, and also from the apostasy of the Messiah. The first dissonance was reconciled when the Messiah, searching for a cure from his sufferings, came to Nathan, who henceforth believed in Sabbatai's vision. He solved the second dissonance by composing his theological treatise *Drusch ha-Tanninim* (A Treatise on Dragons). Here, Nathan recounted, "with explicit reference to Sabbatai's psychotic symptoms, that with the breaking of the vessels the Messiah's soul plummeted into original space and was held captive there in the lowest regions: in the prison of Kelipoth (the dark forces), plagued by snakes that tried to seduce it. In its struggle with the snakes, the Messiah's soul worked to achieve perfection; only when it had achieved perfection could it finally quit its prison and initiate the *tikkun*" (p. 263).

Schönbach suggests that this apologia by Nathan furthered Sabbatai's apostasy, for it contributed a decisive, consonant element— "namely, the 'revelation' that even the extreme sacrilege of a renegation of belief could be demanded of him as a stage in the suffering on the path to his and the world's salvation" (p. 263). Ultimately, Nathan solved the dissonance of apostasy in the *Sefer ha Beri'a* (The Theory of Creation). "In this book, which he completed in 1670, Nathan teaches, taking his earlier theology to the extreme, that it is not sufficient for the devout man to stand beyond evil and attempt to draw Kelipoth's sparks up to him. The last and most difficult phase of the *tikkun* will be completed only when the Messiah descends into the Realm of Impurity to release the imprisoned sparks from within . . . Betrayal by the Messiah is interpreted as the hardest part of his mission; it is only at the end of his path into the dark Realm of Impurity that salvation breaks through" (p. 264).

The significance of the relationship between Sabbatai and Nathan for the problematics of melancholy initially becomes apparent in Gershom Scholem's remarks on myth and Kabbalah. Scholem speaks of the two important powers in Jewish life, Halacha (Law) and Aggadah (Legend), and thereafter of a particular myth:

> The Aggadic myth of the Yalkut Reubeni expresses the historical experience of the Jewish people after the Crusades, and we may say that it is expressed with rather greater force because it is not directly

mentioned at all. The depth of the penetration into the hidden worlds which can be encountered here at every step stands in direct proportion to the shrinking perimeter of their historical experience ... It is characteristic of Kabbalistic theology in its systematical forms that it attempts to construct and to describe a world in which something of the mystical has again come to life, in terms of thought which excludes the mythical element.[5]

This designates primarily behavior in the world that must compensate for loss of world, in this case by means of an attempt at mystical reconstruction. That an atmosphere of melancholy arises, indeed must arise, is something Schönbach likewise hints at:

It is no coincidence that Jewish history provides such an instructive proof of the significance of cognitive dissonance as a motor of historical development. Jews repeatedly suffered at the hands of a fate that said that their field of activity was narrowly confined by both the strictness of the Guardians of Rabbinical Law and the pressures of an inimical environment. The dissonances that arose from this situation could only be reduced by new cognitive orientation and rarely by simple changes of behavior. An early, moving example is the formation of Hasidism—with its ideals of asceticism, ataraxy and altruism—during the first Crusades as the ideology consonant with the suffering of those who, death at the hands of the hordes of crusaders before their eyes, did not relinquish their faith, but rather killed themselves. (p. 266)

Scholem has pointed out that Sabbatai Zevi was psychologically disturbed. "To some extent this truth has of course been suspected before; people have talked of paranoia or hysteria. But a mass of documentary evidence now available shows that his affliction was in fact of a somewhat different nature. He was constitutionally a manic-depressive."[6] Siegmund Hurwitz emphasized this even more strongly: "What is initially to be gleaned from these sparse comments [by Gandor and Laniado] is the fact that at times Sabbatai Zevi suffered from melancholy and depression; at other times he was (as the saying goes) 'filled with great joy.' Laniado terms melancholy a 'suffering imposed by God.' This calls to mind another leading figure of Jewish history, namely King Saul ... In times characterized by melancholy and depression, Sabbatai Zevi was overcome by a paralyzing passivity."[7]

Nathan's attempts to reduce dissonance illustrate how melancholy and mania can be processed within a system. For Nathan, the melancholic phase takes the form of a "shrouding of the face" or a "Fall," and the manic phase that of a "revelation." Melancholy is thus given a negative designation. This negativity is sublated in mystic speculation: "In this doctrine, revelation and melancholy, rise and fall, represent nothing other than stages in the great world process of the *tikkun*. When the Messiah descends into the abyss in a state of depression, the snakes are all-powerful and torture him, whereas during revelation the Messiah's soul succeeds in breaking their power."[8] Here, melancholy is placed in the framework of the order/dis-order dichotomy that has always accompanied the problem. Hurwitz lends this clear expression: "In times of disorientation, of chaos and of disintegration, an attempt is always made from within to generate order, harmony, and unity. The collective expectation for the coming of the Messiah at that time means in psychological terms (that is, viewed from within) nothing other than the gradual engendering of an archetype of wholeness. This external collective hope is joined by an inner demand that Sabbatai Zevi makes on himself—namely, that he realize his own unity. And at this point he fails."[9]

Seen from this vantage point, the phenomenon of cognitive dissonance and its reduction appears to be of general importance for the issue of melancholy. The Aristotelian view of melancholy as something by nature connected with genius already involves such a reduction of dissonance and thus an increase in legitimation. Certainly, this problem cannot be treated solely at the level of individual or social psychology. If we recall the correspondence between Ficino and Cavalcanti, then we can assess the difference in reduction of dissonance in their relationship, as compared with the relationship between Nathan of Ghaza and Sabbatai Zevi. In the latter case, melancholy is considered a phase in a process of order and dis-order, and constitutes—although couched in negative terms—a necessary component of this process. By contrast, Ficino, though personally opposed to the trend to accord melancholy a noble status, subscribes, under pressure, to a view that draws its legitimation solely from tradition. Seen thus, the mystical incorporation of melancholy as a negative but necessary part of a historical process represents a more subtle form of dissonance reduction and legitimation. A more thorough investigation of the relationship that obtains between melancholy and cognitive dissonance, which can be traced only in outline here, would soon reveal the fruitfulness of such an approach. The question of dissonance has already played a major role in our remarks on melancholy in the salon and among the bourgeoisie. The proposition of a loss of world would also have to be inserted into such deliberations. We can hypothesize that with a growing loss of world, dissonance and the pressure to reduce it would likewise increase. In this context, the continuum of a possible reduction of dissonance can lead from ataraxy to excessive action (Montmorency), and can occasionally lead to a linking of both. Among other things, the reference to the intertwining of the problematics of melancholy with cognitive dissonance demonstrates the need both to include history in the analysis and to consider the role of major systems of order (ideologies, world views, religions, mystical currents, myths).

Anthropological Reduction

"Depression is something we cannot leave to the psychiatrists: it is too painful and reaches too far down into the very roots of human existence . . . It should then be clear that, if we inquire as to its meaning, we are dealing not with a psychological or psychiatric issue but with an intellectual and spiritual concern." [10] Thus Romano Guardini writes on the topic of "gloom." He speculates as to its meaning, a question that has always been at the same time an inquiry into the legitimation of depression—for if something is recognized as meaningful, then it is legitimated by that very fact. Judging by the passage quoted, which condescendingly claims from the vantage point of some elitist parapet that psychology and psychiatry have nothing to do with intellectual and spiritual concerns, we are hardly likely to find the meaning of depression in Guardini's investigation. When he speaks of "constitutional mourning," he suppresses the fact that such characteristics of depression are dependent on society, and arrives at a definition that is not lacking in emphatic depth and ambiguity: "Depression is the necessary plight entailed in the birth of the eternal in humankind." And indeed the minor proposition, with its elitist undertones and ideological trimmings, is soon forthcoming: "Perhaps it would be better to say, in certain human beings . . ." [11] Guardini here uncritically adopts what scientific inquiry should first have to test itself against—namely, the withdrawal of melancholic legitimation into the self's inner world, into the individual constitution, into the realm of the anthropological. This reduction, however, has to do less with the nature of melancholics than with the circumstances that prompt such people to term themselves melancholics and to regard themselves as such.

If we survey the focal areas we have thus far treated, we find that an important part has been played by the question of the legitimation of melancholy and melancholic behavior by means of their reduction to anthropology. This was especially true of eighteenth-century bourgeois melancholy. Flight from the world and the inhibition of bourgeois action left no avenue open, other than one that led inward: introversion and melancholy were connected. The normative aspect of this reduction was then used ideologically: the bourgeoisie developed an ethos that was generally valid and that (as is always the case when the legitimation of norms is transposed onto a higher plane of abstraction) was leveled against the reality of the rulers, namely the aristocracy. Friedrich Schiller's drama *Intrigue and Love* succinctly sums up this opposition. Measured in terms of what is considered "human," the aristocracy appears "inhuman."

Melancholy is denounced in utopia: since it constitutes a factor promoting disturbance, it is not welcome in the overall design. At the same time, creators of utopias know full well that the all-embracing nature of their intentions means they have to plan the human being as well. Thus, we already find Burton trying to cure the melancholy of individuals in order to realize his utopia of a melancholy-free England. Planning the human psyche, which was ultimately raised to programmatic status in *Brave New World,* is simply a negative reaction to the knowledge that melancholy can be anchored in a person's inner world and that it is necessary to include this domain in the plan.

The reduction to basic anthropological assumptions seems least pronounced in the melancholy of the salon. Our sketch of La Rochefoucauld clearly demonstrates how he missed the chance to legitimate melancholy by such a reduction; the author of the *Portrait* confessed that he viewed his melancholy as a disposition—intensified by external, exogenous factors. It was the proximity to the world of such melancholy, and of the salon in which it was "processed," that resulted in a lack of any total reduction to anthropological principles—although such a reduction was of course partly in evidence in what was then termed "natural disposition." In addition, the behavioral ideal of the *honnête homme* had a similar effect, for it signified action directed toward the world and did not entail any action that involved withdrawing from it. By complementing each other, proximity to the world and reductive legitimation were mutually determining: the greater the proximity to the world, the less the compulsion to search for a platform for legitimation far removed from the world; the more painful the loss of world, the greater the withdrawal into introversion. Seen in these terms, the melancholy of the salon appears to be the diametrical opposite of its bourgeois counterpart. The utopian exorcism of melancholy confirms this connection: in utopia, a counterworld is being devised and with it a counter to melancholy. The danger for a utopia resides only in the residues of world that might manage to survive and might thus promote melancholy. This is yet another reason for the total nature of utopia: there is no utopia that involves merely little steps taken gradually one by one.[12]

We encounter reduction when Byron speaks of his ennui as a disposition, or when Constant talks of his *humeur* in similar terms, or when Baudelaire makes plans to write the *Lettres d'un atrabilaire*. The process of reduction—which grows stronger with an increasing propensity for reflection—finds clear expression in Maine de Biran's writings:

> The sentiments of the soul that I term "sadness" or "melancholy" differ essentially, in all ways, from feelings of illness or disquiet, which are linked to a poor state of nerves or a certain disposition of the organs. Those sentiments are just as desirable as these feelings are deplorable; all progress of the intellect and the most noble investigations of our faculties are related to the former. Once I experience sadness . . . I fear I might dissolve into that melancholic sentiment, and I find myself within my very self, I surround myself, I seek to penetrate into the depths of my soul, I reflect upon myself . . .[13]

This is reduction, and even if we explicitly ignore his talk of a "disposition of the organs," the phrase "the depths of my soul" means the same thing—the words merely have a greater dignity about them. That Maine de Biran thought of the *homme intérieur* as a type is clear in this context. And if we were to be consistent, we would have to take the process of reduction farther. If we do so, we reach a point at which it turns on itself and no longer provides legitimation. "If melancholy emerges from the depths of the creaturely realm to which the speculative thought of the age felt itself bound by the bonds of the Church itself, then this explains its omnipotence. In fact it is the most genuinely creaturely of the contemplative impulses, and it has always been noticed that its power need be no less in the gaze of a dog than in the attitude of a pensive genius."[14]

The legitimation of melancholy thus returns to its original point of departure, namely speculation on elementals. But legitimation can no longer be achieved. Now it can occur only if the legitimating act is accorded a function that bestows distinction upon people—if legitimation provides recompense for the person who searches for it. If everyone were melancholic (as Burton wrote, with the aim of abolishing melancholy), then there would be no incentive to find legitimation, for there would be no one left to whom an individual would have to legitimate himself. Rather, people must have the possibility of special legitimation; if they do not, then the basis for legitimation vanishes. To be "like everyone else" provides legitimation only as part of the undisturbed accomplishment of an action. If action is inhibited (as it is in melancholy), then special legitimation is needed—particularly since not everyone is thus inhibited. If man is indeed "the unhappiest and most melancholic creature," as Nietzsche suggested, then there is little reason to profess to something that everyone has in common anyway. We can conclude from this that an opportunity to legitimate melancholy arises at the point when people are able to avail themselves of the reduction to anthropology, but also when built-in mechanisms prevent everyone from making use of such reduction to the same extent. There is little consolation to be gained from the insight that each of us is as depressed as everyone else; more is to be drawn from the attitude of someone who feels hurt but who ventures to believe that he or she has been destined for such suffering. This is the most powerful form of legitimation to which we can aspire. It appears independent of factors stemming from the external world and need not fear that it might lose its elitist pretensions. This is also one of the sources for the link between the problematics of genius and those of melancholy.

9 The Climate of Melancholy and Anthropological Reduction: The Philosophy of Arnold Gehlen

> It is time for an anti-Rousseau, for a philosophy of pessimism and seriousness about life.
>
> Arnold Gehlen, *The Image of the Human Being in Light of Modern Anthropology*

In order to understand what the phrase "melancholic climate" means in Gehlen's philosophy, let us look at the first edition of his major work, *Man: His Nature and Place in the World* (1940). There we read that Supreme Leadership Systems represent the *"interests of powerlessness"* in the face of the "existential exposure" of man and his world. They do this "by providing support where power meets its limitations, especially in the face of failure, suffering, chance, and death; by injecting practices to steer destinies (magic, oracles, and so on), solace and hope, and by acting as the agent of communication with the supreme powers, the gods."[1] A further service provided by Supreme Leadership Systems consists of the *"counterwill"* of unbroken life against the impulsive catastrophes consciously experienced or even foreseen by man." A close relationship to melancholy appears here, and is obvious in the following sentence: "The failures of even the most well-considered and urgent actions, the unfulfillability of the elementary demand for 'more life' and the *depression* that must come of it, destinies that strike without warning, diseases, sure and certain death, are all experiences which a conscious being exposed to the world's 'field of surprises' is never spared. These are experiences of powerlessness, and they cannot be removed; they are inherent in the essence of human existence" (p. 457, italics added).

On the other hand, Gehlen calls "man's imagination . . . a force that promotes life, that extends into the future and works against resignation." He says of the primitive mentality: "The tremendous *reserve of resignation,* which is the obverse of the precision of our factual knowledge, has not yet been acquired; the interests opposing powerlessness manifest themselves in primordial power" (pp. 458–459). Supreme Leadership Systems provide the services of "ultimate world orientation, formation of action, and the overcoming of the limits of powerlessness" (p. 461). "The three sources we have distinguished follow clearly from the overall condition of the human being in the world; and this brings us to the conclusion of our anthropology, in accordance with its being an outline for an elementary anthropology" (p. 467).

Gehlen posits depression as constitutive of human beings. Melancholy is no different—or rather, does not see itself as being in any way different. The counter-resignative forces that help to overcome this condition are the Supreme Leadership Systems; humans, who are exposed to the world—the field of surprises—must submit to these systems if they are to keep melancholy at bay. However, a historical distinction has to be made. In the course of history, humans have built up a backlog of resignation which the Supreme Leadership Systems can work off only with greater difficulty than was the case at the time of their original power. In other words, all human beings are, because of the nature of human *being*, destined to be melancholic since they have to suffer the experience of powerlessness inherent in their existential condition. There is no remedy for this, other than the power of the Supreme Leadership Systems to stem the tide of powerlessness. This amounts to asserting a close relationship between the anthropological constitution of the human being and mankind's leadership systems.

This chapter of the first edition is of particular importance because it is one of the few passages Gehlen ever revised. In the preface to the fourth edition (Bonn, 1950) he says, "My reasons for replacing the last chapter with the new version are explained at length in the body of the text. The currently prevalent forms of instrumental and historical-psychological consciousness do not circumscribe the space of the mind. Thus, the last chapter also has the purpose of providing an introduction to research that seeks to pinpoint—via a consideration of the problems involved in the emergence of civilization and elementary social institutions—the laws of the mind that do not appear in those forms." In his most significant modification of the original text, Gehlen discards the teleological view that institutions were founded as the product of a primary form of subjective purposiveness. Instead, he assigns this founding function to ideational consciousness, whose creative power is displayed "in the *founding of institutions,* which, in their essence, are centered in an *idée directrice,* an idea of leadership."[2] Thus, the language Gehlen employs still alludes to the Supreme Leadership Systems, which in the meantime have been replaced by institutions and their *idées directrices*.

What is important for our discussion is that although Gehlen inserts stages (such as ideational consciousness) between the anthropological structure and the institutional superstructure, the original "melancholic" situation is not in the least affected. The human being does not lead his or her life "for fun, or in order to enjoy the luxury of reflection, but out of earnest need" (p. 17). The individual is "the being who is threatened or 'put at risk,' and who, in terms of constitutional structure, may come to harm" (p. 32). The historical distinction is not missing, for "the general feature of *subjectivity*" is "the stigma affecting the human being during an age in which institutions are in decline." Gehlen would agree with Winston Churchill on this point: "No matter what it is, a man's life must be nailed to a cross, be it that of thought or that of deed."[3]

This provides us with an implicit description of the "melancholic climate" that forms the point of departure for Gehlen's philosophy. Before turning to the institutions, which are totally inconceivable without this climate, we must mention the connection between action inhibition and reflection, which appeared to characterize the issue of melancholy. Even in Gehlen's early works, concepts of nonaction, especially the notion of reflection, are treated as residual concepts. Even in his works that do not yet show the influence of the pragmatists (his *Theory of Freedom of the Will* (1933) or his article of the same year, "The Concept of Reality in Idealism"), reflection is presented as action inhibition. Reflection is not understood exclusively in terms of action inhibition, because the concept of action becomes decisive for the anthropology he advocates here; all problems must therefore be resolved from the point of view of action, and not vice versa. The human being, owing to the unreliability of his instincts, must bend the world to his will and change it, and is able to accomplish this only by means of the life-securing process of activity. To a life-securing process, every reflection—that is, every moment spent thinking about problems instead of directly tackling them—is inhibiting. Reflection can thus also be regarded as "loss of world."

In this light it seems difficult to establish a link between the original anthropological situation Gehlen describes as melancholic—namely, that of *constitutional* powerlessness and depression[4]—and the concept of reflection as action inhibition, which is held to be characteristic of melancholy but which Gehlen must reject in the framework of his theory of action. The polemic against reflection would indeed be incompatible with an underlying melancholically oriented climate, were it not for the theory of institutions, which binds the two concepts together and is in fact based on them. Without institutions, external stabilization would not be guaranteed: "In view of the human being's openness to the world and liberation from instinct, there is nothing to ensure that concerted action will ever come about or that, once having come about, it will not fall apart tomorrow. *The institution fills precisely this gap.* It takes the place of the automatic link missing between people, and thus establishes its validity as something imperative, as we have described at length." Gehlen also says, "It is only through the agency of institutions that social action of any kind becomes effective or lasting in nature, subject to norms, quasi-automatic and predictable."[5] In this way institutions also supply, via the detour of external invariances, internal stabilization for "the unstable, plastic, and variable domains which, by nature," are part of the human condition.

This is why society, through its institutions, is seen as designed to fulfill the anthropological demands that arise from the essence of the human being. Since human beings are destined to act, society has the task of realizing this purpose and stabilizing action. The fact that institutional mechanisms "suddenly acquire an entelechy of their own" and ultimately impose their new "quality of imperative validity" on human beings is not something opposed to the individual but instead relieves him of part of his burden: "What we now wish to demonstrate is, namely, that a formation of motives which is actually personal in nature and intervenes in existing institutions in a creative and superelevating manner presupposes precisely the type of relief that was described in institutionalized behavior."[6]

At this point, we must note a special characteristic of Gehlen's concept of action: it appears in connection with the concept of labor and, moreover, is often used as a synonym for it.[7] If we recall what we have said about bourgeois melancholy, a decisive connection comes to light here. We saw that labor was a means of counteracting the bourgeois melancholy that developed after the economic emancipation of the bourgeoisie. It permitted the space of introversion to be left to those who could not or would not become economically active, namely the free-floating intelligentsia. The concept of labor in the present case appears to be fused in a similar way to that of action: it is a medicine against constitutional depression, an antidote to melancholy. Reflection is defused in action, and with it the incentive to become melancholic; conversely, action (labor) can counteract melancholy. However, action is a sure means of defense only if it is guaranteed by institutions that stabilize action. Here a second antimelancholic factor comes into play: the concept of order. If we consider humans' original state to be insecure and unbound by instincts, we supply corresponding metaphors for dis-order; a phrase such as "frightful naturalness" implies a primordial chaos. On the other hand, institutions are agencies of order: they prescribe preferences toward which human action can orient itself. Both action and institution are thus effective in equal measure and counteract the seeds of dis-order and constitutional melancholy: they tend to create order and thus dissipate melancholy. By means of actions and institutions that call for action, action inhibition and thus the inclination to engage in reflection are also eliminated. In this manner, an "atmospheric" precondition of melancholy is removed. Gehlen's anthropological design is thoroughly "melancholic" in conception, and his institutional doctrine is the antimelancholic remedy for melancholy.

If Gehlen's philosophy remained within these parameters, which are certainly not narrow, we could demonstrate its similarity to a view oriented toward melancholy, to a state of the human constitution— namely, the predisposition toward depression and dis-order. The parallels do not stop here, however, because Gehlen goes on to provide an elaborate interpretative framework which he develops into a cultural critique. He orients this, in turn, toward the concept of action and reflection. Since institutions, and thus also the society that is necessary for their authentication, have to be bolstered, Gehlen condemns reflection because it keeps the human being from acting. Thus, he regards reflexivity as "lost innocence," and reflection as "originally the high art of positing ambiguity," as "the functional form of subjectivity," as fashionable "passions à la Werther or à la Kierkegaard" (!), as "a chronic state and characteristic . . . of mass consciousness"—in short, as the sympton of an age whose asserted subjectivity Gehlen chooses as the target for his attack. The determination of the negative side of reflection on the basis of his fundamental anthropological argument proceeds along these lines, extending all the way to the superstructure of cultural critique; and we can safely assume that we are dealing with a polemic against melancholic attitudes when the targets of attack are such decidedly melancholic "types" as Werther and Kierkegaard. Gehlen draws up a counterimage of a society that is a matrix of tightly welded institutions and that in the course of time may, if anything, be changed and rearranged but not overthrown. The concept of action thus gradually acquires an ambivalent coloring: it provides for change only in the area of interpersonal relations, but otherwise expects human beings to "allow themselves to be consumed by a life of action, which is, after all, only as it should be"[8]—unless they want to be dismissed as introverts.

In his essay "The End of the Personality" (1956), which is important for an understanding of his cultural critique, Gehlen writes:

> When in the age of Hellenism the endless victories and defeats, the cultural flood and cultural subversions, made it impossible to entertain the thought that man is a perpetrator of deeds, people nevertheless did not give up this conviction but used deeds to change themselves: the alert thinker carved out of himself a counterfigure to existing conditions. The stoic and cynic were plastic figures who showed how the individual could nevertheless juxtapose a freedom of action to the chaos of circumstances, and how he could aim at developing his own immunity to events and destinies. The fact that there is no longer any stoic gesture or any aggressive cynical literature, not even in England, shows that the reserves of indignation have been exhausted; they have made way for the ill humor of boarders in the house of existing conditions. On the other hand, we have cultural "critique" galore . . .[9]

Up to this point we have found only a connection between humans' constitutional melancholy and a design based on institutions and action systems to banish this melancholy. Let us now add a new element that for the first time makes cultural critique possible: a view of current conditions. We must describe these conditions if we are to summarize and perhaps even expand on Gehlen's philosophy. The best point of reference is found in *Man in the Age of Technology*. Here Gehlen presents his theories of the "disparagement of real contact" and of "subjectivism as processing of the self and refinement of the isolated soul," deriving them from a historical constellation that has also proved important for our own study. This is particularly true if we consider that Gehlen's point of departure is the observation that "around the middle of the eighteenth century, three phenomena arose simultaneously: European industrialization, the science of psychology, and sentimental-psychological literature such as Richardson's novels (or *Werther* in Germany)."[10]

Gehlen draws on this period for certain premises of his cultural critique. It is the source of, among other things, his notion that the opaqueness of the modern world teaches people to become resigned. The sentence clearly brings to mind those formulations in the first edition of *Man* that dealt with history's growing reserves of resignation and the Supreme Leadership Systems' increasing difficulty in coping with them. Finally, Gehlen discerns a phenomenon that might be called "bourgeois melancholy":

> The Enlightenment era appears to us at an end; its premises are dead. Yet its consequences are still with us, in particular a deeply rooted tendency to consider a certain number of things as obvious. We repeat, the Enlightenment premises are dead. For instance, today we are not as likely to believe that reason, equally present in all men, can from its own resources attain nontrivial knowledge; or that nature is "reasonable," i.e. knowable through and through, and incapable of contradicting the criteria posited by an educated and right-minded humanity. *And today, when the bourgeoisie of the whole world often seems secretly to consider itself beaten, it is worth recalling that it considered as utterly certain that what it considered rational would ultimately triumph in history.*[11]

Utopian thought had been regarded as a chance to eliminate melancholy through planning and to draw up an antimelancholic counterplan. In taking leave of history, Gehlen reinforces the intentions of his anthropology and cultural critique. Initially, Gehlen rejects the historical viewpoint for methodological reasons: "Man is the most complex object of all. It is impossible to treat all aspects of him at the same time, and thus we have had to generalize to a very large extent from such fundamental facts as those that lie in the *historicity* of the human being and in his constant integration into specific, historical *commmunities,* in order to arrive clearly at equally fundamental *other* facts."[12] If historicity vanishes from anthropology for methodological reasons, then history, too, disappears down the anthropological drainpipe. Gehlen adopts Pareto's concept of "cultural crystallization" (Cournot's concept of *"post-histoire"*) and uses it to refer to "the state of affairs in any given cultural realm . . . that occurs when the possibilities there are all developed in terms of their basic properties."[13] In 1961 he dared to predict that "the history of ideas has come to a conclusion, and that we have arrived in *post-histoire,* so that Gottfried Benn's advice to the individual—namely, 'Count on using your own reserves'—should now apply to mankind as a whole."[14] Hendrik de Man claimed that *"post-histoire* does not mean the lethargy of a culture whose vitality has dried up; it means the entry into a phase of world events that does not fit into history at all, because the otherwise historically verifiable connections between causes and effects are not forthcoming."[15] Gehlen shared such views, which probably also served to water down the similarity between his ideas and theories such as Spengler's.

Here lies the key to Gehlen's actual conception of melancholy. Anthropology and the doctrine of institutions both describe man's constitutional depression, even as they both indicate the means of combating it: action and labor. However, with his adoption of a view of *post-histoire*, the future vanishes from Gehlen's conception. Its absence and the recourse to the past are essential signs of the "melancholic climate." This results in a paradox. In the area of anthropology, Gehlen discerns possibilities for diminishing melancholy—possibilities that, in the large framework of his philosophy of history, put an end to history and prove to be grandiosely futile; because in a state of *post-histoire*, very little of import can be changed—one can count on nothing but that which already exists. However, this insight is available only to a privileged few. Whoever is not privy to it manifests the attitude that Gehlen, like Scheler, refers to as "pleonexia":

> The word "pleonexia" means greediness, overbearingness, and a domineering thirst for power. The word can hardly be dispensed with these days from a socio-psychological viewpoint. It can be used to define the masses, particularly since the already standardized meaning of this term, which is burdened with ideas about the "primitive person" and such, has long become unsatisfactory. It makes no difference what kind of education or social status the individual has: if he manifests pleonexia, he belongs to the masses, whereas, by the same token, anyone who practices self-discipline, self-control, has distance from himself and some idea of how he can grow, and should be considered part of the elite.[16]

A number of things could be said to contest this. Not the least of them is that the traits demanded here can be imparted only by means of a specific upbringing in the family and at school, and already mirror a particular position in the system of rule: it is not easy for someone who has everything to manifest greediness. The point, however, is more that this is a behavioral ideal which is blatantly elitist and a product of the *post-histoire* conception. The "All is vanity" motto plays a role here, and whoever does not know it should simply continue trying, practicing greediness and thereby documenting his mediocre rank. Here we can see a worthy conservative pattern. As early as 1433, in the treatise *De Concordantia Catholica*, which Nicholas of Cusa wrote for the Council of Basel, the state was compared with a body that is damaged most by melancholy: "Yet not only the expressions used, but the whole construction of Nicholas of Cusa's sentences, make it plain that the indolence of the phlegmatic, the

contentiousness of the choleric and the ostentation and voluptuous-
ness of the sanguine were in his view far less weighty matters than
the 'pestilential' vices of the avaricious, thievish, usurious, pillaging
melancholic with his ill-gotten gains, whose picture seems to have
been drawn with the most lively repugnance."[17] This coincides for
the most part with Gehlen's description of pleonexia; and when
Klibansky, Panofsky, and Saxl speak of the doctrine of temperament
as being "in some respects one of the most conservative parts of
modern culture," Gehlen profits from this conservative background:
descriptions such as those of the masses ossified in pleonexia always
have an air of being definitions per se—a feature also true of the
doctrine of temperaments.

Gehlen's description of boredom likewise fits into this elitist
framework:

> [Boredom] is no minor subject. Schopenhauer said, and rightly so,
> that in the end it paints true desperation on people's faces and is a
> calamity against which public measures for prevention have been
> taken. Probably we can include in the context of these phenomena
> the unhappy overall veneer of mankind today, which is condemned
> to passing the time outside the bustle of work, and among whom
> even the young girls cultivate an impudent style. At any rate, educa-
> tion does not help against boredom either, since it too becomes bor-
> ing. Only *reality* would help—namely, experiences that are intrinsi-
> cally coherent and that one could allow to ripen within oneself and
> then digest morally.[18]

This conception of boredom is aristocratic through and through, for
it insists on the diminution of boredom; and even if Gehlen usually
declares such a reduction to be impossible, he does not transform
boredom into some means for secondary elitist feelings, as Leopardi
does, for example. We can now link the "melancholy climate" with
the interconnections we have constantly drawn on in our study. At
the outset, Gehlen considers the human constitution to be depressive.
This "impotence" was originally reduced directly through the
Supreme Leadership Systems, which created a balance in anthropologically conditioned factors of melancholy and thus made human
stability—which, in fact, means order—possible in the first place. In
this connection, the imagination is accorded a particular significance
as a force opposing resignation. This sharply contoured teleological
context is jettisoned in Gehlen's later conception: the category of
"secondary objective purposiveness" now gains importance, and
institutions are created by an ideational consciousness whose function

is to found institutions. From this point on, we can no longer term Gehlen a pessimist if we wish to link pessimism and determinism in the manner, for instance, that Stenderhoff adopted.[19] For the category of "secondary objective purposiveness" introduces chance into the system. The ideational consciousness precludes any fatalism. The concept of elites is to be found concealed here as well—if, that is, we are not to assume that we are dealing with some successor to the notion of a "national spirit" [*Volksgeist,* a term that has over- tones of National Socialism.—*Translators*]. Yet even such a spirit would not have to appear as a ghost wherever it wishes and could select the members of an elite as its bearers. By virtue of his convic- tion that he is living in *post-histoire,* Gehlen cannot proceed down an avenue that would involve juxtaposing an Enlightenment project to the anthropologically melancholic condition of human essence. The past thus comes to predominate. This view and the impossibility of utopia in the absence of a category of the future go hand in hand with the stores of resignation that build up, or so Gehlen would have it. History comes to a standstill at the conclusion of a melancholic trend that reaches a peak in Now-Time, or *Jetzt-Zeit.* [The notions of "history at a standstill" and of *Jetztzeit* are both main categories of Walter Benjamin's later philosophy.—*Translators*] In the process, imagination becomes a category that "carries through" only as far as the institutions, but then is no longer able to alter any aspect of post- history.

This conception attests to a heroic attitude that reminds us of Montmorency and slightly of Don Quixote, because it too is practiced by a citizen who covertly and quietly regrets not *being* an aristocrat and therefore at least *feels* like an aristocrat. Gehlen's philosophy is thus imbued with the air of tragedy that surrounds the aristocracy, certainly after the discovery of post-history, which is first called by its name in 1952 but is implicitly present as early as 1935[20]—just as it is impossible to conceive of the plays of Corneille and Racine in a bourgeois setting, if, that is, the bourgeoisie even understands them. In 1934, Gehlen wrote in his essay "The Structure of Tragedy": "Re- flexiveness and the lost innocence of a complete era, such as moder- nity, provide no ground for fates; it must remain impossible for people to excuse themselves from a tragic conflict, and herein resides the deep harmony of the preconditions involved. For man, animated by objective and stringent systems of order as well as by concrete ethical life, is always himself naive and unconscious, whereas the powers withdraw from someone who is reflexive."[21]

Gehlen has, by using the notion of post-history, discovered a way of proving modernity worthy of tragedy. Such a conception can accommodate an image of human beings in which they are but disciplined beasts, consumed in institutions and devoted to a "this-worldly" transcendence. And it is here that we find the aporia of the attempt to rescue the tragic stance, an aporia composed largely of the naiveté of the individual who acts and allows himself to be sacrificed with the same matter-of-factness. The "dilemma of conservatism" (Greiffenhagen) is very similar in composition: it can but condemn reflection reflexively.[22] Mannheim distinguished conservative, bourgeois, and proletarian modes of thought according to their respective relation to the moods of time, construing the first to focus chiefly on the past, which constitutes the present. He also referred to the cyclical nature of conservative thought and emphasized that here the historical image of time receives a sense of "imaginary spatiality." These are all syndromes that we have already encountered in the history of melancholy and that help complete the picture. Thus, by speaking of it, Gehlen already forfeits the naiveté that would grant true dignity. The conservative who writes has already reflected on his subject and is caught in the conservative dilemma—namely, that he who condemns reflection has already been convicted of that which he polemically attacks.

Despite the aristocratic associations that Gehlen attaches to the melancholy climate (and this involves clear antibourgeois affects in statements such as those concerning the natural desire for a Land of Milk and Honey, a desire that must be suppressed),[23] it also exhibits affinities to Idealism, reminding us that it is rooted in this philosophy. These affinities are evident in the passages in which Gehlen admits to having worked with the "abstraction of the individually acting human,"[24] and in so doing reveals that his theory of action in large part functions with a conception that excludes any partners and is almost solely oriented toward solitude. This is expressed even more openly in *Original Man and Late Culture:* "Institutionalization—for example, in universities—is a chance component of philosophy; it is not intrinsic to philosphy, which is ultimately a solitary process."[25]

Despite the obvious distance, this brings to mind the conception of introversion that accompanied melancholy in eighteenth-century Germany. At times it appears as if Gehlen permits philosophy and the philosopher something that must be denied to the individual as actor: the withdrawal into introversion. This is intimated by the concluding sentences of *Original Man and Late Culture,* which draw a picture of a cheerful and free philosophy along classical lines. The lament that today a long-discarded stoic or cynical stance has had to yield pride of place to moroseness attests to this. Gehlen's plea for an attitude that takes classical philosophy as its model remains as embedded in the realm of a melancholy climate as do his anthropological views. It is but a small step from mourning the loss of a cynical stance to resignation. Klaus Heinrich has trenchantly pinpointed this link. He describes the "reduction to the animalist" as a form of resignation— although the thrust of this hardly touches Gehlen. Another argument is better suited to this purpose, namely that "resignation first becomes cynical when one accepts disappointment,"[26] if only we expressly remember what serious consequences are connected with Gehlen's assumption of the presence of *post-histoire*. He declares that he does not accept it, yet he considers the recognition of the end of history (which already permits making an elitist classification of his own) and the stoicism or cynicism this engenders as the stance that should preferentially be adopted.

The melancholy climate can be traced back to Gehlen's work *Real and Unreal Spirit: A Philosophical Investigation into the Method of Absolute Phenomenology*, which appeared in 1931. It is among the few books from which the author later dissociated himself: "Today we would probably call the manner of thinking and pathos of this book 'existentialist,' although the author did not understand himself to be such. At any rate, he abandoned this position the minute he realized how easy it was to adopt and defend it: there are no arguments that can be leveled against unreserved self-presentation. At least he realized that he had to burn the bridges between himself and existentialist philosophy, which was just being born."[27] The thrust of this self-interpretation was borne out by critics of the early Gehlen, who were of the opinion that the ingredients of this form of philosophical thought would disappear "once Gehlen turns to providing justifications for his anthropology, which is, as it were, constructed from below."[28] We wish to rebut such a view. Our rebuttal draws first of all on Gehlen himself, who in the context of his early writings spoke of a renaissance "in the true sense of the word, which includes the hopelessness of that which one first strives for, as well as the possibility of unexpected fecundity."[29] A further argument can be added to this arbitrarily legitimated one. Let us recall Gehlen's own rejection of *Real and Unreal Spirit*. The book was admittedly (as Gehlen himself said) understood to be existentialist, but this was not the author's actual intention; once adopted, the position was abandoned not because it had proven to be false or at least untenable, but because it was easy to adopt and could free itself from the clutches of criticism without any difficulty. Here, heroism enters into science: we could describe Gehlen's further development as the attempt to take up forward positions on a limb and defend them against the enemy—an attempt in which he succeeded.

Elsewhere, Gehlen termed his early book "praxis-related" and linked it to pragmatism.[30] Here again we can sense the touch of coquetry in Gehlen's repudiation of his own work. *Real and Unreal Spirit* cannot be conjured away, as its author would like—neither by himself, nor by more recent interpreters of his work who begin their description of the doctrine of institutions with the book's famous sentence concerning our modern age, namely that "it makes it a duty to distrust the spirit irrespective of the ideas in which it moves."[31] The spirit of 1966 is the same as that of 1931. In addition to the above-mentioned arguments, we would do well to examine Gehlen's early book because it focuses ostensibly on problems that have been central to our study: gloom and boredom. Admittedly, the latter phenomenon recedes into the background when compared with the former, which could also be described as melancholy.[32]

Gehlen initially presents the opposition between being and gloom in very general terms: "The basic phenomenon is thus the pure condition of intrinsicness of a higher or lower *reality,* in a quite general and completely untheoretical sense. The contrasting determination of the condition of being is the one described above—namely, that of a state of having essentially gone astray, of gloom, of temporariness" (p. 24). Gehlen then renders this conception more specific: "Finally, the stage of being and the stage of happiness coincide. Gloom is the sign of inner insecurity and of the substantive inner turmoil of the lower stages of being" (p. 26). It must strike us as paradoxical when Gehlen later writes that he wishes "to expend the utmost energy in avoiding the notion that an ontology is being produced here" (p. 149). With a view to the later "anthropological shift," we must ask at this juncture how human beings behave in such situations,[33] given that the lower stages of being signify gloom. Gehlen initially gives an answer that appears to differ considerably from the solutions he proposes later. He points to the decisive role of the Other. "A human being's sole adequate object is the Other, and Being realizes itself in its substantive forms in the relations between human beings" (pp. 30–31). This reciprocal reference leads to a higher stage of being and consequently is a means to combat gloom. The "phenomenal forlornness of the single person" (p. 37) and the dialectical side of individuation accord with this: "This is the abyss of consciousness: without the Other, I would be nothing and would not be; my actions are aimed at him and yet lead me to myself; my characteristics are only in my expressing-myself to him" (p. 37). Gehlen does not, however, pursue this path very far. "Human beings do so little for one another for the same reason that they think so little of one another: they are blocked off from their own reality. This, I believe, is to be found today only in the most elementary of human relations: in the family, among a few intimate friends. This is the untiring location of our life: here we attain ourselves" (p. 31). Yet from this he does not subsequently develop a theory that, for example, describes the family as a mediating agent. Instead he remains at the general level of cultural criticism. For what he expresses here is but the "inclination of our deeply diseased and unreal Existence—our 'culture'— to find itself again in the act of grasping the simplest and most basic realities" (p. 31). This dashes the assumption that, in principle, the lower stages of being (which are revealed in certain situations) could be transformed by the agency of social authorities out of their "gloom" to higher stages: to states of world affinity.

This attempt was to succeed in quite a different manner, and Gehlen describes it in his chapter "On the Negative and Relinquishing Cognition" (pp. 125–131). In view of the negative, "the self-sublimation of consciousness is now the location" (p. 126):

> It is, then, only the conviction that the previous deep logic of our life has led us here which keeps us afloat; and a sort of belief in ourselves, a need to yield up the tiller to our life and to leave it to fate, which confronts us usually in the inconspicuous guise of chance. And everything depends on not delaying reflection unduly, out of fear; happiness, which is concealed in the Negative, waits for us, but only for a certain time. Life, in order to be completely itself, must search out the Negative and stand the test of it, and if Spirit is to be an immanent property, it must renounce itself. (p. 126)

If we were to decode these sentences, which remind us of Nicolai Hartmann in their ontological orientation, formally of Hegel in their "negative dialectics," and of Kierkegaard in their pathos of risking the self ("situation," "moment," "leap"), we would be able to prove that they incorporate Gehlen's later position. Let us first briefly review his stance. "In other words, we shall claim here that the Negative is one of the positive contents of reality as such" (p. 131): this is the underlying thought that prevents Gehlen from further examining the phenomenon of the *reciprocal* relations of *humans beings*. It also forms the basis for his cultural criticism, which censures less the "Negative" in the state of culture than the extant possibilities for easily coping with the "Negative." Our age is "bereft of community" (p. 63); the world consists of "agents and canvassers, whose only object is money" (pp. 66–67). For this reason, "contemplation is one of the high points in the life of a primitive person; and therefore the desire to travel, which flourishes only in large cities, is a wish to come to oneself in a more real environment" (which means, however, one with higher, more gloom-*free* stages of being). "The false life we all lead" (p. 108), "the effeminization of our intellect" (p. 187), the "loss of reality (in the intensive meaning of 'reality') among people today, which is widely spoken of as degeneration and decline, to the extent that they are unable to attain such a meaning" (p. 187)—all of these are ultimately the consequence of progress, a product of civilization: "Lessons by radio are the end of science in the form Galileo gave it in the face of the Inquisition" (p. 105).

In other words, the individual can overcome the "Negative" (gloom, the lower stage of being) only if he bears the burden of the Negative—which results in its dialectical position as something secondarily positive. This "processual" conception results in the view that "such a form of science as is last reflected, under the idea of being, as the highest . . . is condemned to perpetual disappointment, because Being remains unattainable in extensive terms and, above all, because Being *is not an empirical concept*" (p. 161). This characterization does not, however, hold true for philosophy, which, following Schopenhauer, saves itself from disappointment by wishing not to *know* the essence of being-as-becoming, and by instead wishing to depict it and to enable the individual to experience it in every single thing. Hence the apodixis of the statement that absolute phenomenology follows from the "impossibility of resignation in existential questions" (p. 188), and hence the emphatic exclamation that "reality and with it happiness is attainable in every moment" (p. 194).

The path of phenomenological development from unreal to real spirit can thus be represented as follows. Human beings originally live in lower stages of being, in gloom, solitude, and abandonment; this is a motif in existentialist philosophy. They liberate themselves from such conditions by self-estrangement: they devote themselves to negation, and experience happiness in such devotion. Here we find motifs anticipated that are later to determine Gehlen's view of the "birth of freedom from estrangement." Yet here we can also perceive the difference. Even if this is only intimated, the element in the lower stages of being that surmounts these—the will to estrangement—is originally the relation to the Other, and this is, in substance, the decision to merge with the Negative, from which the liberation into real spirit then supposedly ensues. It is the institutions that are lacking here; later they are to bring about that which is attributed to the reciprocal relationship and, even more strongly, to "chance." The latter, in fact, never dwindles in significance: indeed, it is concealed in the influence of ideational consciousness and the creative power of the *idées directrices*. It is an element of resignation and of potential decisionism, as well as a badly disguised elitist claim. Cultural criticism exists in both, and we even find a pleonasm: *The Soul in the Age of Technology*. Gehlen never gave up his polemic against civilization.

What is lasting in Gehlen's eyes resides essentially in humankind's underlying constitution, or in the human situation. Originally he conceives this as a lower stage of being—as gloom, among other things. It could also be termed "melancholy"[34]—seen formally in terms of the loss of possibilities (of "higher" being). At a later date, Gehlen gives anthropological strength to the foundations for this: having already described them as melancholic, he derives them from the constitution of a "defective being" released from its instincts which, in order to save itself, allows itself ultimately to be consumed by institutions. Although Gehlen boasts that his thought did not operate "with ontological hypotheses," his early position must nevertheless be termed ontological, just as his later one ossifies into metaphysics. Ontology is to be understood in this context not only philosophically, as the endeavor to "explore existence as existing, that is, the principles, regularities, and structures attributable to existence as such,"[35] but also as the assumption of the existence of a prioris as such, an assumption that uses the concept of being.[36] The melancholy in this theoretical stance shifts from being to the psyche, from the domain of ontology to that of metaphysics. Gehlen makes a plea for the abolition of melancholy, initially via a dialectical principle that proves its worth in tolerating the Negative, and later via the stabilizing power of institutions that appear to have metaphysical foundations, namely through the agency of the *idée directrice*.[37] The dialectical moment in both conceptions appears initially to involve viewing the antithesis between the negative in being, on the one hand, and the disconcertedness of the psyche owing to openness, on the other, as positive, compared with the claim to "happiness," security, and legitimation. Gehlen's position, however, is characterized less by the dialectical estimation of the negative moments than by the formal trend toward rigidification, which remains constant.

Gehlen's intention is both to overcome gloom as a negative moment and a lower stage of being and to stabilize humankind's

unstable constitution. The negativity of these two elements is, however, the precondition for the dignity that the individual demonstrates by enduring situations and by giving himself over to institutions. Institutions gain validity only because they *must* fulfill a
stabilizing function. The insufficiency of the initial situation is
intrinsic to them; without this, institutions would, for example, have
no claim to validity, because they would not be expected to achieve
anything. In other words, the *changeability* of the initial situation is
what offers institutions the chance to legitimate themselves. Their
"negative" *constancy*, however, and the unchanging necessity for a
stabilizing agency first provide a guarantee of legitimation. This is
the reason for the unalterable climate of melancholy that also characterizes Gehlen's anthropology. The abolition of history corresponds
to this, as does the retrospective cultural criticism.

At this juncture, we should relate Gehlen's "melancholic" position
to other currents in philosophical conceptions of the present.
Adorno's position could fulfill this function—from the *Dialectic of
Enlightenment* to *Negative Dialectics.* In this connection, we would do
well (if we had the space) to cast a glance at Heidegger's work. And
in the context of Adorno, this would probably best be accomplished
by undertaking a critical analysis of language; in the context of
Gehlen, by comparing the ontological safety mechanisms: "This book
was written before I became acquainted with Heidegger's *Being and
Time,* which in some respects processes similar thoughts" (*Real and
Unreal Spirit,* p. 84, n. 59).

For Adorno, the observations gathered in his *Minima Moralia,*
which he dedicated to Max Horkheimer, constitute signs of the
"melancholy science" (p. 15, and see the end of the present study).
He declares that these signs show the "sickness proper at the time
[to] consist precisely in normality" (p. 58), and he views the dialecti-
cian as similar to the court jester: "Sense can only endure in despair
and extremity" (p. 200). What remains is the recourse to theology:
"The only philosophy which can be responsibly practised in face of
despair is the attempt to contemplate all things as they should present themselves from the standpoint of redemption" (p. 247).

The question Adorno later posed—"What purpose is there left for
philosophy?"—draws its answers from the same realm. The state of
philosophy in "society, which the former is intended to penetrate
and not to deny, accords with philosophy's own desperate situation:
the necessity of formulating that which has itself already been
embraced by the machinery of society under the heading of the
absurd."[38] Philosophy remains "as if it were a powerless attempt by

194 THE PHILOSOPHY OF ARNOLD GEHLEN

thought to retain power over itself and to convict some fobbed-off mythology and blinkered resigned conformism of being untrue according to philosophy's own standards" (pp. 17–18). Overall, Adorno speaks of a "desolate chain of philosophies" (p. 18) that will most probably not be broken in the "state of a world drifting toward catastrophe" (p. 23) in which it appears to be "too late . . . for contemplation" (p. 24).

Cultural critique that makes a case for subtlety and turns against itself as if against its object fits this situation: "To accept culture as a whole is to deprive it of the ferment which is its very truth: negation" (*Prisms,* p. 28). In a world that has become an "open-air prison" (p. 34) in which everything is one and the same, all that remains is thought.

Here again we encounter an elitist claim, though it is phrased more dialectically than was the case in Gehlen's work: "The moment an elite knows and declares itself to be such, it transforms itself into the opposite of what it claims to be, and draws its irrational rule from conditions that perhaps grant it some rational insights. In God's name [!], one may be an elite; but one should never feel oneself to be such."[39] Here, the Prussian maxim of "being more than one seems to be" is transplanted into philosophy, as if the elite's claim to *being* were not itself grounds for critique. One cannot help noticing the similarity between this position and a stance that unmasks itself by taking care not to indulge in uninhibited demonstrations of its privileged state—and thus all the more surely enjoys it. Times are too subtle and relations of rulership have become too fragile to make any "demonstrative leisure" (Veblen) worthwhile.

The above conceptions culminate in *Negative Dialectics* (1966). Adorno now understands ontology ironically as the "epitome of negativity" (p. 121). "If one were drafting an ontology in accordance with the basic state of facts, of the facts whose repetition makes their state invariable, such an ontology would be pure horror" (p. 122). The negative dialectics that plans to emancipate itself from the Hegelian variant is linked to a "logic of disintegration" (p. 144). Adorno states in a note appended to the German edition that the idea of this logic is one of the oldest of his philosophical conceptions, stemming from his student days.

Taking up the anthropological strand in the separation of mind and body, Adorno says that "an unhappy consciousness is not a delusion of the mind's vanity but something inherent in the mind, the one authentic dignity it has received in its separation from the body" (p. 203). A dialectics that lodges a complaint against the enforced melancholy of thought as a moment of happiness becomes apparent in a passage that is closely related to the themes treated here:

> The current objection, extrapolated from the "Feuerbach Theses"— that a happy spirit is impermissible amid the growing misery of the exploding populations of poor countries, after the catastrophes that have occurred, and in view of those that are impending—has more against it than the fact that it mostly makes a virtue of impotence. True, we cannot really enjoy the spirit any more, because a happiness bound to see through its own insignificance, through the borrowed time it has been granted, would be no happinesss. Subjectively, too, it is undermined even where it keeps stirring. There is much to indicate that a knowledge that is crippled, temporarily at least, in its possible relation to practical change is not a blessing in itself either. Practice is deferred and cannot wait; this is what ails even theory. But when a man can do nothing that does not threaten to turn out for the worst even if meant for the best, he is bound to start thinking—and this justifies him, as well as the happy spirit. (pp. 244–245)

Certainly, differences between Adorno and Gehlen exist, perhaps of an insurmountable nature. Nevertheless, the closeness of Adorno's ideas to the conceptions of the early Gehlen is clear here: it is to be found not just in the notion of happiness withdrawn from the negative, but also in the individual aspects of the "renunciation of cognition" in Gehlen. The reservations toward anthropology seem doubtful: "That man is 'open' is an empty thesis, advanced—rarely without an invidious side glance at the animal—by an anthropology that has 'arrived.' It is a thesis that would pass off its own indeterminacy, its *fallissement,* as its determinate and positive side . . . That we cannot tell what man is does not establish a peculiarly majestic anthropology; it vetoes any anthropology" (p. 124). What this position fails to recognize is that the thesis of openness is by no means "invidious" toward the animal, but was conceived of by man as he gazed full of jealousy at the animal's instinctually secured legitimacy.

Adorno never provided the "major" argument against anthropology, and the above remark would therefore seem to be peripheral to his work; others, such as Habermas, have gone farther.[40] Following *Negative Dialectics,* we can confidently assume that any discussion that might have reached farther would have been blocked by the presence of the elementary affinities we have outlined here.

A thought that is central in Gehlen's work, such as that of giving oneself over to institutions, may admittedly, be far from Adorno's mind. "The trouble is with the conditions that condemn mankind to impotence and apathy and yet would be changeable by human action; the trouble is not primarily with people and with the way conditions appear to people" (p. 190). His standpoint admittedly distances itself from that of Gehlen's ontology, which is intended to support an anthropology; in Adorno's work, there is no counterpart to Gehlen's verdict on reflection as inhibitive of action; yet the two agree on the value of the negative (Adorno sees it formally, as the movement of thought) in the conception of the world's unchangeable condition, which makes philosophy necessary as critique and makes it possible in the first place. Both raise elitist claims and courageously suppress their longing for something better: melancholy appears as the atmosphere in which critique leaves things as they are. The comfortable "Hotel Abyss," which Georg Lukács referred to so viciously, offers rooms to both thinkers.[41]

Adorno's claim can be interpreted in terms of the metaphors he uses, and in the manner in which he attempted to discuss Kant's work: "Yet he who claims that literal, sensual happiness is better than the impermissible happiness of the spirit misunderstands that once historic sublimation comes to an end, detached sensual happiness will have a similarly regressive touch, like the relationship of children to food, which disgusts the adult. Not to be like children in this sense is a bit of freedom" (p. 245). Here, dialectics becomes as impotent vis-à-vis real conditions as it is subtle. No longer are satiation and hunger thrown into question; rather, attention is paid to the table manners of those who do not need to worry about food.

It is not just Gehlen's melancholy that is characteristic of someone barred from living the life of an aristocrat, infused with the nobility of the spirit. The elitist claim and the pathos of the special are combined with retrospection and with the dignity that draws its glory from dedication and sacrifice. By way of contrast, and after what we have already said about melancholy, it now remains to show that the stances behind these supposedly invariable positions are actually only historical in nature. Rather than viewing melancholy as an anthropological quality, we should ask whether it is not in fact the condition for *an* action-oriented anthropology and *a* philosophy of history that cannot harmonize except by assuming the existence of "underlying" gloom and the opportunity that arises from this of stylizing such gloom as a stance one supposedly wants for oneself. Gehlen's philosophy, with the fundamental claims it makes, appears to contain what has been described as an ingredient of melancholy. This speaks in favor of both the particular atmosphere of Gehlen's anthropology

and of a potentially wider applicability for the concept of melancholy—a concept then detached from the cherished trove of
bourgeois intellectual metaphors.

In the introduction to his *Studies on Anthropology and Sociology,*
Gehlen writes that "here the reader will not come across any appeals
(so obtrusive nowadays), notions of oscillation, didacticisms, or
utopias [!]. The author does not wish to belong to the group of wise
men Luther admonished (in his "Scholion to the Lectures on the
Epistle of Saint Paul") for skimming a comfortable science off the
top of sorrowful things." Gehlen cannot lay sole claim to this confession; for it expresses a relationship to reality that has, with the loss of
naïve Enlightenment optimism, forfeited the Enlightenment impulse
to improve the world. The absence of such an attempt, or people's
loss of faith in its possibility, has consequences that go beyond the
confines of science into the world of politics. The heroism of standing
still, of arrested motion, knows that it has "sorrowful things" on its
side. And thus the melancholy science flourishes in a climate of
melancholy.

Notes

2. Order and Melancholy

1. Robert King Merton, *Social Theory and Social Structure*, 9th ed. (Glencoe, Ill., 1964), pp. 131–194.
2. If we speak here of Merton's "system," we do not mean to designate anything more than the general referential framework in which the concept of melancholy is placed. That a concept of system has an influence on the frame of reference, which is supposed to correspond to that middle-range theory, is something that will be demonstrated later.
3. Ralf Dahrendorf's "unsociety" likewise reflects the absence of all action. The term "resignative behavior" would also have been suitable, were it not for the fact that it is used in a different context in the present study. To translate "retreatism" by the German *Weltflucht* ("flight-from-the-world"), as Hartmann does, may appear brilliantly convincing, particularly if one tackles the problematics of a loss of world. But here we are not dealing with a loss of world (compare Freud on melancholy), and the term "flight" is itself still too "active" in nature. It would be suitable if one understood it as a sort of *compulsion to flee*, enforced from outside. See H. Hartmann, "Stand und Entwicklung der amerikanischen Soziologie," in *Moderne amerikanische Soziologie: Neuere Beiträge zur soziologischen Theorie* (Stuttgart, 1967), p. 35.
4. Ralf Dahrendorf, *Society and Democracy in Germany* (London, 1968). The concept refers here specifically to German society after the abdication of Kaiser William II.
5. Merton, *Social Theory*, pp. 176ff.
6. Zena Smith Blau, "Old Age: A Study of Change in Status" (diss., Columbia University, 1956). The form of "retreatism" Merton traces corresponds to an involution melancholy, which would appear to be more open to sociological analysis for the simple reason that the exogenous, triggering factor occurs far more frequently than it does in all other variants of depressive behavior. See Hans Hoff, "Das veränderte Erscheinungsbild der Melancholie," *Wiener Klinische Wochenschrift*,

68 (1956), pp. 730ff. However, Hoff also gives a reason for the difficulties facing sociology when tackling this area. He writes that melancholy today appears in syndromes "which, compared with the classical forms, are less clear and seem to be better adapted to life." Acultural and asocial behavioral mechanisms thus do not lend themselves to analysis by forming self-evident extracultural and extrasocietal truths!

7. Sociologically oriented endeavors that take this tack are far from new; a good example—also for the naïve statistical "approach," which at the time was the only one possible—is Ludwig Stern, *Kulturkreis und Form der geistigen Erkrankung* (Halle a.d. Saale, 1913). Stern believes that he can prove the strata-specific distribution of melancholy (more frequent among the lower than among the upper strata; stronger among rural communities than among city dwellers) and creates a "psychopathological cultural index" which is arrived at by multiplying the quotients of functional and organic psychoses by one hundred. The minimal influence of such efforts is obvious, especially if the standard is intended to reflect the "strength of the pathological effect of culture on the psyche" and "the heights of culture" (ibid., p. 59). As late as 1961, a statement such as the following could still be written: "We may well begin with the fact that the depressive syndrome, as we see it every day in practice, in spite of its variety, shows no definite characteristics attributable to linguistic groups, ethnic groups, nations, races, religious, political, or ideological affiliations, or social status." H. J. Bochnik, "The Methodological Problem Involved in the Delimitation of Depressive Syndromes in European Psychiatry," in *Depression: Proceedings of the Scandinavian Symposium on Depression* (Copenhagen, 1961), p. 210.

Few new insights are to be gained from the exceptionally broadranging attempts at a sociological classification, such as that made by F. Müller-Lyer in his *Soziologie der Leiden* (Munich, 1920).

8. Merton, *Social Theory*, p. 189.
9. Pierre Janet, "The Fear of Action," *Journal of Abnormal Psychology and Social Psychology*, 16 (1921–22), pp. 150ff; and idem, "Fear of Action as an Essential Element in the Sentiment of Melancholia," in *Feelings and Emotions*, ed. Martin L. Reymert (Worcester, Mass., 1928), pp. 297ff.
10. Dieter Claessens, "Rationalität revidiert," *Kölner Zeitschrift für Soziologie und Sozialpsychologie*, 17 (1965), p. 474.
11. Merton, *Social Theory*, p. 183.
12. Compare Erwin Panofsky and Fritz Saxl, *Dürers "Melencolia I": Eine quellen- und typengeschichtliche Untersuchung* (Leipzig and Berlin,

1923), pp. 30ff. See also Panofsky, *Albrecht Dürer* (London, 1948), pp. 284ff.

13. See Eric Voegelin, "Was ist politische Realität?" *Politische Vierteljahresschrift*, 7 (1966), pp. 2ff.

14. *Oxford English Dictionary*, vol. 1 (Oxford, 1933), s.v. "Anomy."

15. Merton, *Social Theory*, p. 162.

16. Albert K. Cohen, "The Sociology of the Deviant Act: Anomie Theory and Beyond," *American Sociological Review*, 30 (1965), p. 6.

17. R. M. MacIver, *The Ramparts We Guard*, 3rd ed. (New York, 1952), pp. 77, 85, 87.

18. Gordon Rose, "Anomie and Deviation: A Conceptual Framework for Empirical Studies," *British Journal of Sociology*, 17 (1966), p. 31.

19. Byron, *Journals and Letters*, vol. 1 (London, 1830). In his *Bibliographia Burtoniana* (Stanford, Calif., 1931), Paul Jordan-Smith takes Mortimer Clapp's pathos-laden sentence as the dedication: "The *Anatomy of Melancholy* is the Notre-Dame of literature" (*Scribner's Magazine*, 87, p. 221).

20. Friedrich Engels, letter to William Lamplugh of London, 10 January 1894, in Karl Marx and Friedrich Engels, *Über Kunst und Literatur* (East Berlin, 1967), vol. 1, pp. 404–405.

21. Harold Nicolson, *Journey to Java* (London, 1957), p. 13.

22. Walter Jens, *Herr Meister: Dialog über einen Roman* (Munich, 1963), p. 114. The list of people influenced or impressed by Burton could be extended at random; in addition to those already mentioned, certainly Coleridge, Southey, Keats, and Thackeray belong on it. See Edward Bensly, "Robert Burton, John Barclay and John Owen," in *The Cambridge History of English Literature*, ed. Ward-Waller, vol. 4 (Cambridge, 1950), pp. 242ff.

23. Raymond Klibansky, Erwin Panofsky, and Fritz Saxl, *Saturn and Melancholy: Studies in the History of Natural Philosophy, Religion and Art* (London, 1964), p. 134, n. 19.

24. Pierre Mesnard, "Robert Burton: Théoricien et clinicien de l'humeur mélancolique," *La Vie médicale*, special no. entitled *Humeur et angoisse* (Christmas 1962), pp. 69–74. For personal details, see in particular Jean Robert Simon, "Robert Burton (1577–1640) et l'*Anatomie de la Mélancolie*," *Etudes Anglaises*, 19 (1964), p. 11: "Esquisse d'une biographie." For a bibliography see Jordon-Smith, *Bibliographia Burtoniana*.

25. Frank Percy Wilson, *Seventeenth-Century Prose: Five Lectures* (Los Angeles, 1960), p. 30.

26. Compare J. Max Patrick, "Robert Burton's Utopianism," *Philological Quarterly*, 27 (1948), pp. 345ff.

27. Simon, "Robert Burton," p. 416, n. 111.
28. Mesnard, "Robert Burton," p. 77.
29. Patrick, "Robert Burton's Utopianism," p. 346.
30. Patrick sets out to "determine its literary and sociological importance," ibid., p. 346.
31. W. R. Mueller, *The Anatomy of Robert Burton's England* (Los Angeles, 1952), p. 35, quoted in Simon, "Robert Burton," p. 412, n. 97.
32. Cf. Jordan-Smith, *Bibliographia Burtoniana,* p. 23. Melanchthon also took up Democritus in his description of melancholy: see Klibansky et al., *Saturn and Melancholy,* pp. 98f.
33. The pseudonym refers to an anecdote told by Hippocrates. Democritus ridiculed the life of his fellow citizens in Abdera, and "was so far carried with this ironical passion" that they thought him mad and sent him to Hippocrates to be cured. The latter found him "in his garden in the suburbs all alone, *sitting upon a stone under a plane tree, without hose or shoes, with a book on his knees, cutting up several beasts, and busy at his study.*" When Hippocrates asks him what he is doing, Democritus answers that he is cutting up animals in order to find the causes of madness and melancholy. See Robert Burton, *The Anatomy of Melancholy,* ed. A. R. Shilleto, 3 vols. (London, 1903), vol. 1, p. 48. This edition, from which all citations will be taken, is based on the sixth edition of 1651–52.
34. Ibid., p. 17.
35. Ibid., pp. 87 and 90.
36. Erwin Panofsky and Fritz Saxl, *Dürers "Melencolia I,"* p. 14.
37. Hellmut Flashar, *Melancholie und Melancholiker in den medizinischen Theorien der Antike* (Berlin, 1966), p. 21 and passim.
38. Ibid., p. 43.
39. See Flashar's edition and translation of *Aristotle: Problemata Physica* (Darmstadt, 1962), p. 309, n. 2. At a later date Flashar attempted to prove that the passage from *Problemata,* 30, 1, must be linked to Aristotle's successor Theophrastus (Bombast of Hohenheim), whose treatise on melancholy has been lost. See ibid., pp. 322 and 335, and also Flashar, *Melancholie,* p. 61. This formulation—pseudo-Aristotelian in nature, according to Flashar—was influential above all because it was spread by Cicero and Seneca.
40. Hubert Tellenbach, *Melancholie: Zur Problemgeschichte, Typologie, Pathogenese und Klinik* (Berlin, Göttingen, and Heidelberg, 1961).
41. Panofsky et al., *Dürers "Melencolia I,"* pp. 29f. They term one strand "negative-gnostic" (already taking into account its later development) and the other strand "positive-neoplatonic." See also Klibansky et al., *Saturn and Melancholy,* pp. 42, 217ff.
42. Mesnard, "Robert Burton," p. 78.

43. "And who is not a fool? Who is free from melancholy? Who is not touched more or less in habit and disposition?" Robert Burton, *The Anatomy*, p. 39. This form of argument is typical for Burton. Thus, he writes of prisoners: "They lie nastily among toads and frogs in a dark dungeon . . . They live solitary, alone, sequestered from all company but heart-eating melancholy" (ibid., p. 398), although the sting is later taken out of this image, which accordingly becomes affirmative: "What I have said of servitude, I say again of imprisonment. We are all prisoners. What's our life but a prison?" (ibid., vol. 2, p. 200).

44. Ibid., p. 87.

45. Ibid., p. 91. Burton does not refer directly to the Aristotelian linking of genius and melancholy; but his reference to the tutor at the Macedonian court (Aristotle became Philip's tutor under Amyntas of Macedonia) seems to show that he at least thought such a link existed.

46. "Hardly another thinking man of his time can have been so little concerned or affected by its political or religious controversies." J. W. Allen, *English Political Thought*, vol. 1 (London, 1931), p. 88, quoted in Simon, "Robert Burton," p. 104, n. 1.

47. Simon, "Robert Burton," p. 110.

48. Patrick, "Robert Burton's Utopianism," p. 357.

49. Mueller, *The Anatomy*, p. 45; quoted in Simon, "Robert Burton," p. 413, n. 100. On the closeness of Burton's utopia to the reality of his day, compare also Douglas Bush, *English Literature in the Earlier Seventeenth-Century, 1600–1660*, in *The Oxford History of English Literature*, 2nd ed. (Oxford, 1962), vol. 5, p. 297.

50. Burton, *The Anatomy*, p. 109. As mentioned, our intention here is not to provide some sort of reductive biographical "psychology of knowledge"; yet Simon's remark is nevertheless worth quoting, namely that Burton "was the youngest son of a family which considered itself to be of patrician ranking, even if it had no title." Simon, "Robert Burton," p. 389.

51. Simon, ibid., p. 389.

52. Burton, *The Anatomy*, p. 114.

53. Ibid., p. 92.

54. W. Osler has stated: "An eager interest in human character and activity consorted with something that is hard to distinguish from pedantry . . . a great medical treatise, orderly in arrangement, serious in purpose." Quoted in Bensly, "Robert Burton," pp. 242 and 245.

55. "Physical, mental and social causes of melancholy are carefully classified." Jordan-Smith, *Bibliographia Burtoniana*, p. 6.

56. Patrick, "Robert Burton's Utopianism," p. 356.

57. Simon, "Robert Burton," p. 410.

58. Wilson, *Seventeenth-Century Prose*, p. 37.
59. Simon, "Robert Burton," p. 400.
60. Paul Foriers, "Les Utopies et le droit," in *Les Utopies à la Renaissance* (Brussels and Paris, 1963), p. 233. "They have few laws; for to people so instruct and institute [sic] very few do suffice . . . Furthermore, they utterly exclude and banish all attorneys." Thomas More, *Utopia* (London and Melbourne, 1988).
61. Emeric Crucé, *Le Nouveau Cynée, ou discours d'état représentant les occasions et moyens d'establir une paix générale, et la liberté du commerce par tout le monde* (1623), pp. 166 and 167. Quoted in Foriers, "Les Utopies," p. 240.
62. Alcmaon of Croton. See Klibansky et al., *Saturn and Melancholy*, pp. 5ff.
63. It is worth mentioning that the names of the temperaments "were initially laid down in the first half of the twelfth century, in a text entitled *De Philosophia Mundi*, which is entered in the *Patrologia Latina* (172, pp. 39ff, *Migne*) under the works of *Honorius of Autun*, yet whose author is given in the manuscripts under two further names, including Wilhelm von Conches, from whom the text actually stems." Flashar, *Melancholie*, p. 115. See also Klibansky et al., *Saturn and Melancholy*, p. 15.
64. Klibansky et al., *Saturn and Melancholy*, p. 15. Both elements are united in Christian cosmology; the names of the four temperaments appear as "deficient forms *(quia corrumpitur natura)*," as Flashar terms them in his *Melancholie*.
65. As with all statements on Burton's work, this holds true explicitly for the utopian preface: the *Anatomy* contains both levels, the "physiological" and the "cosmological."

    Bombast launched a polemic against the micrological restriction of the medieval, medicinal concept of "melanckoly": "from what element does the illness come? from fire, not cholera; from the earthly realm, not from melanckoly; . . . and this is the reason why, not the saying that that is melanckoly, for neither Heaven nor Earth know melanckoly . . . it is from the generatis, procreatis, fillius and filiabus of the elements that the physikal body is to be seen in terms of its illnesses, discerned and adjudged." Paracelsus, *Labyrinthus Medicorum Errantium* [On the Mistaken Path of Doctors] (1537–38), in his *Sämtliche Werke*, ed. Karl Sudhoff (Munich and Berlin, 1928), vol. 11, p. 180. On the other hand, Bombast mediates the micro- and macrological conceptions. See ibid., p. 195.
66. Wilson, *Seventeenth-Century Prose*, p. 29.
67. Lawrence Babb, *The Elizabethan Malady: A Study of Melancholia in*

English Literature from 1580 to 1642 (East Lansing, Michigan, 1951), p. vii.

68. Don Cameron Allen, "The Degeneration of Man and Renaissance Pessimism," *Studies in Philology*, 35 (1938), pp. 202ff.

69. *Nouvelle Biographie Générale*, vol. 1 (Paris, 1840).

70. Allen, "The Degeneration," p. 206.

71. Norbert Elias, *The Civilizing Process: The History of Manners*, tr. Edmund Jephcott (Oxford, 1978); and idem, *State Formation and Civilization* (Oxford, 1982), in particular in this context the latter volume. The word "unstable" reflects the state of a society in flux. Elias' proof of the corresponding socio- and psychogenesis, the relation of the human being's "structure of affects" to the respectively valid constitution of society, is of particular importance in connection with the topics dealt with in the present study. We have already seen that the cosmological and physiological approaches blend in Burton's concept of melancholy, and that "melancholy" therefore seems to be an appropriate term for describing the human psyche *and* society.

72. Arnold Williams, "A Note on Pessimism in the Renaissance," *Studies in Philology*, 36 (1939), pp. 243ff.

73. Bush, *English Literature*, p. 296.

74. Hermann Glockner, *Die europäische Philosophie von den Anfängen bis zur Gegenwart*, 2nd ed. (Stuttgart, 1960), pp. 396 and 457.

75. Helmuth Plessner, "Die Emanzipation der Macht," *Merkur*, 16 (1962), pp. 907 and 910.

76. Georges Duveau, *Sociologie de l'utopie et autres "essais"* (Paris, 1961), p. 189 ("Fragments"). Judith Shklar points to the fundamental link between melancholy and utopia: "Its esthetic and intellectual tension arises precisely from the melancholy contrast between what might be said and what will be." Judith Shklar, "The Political Theory of Utopia: From Melancholy to Nostalgia," *Daedalus: Journal of the American Academy of Arts and Sciences* (Spring 1965), p. 367. See also ibid., p. 372. Klibansky et al., *Saturn and Melancholy*, p. 134, shows how Kronos appears in classical Greek comedy—the counterpart to the Romans' Saturn, of whom we have already spoken—as the "lord of Utopia."

77. Emile Dermenghem, *Thomas Morus et les utopistes de la Renaissance* (Paris, 1927), p. 34.

78. The inhabitants of Burton's utopia should all be encouraged to marry rather than prevented from doing so, "except they be dismembered, or grievously deformed, infirm, or visited with some enormous hereditary disease in body or mind; in such cases, upon a great pain or mulct, man or woman shall not marry, other order shall be taken for them to their content." Burton, *The Anatomy*, p. 120.

79. See Wilhelm E. Mühlmann, "Der revolutionäre Umbruch," in *Rassen, Ethnien, Kulturen* (Neuwied and Berlin, 1964), pp. 321ff; and idem, *Chiliasmus und Nativismus: Studien zur Psychologie, Soziologie und historischen Kasuistik der Umsturzbewegungen,* 2nd ed. (Berlin, 1964). The distinction between utopias presented above would suggest itself here. If one thinks of Scheler's "typology of class-determined forms of thinking," in which an optimistic view of the future and pessimistic retrospection are attributed to the lower class and a pessimistic view of the future and optimistic retrospection are ascribed to the upper class, then one could conclude, without accepting Scheler's global dichotomy, that "utopias of the upper class" can only be reactionary. See Max Scheler, *Problems of a Sociology of Knowledge,* tr. M. S. Frings (London, 1979).

80. Elias, *The History of Manners,* p. 197. Elias is quoting H. Dupin, *La Courtoisie au Moyen Age* (Paris, 1931), p. 77. On the link between the label "mournful and pensive" and the tradition of melancholy, see Klibansky et al., *Saturn and Melancholy,* p. 222. In 1881, Maupassant gave the following advice to a young man who wished to enter the diplomatic service: "Be beautiful, young man; acquire the habits of the salons, know how to converse with and seduce women. This is the path taken by a man or woman of the world, to know how to say everything in an interesting manner, never to be boring and to avoid monologues." Quoted in Laure Rièse, *Le Salons littéraires Parisiens du Second Empire à nos jours* (Toulouse, 1962), p. 11.

81. Elias, *The History of Manners,* p. 201. The concluding phrase also alludes to the fact that the cleric was allowed the strata-specific permission to be melancholy, since his "profession" was not this-worldly. This phenomenon, namely the link between melancholy and a circle of persons predestined for it, will be discussed further in a later section. We have already touched on it in our tangential remarks on genius in Aristotle's supposed *Problemata.*

82. Tommaso Campanella, *The City of the Sun,* tr. D. J. Donno (Los Angeles, 1981), p. 55. The mythological theme of the topsy-turvy world can be seen here in the reference to an inverted order. See Mühlmann, "Der revolutionäre Umbruch."

83. Campanella, *The City of the Sun,* p. 101. On this topic, see Karl Popper, "Utopia and Violence," in *Conjectures and Refutations,* 2nd ed. (London, 1965), pp. 355ff.

84. Campanella, *The City of the Sun,* pp. 41 and 89. [The older, 1885 translation edited by Henry Morley, p. 251, more accurately reflects the German rendering.—*Translator.*] The last sentence of the passage appears to introduce a streak of utopian randomness into the argument, as part of a hodgepodge which in the utopian system can be

combined all too easily with rigorous order. Indeed, this is one of those passages which keep cropping up in the history of melancholy—passages in which speculative thinkers correctly guessed the existence of something that scientists later discovered. Thus, Campanella here anticipates that disturbance of the oral senses which is so important for the melancholy complex Tellenbach remarked on: "The melancholic knows himself to be shut off from the world, with his faulty sense of smell" (Hubert Tellenbach, "Zur Klinik der Oralsinn-Störungen in endogenen Psychosen," *Jahrbuch für Psychologie, Psychotherapie und medizinische Anthropologie,* 18 [1965], p. 193). Campanella probably borrowed this link from mythology. Vettius Valens mentions "the melancholic with a faulty sense of smell" in his writings; and ancient Rome's God of Fertilizers was "Saturnus Sterentius," or "Sterenbus." See Klibansky et al., *Saturn and Melancholy,* pp. 146–147, n. 66. Christian Enzensberger thus draws on a long tradition when linking *acedia,* a deadly sin, with dirt. See Enzensberger, *Smut,* tr. Sandra Morris (London, 1972).

85. Campanella, *The City of the Sun,* pp. 130 and 135.

86. Quoted from Paul Lafargue, "Thomas Campanella," in *Vorläufer des neueren Sozialismus,* vol. 3, *Die beiden ersten grossen Utopisten* (Stuttgart and Berlin, 1921), p. 117. The assignation of the color black and a melancholy "complexion" as traits seems particularly widespread; see Klibansky et al., *Saturn and Melancholy,* p. 118.

87. H. J. Krysmanski, *Die utopische Methode* (Cologne and Opladen, 1963), p. 3.

88. Heinz Höhne, "Der Orden unter dem Totenkopf: Die Geschichte der SS," part 14 of a series, *Der Spiegel,* 21 (1967), p. 55. The argument was between Himmler and Otto Ohlendorf, whose "Meldungen aus dem Reich" were intended to convey the real mood in Nazi Germany to a select few; they were forbidden in 1944.

89. Halle, undated. Hereafter page numbers are given in parentheses in the body of the text.

90. Christa Baumgarth, *Geschichte des Futurismus* (Reinbek bei Hamburg, 1966), pp. 23 and 9.

91. Ibid., pp. 26–27. The Futurists seized the opportunity offered by the First World War to put this program into practice: "When Italy entered the war on 24 May 1915, some of the Futurists volunteered for a bicycle batallion and went through their baptism of fire in October of the same year" (ibid., p. 108).

92. In an interview with the Paris journal *Comoedia.* See Baumgarth, *Geschichte,* p. 35.

93. Ibid., documentary appendix, p. 156.

94. Ibid., p. 155. On 20 February 1909, the critic Enrico Thovez termed

Futurism a "deeply melancholy play" (*La Stampa*, Turin, 20 February 1909; quoted in Baumgarth, *Geschichte*, p. 34). On the Futurists' animosity toward melancholy, which not only involved a rejection of the melancholy temperament but also found direct expression in the poetry, see Paer Bergman, *"Modernolatria" et "Simultaneita": Recherches sur deux tendances dans l'avant-garde littéraire en Italie et en France à la veille de la première guerre mondiale* (Stockholm, 1962), especially pp. 103–105.

95. Maurice Nadeau, *The History of Surrealism*, tr. R. Howard (London, 1964), p. 70. The yearning for a lost paradise is anti-Futurist and corresponds to the melancholy turning toward the past, which essentially inhibits utopia. Surrealism and Futurism unite in combating boredom; Breton speaks in the *Manifesto* of how difficult it is to "ne plus s'ennuyer en compagnie." *Manifeste du Surréalisme*, 3rd ed. (Paris, 1924), p. 49.

96. Nadeau, *The History of Surrealism*, p. 101. See also Breton: "Assurément, il en va de la production artistique et littéraire comme de tout phénomène intellectuel en ce sens qu'il ne saurait à son propos se poser d'autre problème que celui de la *souveraineté de la pensée*." *Second Manifeste du Surréalisme* (Paris, 1930), p. 45.

97. Nadeau, *The History of Surrealism*, p. 140.

98. The text in question is the *Grand Jeu*, edited by Gilbert-Lecomte, Daumal, Vaillant, and Sima. Quoted in Nadeau, *The History of Surrealism*, pp. 123–124.

99. "Naturally, the history of utopia is inextricably bound up with the history of utopian thought. Utopian thought crystallizes into utopia, and therein takes on the form of a literary genre. The precondition for the emergence of utopia is thus that utopian thought come to understand itself as utopian." Werner Krauss, "Geist und Widergeist der Utopien," in *Perspektiven und Probleme: Zur französischen und deutschen Aufklärung und andere Aufsätze* (Darmstadt and Neuwied, 1965), p. 331. As this position centers on "reflexivity" in utopian thought, we shall return to it in our discussion of action inhibition and reflection.

100. Georg Simmel, "From His Post-humously Published Diaries," *Logos*, 8 (1919–20), p. 123.

3. Surplus Order, Boredom, and the Emergence of Resignative Behavior

1. A. Vinet, *Moralistes des seizième et dix-septième siècles* (Paris, 1895), p. 7.

2. Immanuel Kant, *Anthropology from a Pragmatic Point of View*, tr. V. L. Dowdell (Carbondale, Ill., 1978).

3. Walter Muschg, *Tragische Literaturgeschichte*, 2nd ed. (Berne, 1953), p. 446.

4. Krysmanski, *Die utopische Methode,* p. 8.

5. Arnold Gehlen, "Genese der Modernität—Soziologie," in *Aspekte der Modernität,* ed. Hans Steffen (Göttingen, 1965), pp. 31ff., 45.

6. Voegelin, "Was ist politische Realität?" pp. 26 and 37. Compare how carefully Gehlen extricates his favorite authors, Proust, Musil, Flaubert, and Dostoyevski, from the domain of sociology by assigning them to the field of psychology, though not in a scientific sense. Arnold Gehlen, *Urmensch und Spätkultur: Philosophische Ergebnisse und Aussagen,* 2nd ed. (Frankfurt am Main and Bonn, 1964), p. 19.

7. Leo Lowenthal, *Literature, Popular Culture and Society* (Englewood Cliffs, N.J., 1961), p. xvi.

8. Theodor W. Adorno, *Minima Moralia: Reflections from a Damaged Life,* tr. E. Jephcott (London, 1979), p. 175.

9. See Karl Giehlow, "Dürers Stich 'Melencolia I' und der maximilianische Humanistenkreis," *Mitteilungen der Gesellschaft für vervielfältigende Kunst* (Vienna, 1903), pp. 29–41; Panofsky et al., "Dürers 'Melencolia I'"; Klibansky et al., *Saturn and Melancholy;* and G. R. Meyer, "Dürers Melancolia und ihre Symbolik," *Eranos-Jahrbuch* (Zurich, 1934; 2nd ed., 1935), pp. 231ff.

10. Johan Huizinga, *The Waning of the Middle Ages,* tr. F. Hopman (Harmondsworth, 1976), p. 31. The theme of the world's aging continued to be the source of pessimistic worldviews until the Renaissance. In this view, melancholy and an aversion to history were linked, and writers adumbrated that form of *post-histoire* which would later concern Cournot, de Man, Gehlen, and others. See Don Cameron Allen, "The Degeneration," p. 213.

11. Du Laurens (1599, p. 98). Quoted in Babb, *The Elizabethan Malady,* p. 46.

12. Wiliam W. Ireland, *The Blot on the Brain: Studies in History and Psychology* (Edinburgh, 1885), p. 158. On these questions, compare Hans von Hentig, "Über den Cäsarenwahnsinn: Die Krankheit des Kaisers Tiberius," *Grenzfragen des Nerven- und Seelenlebens,* vol. 119 (Munich, 1924).

13. Mühlmann has spoken of "minimal social differences" which "dislodge the revolutionary thorn." See "Der revolutionäre Umbruch," p. 366.

14. Elias, *State Formation,* vol. 2, p. 176.

15. Ibid., p. 193. On the overall issues involved, see Lucien Goldmann, *The Hidden God: A Study of Tragic Vision in the "Pensées" of Pascal and the Tragedies of Racine,* tr. P. Thody (London, 1964).

16. Elias, *State Formation,* p. 196.

17. Jean Hippolyte Mariéjol, *Henri IV et Louis XIII* (Paris, 1905), p. 390. Quoted in Elias, *State Formation,* p. 195.

18. Emile Magne, *La Vie quotidienne au temps de Louis XIII d'après des documents inédits* (Paris, 1942), p. 55. On the issues (such as the "pensioning off" of the aristocracy), see also Ernst Wilhelm Eschmann, *Die Führungsschichten Frankreichs*, vol. 1, *Von den Capetingern bis zum Ende des Grand Siècle* (Berlin, 1943).

19. La Rochefoucauld, *Mémoires*, in *Oeuvres complètes*, rev. ed. (Paris, 1957), p. 47.

20. Magne, *La Vie quotidienne*, p. 79.

21. La Rochefoucauld, *Mémoires*, p. 53.

22. The only similarity to Freyer's "secondary system" is the terminology. What is involved is not a lack of preconditions, but the fact that the secondary system of order is derived from the first.

23. Vinet, *Moralistes*, p. 191.

24. W. G. Moore, "The World of La Rochefoucauld's 'Maximes,'" *French Studies*, 7 (1953), p. 338.

25. "Portrait de La Rochefoucauld fait par lui-même," in *Oeuvres complètes* (Paris, 1957), p. 12. Grandsaignes-d'Hauterive therefore opts for an interpretation which runs counter to La Rochefoucauld's own when he puts excessive emphasis on "endogenous" factors: "En résumé, La Rochefoucauld, par son naturel mélancolique, montre des dispositions innées pour le pessimisme." *Le Pessimisme de La Rochefoucauld* (Paris, 1914), p. 48.

26. J. Bourdeau, *La Rochefoucauld* (Paris, 1895), p. 18.

27. Ibid., p. 22.

28. Maxims 304 and 352 of the 1678 edition. Quoted in *Oeuvres complètes*, pp. 448 and 454.

29. Maxim 532 of the "Maximes Posthumes," *Oeuvres complètes*, p. 483. It should not be forgotten that in those days a concept such as boredom covered a much "greater" depth of psychological affects: in the sixteenth century, *ennui* signified above all "affliction, douleur, tristesse," and the examples offered by Huguet could equally well use "melancholy" instead of "boredom": "Pensant venger l'ennuy qui entra en mon ame le jour propre que feu mon seigneur et mary deceda ..." (*Amadis*, vol. 5, p. 5). Edmond Huguet, in *Dictionnaire de la langue française du seizième siècle*, vol. 3 (Paris, 1946), p. 464, s.v. *ennuy*.

Le Savoureux also pointed to the reduction in the concept's applicability: "On sait que la signification du mot *ennui* a peu à peu perdu de sa force. Tandis que, même au singulier, il exprimait encore au XVIIe siècle le chagrin et la douleur morale vive, de nos jours, lorsqu'on parle d'ennui, on entend soit un tracas, une peine légère, soit un sentiment de manque d'intérêt aux choses, tel qu'on éprouve quand on est oisif par example." H. Le Savoureux, "L'Ennui normal et l'ennui morbide," *Journal de psychologie normale et patho-logique,* 11 (1914), p. 131. See also Ulrich Weber, "Ennui: Die Bedeu-tung des Wortes in der französischen Romantik" (diss., Freiburg Uni-versity, 1949), especially the section entitled "On the Relation between *Ennui* and *Mélancolie,*" p. 98. With respect to the close link between the concepts of boredom and melancholy in English after 1340, see the *Oxford English Dictionary,* vol. 6 (Oxford, 1933), p. 312. Herbert Plügge speaks of the "uncanny relatedness of ennui, melan-choly, and despair," in his essay "Pascals Begriff des Ennui und seine Bedeutung für eine medizinische Anthropologie," *Wohlbefinden und Missbefinden: Beiträge zu einer medizinischen Anthropologie* (Tübingen, 1962), p. 7.

30. Madame de Sévigné, "Letter to Mme de Grignan, her daughter, of October 25, 1679," in Sévigné, *Lettres,* vol. 2 (Paris, 1955), p. 484.

31. As a consequence, in the eighteenth century we see the establishment of the first salon that "has emancipated itself from Versailles"—at the home of the Duchess of Maine in Sceaux. The behavioral maxims still apply, however: "No one was allowed to be bored, inactive, dull." A. von Gleichen-Russwurm, *Das galante Europa: Geselligkeit der grossen Welt, 1600–1789* (Stuttgart, 1910), pp. 250ff.

32. Letter of La Rochefoucauld to Jacques Esprit, undated, in *Oeuvres complètes,* p. 603; letter of La Rochefoucauld to the Marquise de Sablé, ibid., p. 612.

33. Gerhard Hess, *Zur Entstehung der "Maximen" La Rochefoucaulds,* (Cologne and Opladen, 1957), p. 11. On a certain prejudice with respect to theories that attempt to explain the emergence of maxims from social conditions, see Margot Kruse, *Die Maxime in der französis-chen Literatur: Studien zum Werk La Rochefoucaulds und seiner Nachfolger* (Hamburg, 1960). Even Kruse eventually concludes that one of the sources of the pessimism exhibited by the maxims is "to be found in the melancholic trait in La Rochefoucauld's nature . . . , which was strengthened by the disappointments he suffered in his life and made him sensitive to trends that were both misanthropic and inimical to the world, tendencies that crop up ever more strongly in the mid-seventeenth century in France, usually owing to religious impulses" (p. 33). However, if the development of the concepts of boredom and melancholy is taken as the point of departure, then in the case of La Rochefoucauld and the salons of his day some misanthropic or world-inimical impulse is of less interest than the compulsion to turn this impulse into a social quality and conceal it. When Barthélemy speaks of what the *précieuses* contributed to society, the same holds true for the salons, namely "le goût des réunions, de la conversation,

de la délicatesse, de la sociabilité, en un mot." Edouard de Barthélemy, *Les Amis de la Marquise de Sablé: Recueil de lettres des principaux habitués de son salon* (Paris, 1865), p. 42.

34. "Demi-disgrâce," according to Bourdeau, *La Rochefoucauld,* p. 84; see also Vinet, *Moralistes,* p. 193.

35. Bourdeau, *La Rochefoucauld,* p. 79.

36. Magne, *Le Vrai Visage de La Rochefoucauld,* p. 157.

37. Georg Misch, "Die Autobiographie der französischen Aristokratie des siebzehnten Jahrhunderts," in *Deutsche Vierteljahresschrift für Literaturwissenschaft und Geistesgeschichte,* 1 (1923), p. 192. Admittedly, Sainte-Beuve already believed he had found among the authors of the maxims that form of introversion which resists action: "L'Ajax de l'Iliade, portant, pendant l'absence d'Achille, le poids de l'armée troyenne, ou Ney dans le feu de la mêlée à Friedland, laissez-les faire! Et vous, Fontenelle, ou monsieur de la Rochefoucauld, en ce moment, n'approchez pas!" Charles-Augustin Sainte-Beuve, "Préface pour les Maximes de La Rochefoucauld" (Edition elzévirienne de P. Jannet, 1853), in *Causeries du lundi,* vol. 11 (Paris, 1948), p. 410.

38. Arnold Hauser, *The Social History of Art,* tr. Stanley Godman (London, 1951), p. 439. See also Carl J. Burckhardt, "Der Honnête Homme: Das Eliteproblem im siebzehnten Jahrhundert," in *Gestalten und Mächte: Reden und Aufsätze* (Munich, no date), pp. 71–96.

39. Translated by François Salignac de la Mothe-Fénelon, *Les Aventures de Télémaque, fils d'Ulysse* (Paris, 1807). The formulation "valeur discrète et prévoyante" (ibid., pp. 149–150) stems from the vocabulary of the civilizing process!

40. According to Misch, "Die Autobiographie," p. 175.

41. On this point see Saint-Simon, in the collection *J'ai lu l'essentiel,* ed. Geneviève Manceron and Michel Averlant (Paris, 1965), pp. 54ff. ("Tous les ans au mois de mai, la guerre"). See also Frantz Funck-Brentano, *La Cour du Roi Soleil* (Paris, 1937).

42. Misch, "Die Autobiographie," p. 197.

43. Hauser, *The Social History of Art,* p. 440.

44. Harold Nicolson, *The Age of Reason* (London, 1960), p. 3.

45. Quoted from Misch, "Die Autobiographie," p. 199. Here, the focus is almost exclusively on the boredom of the aristocracy. A more thorough study would presumably reveal the existence of a bourgeois boredom which also played a role in the Fronde and was motivated not least by financial considerations. Evidence of this is to be found in a passage in Aynard: "La milice bourgeoise était devenue une sorte de garde nationale qui prit peu à peu l'habitude de sortir *dans la rue* pour s'amuser, se 'désheurer' comme dit Retz, qui connaissait bien

ses moeurs." Joseph Aynard, *La Bourgeoisie française,* 2nd ed. (Paris, 1934), p. 248. Littré, who quotes this piece from Retz's memoirs, defines *se désheurer* as "être hors de ses heures habituelles"—which refers us back again to the issue of order and dis-order. Emile Littré, *Dictionnaire de la langue française,* vol. 2 (Paris, 1956), p. 1734.

46. Ivanoff has adopted an example of maximal affect modeling from Chapelain, whereby it is unclear whether the irony is intended by the author, since the Marquise de Sablé, who is being referred to, was not exactly happy in her marriage: "Mme la Marquise de Sablé doncques est vefve et une des plus honnestes vefves qu j'aye jamais connue; elle ne rit, ni ne pleure et sans grimacer son deuil n'y monstrer une constance scandaleuse dans un aussi important change-ment que celuy la, elle garde le vray tempérament necessaire pour ne donner aucune prise sur soy . . . on dit que cette condition luy sied si bien, que c'est dommage qu'elle ne lui est plus-tost arrivée." Chapelain, *Lettres,* vol. 1, p. 640. Quoted in N. Ivanoff, "La Marquise de Sablé et son salon" (diss., Paris, 1927), p. 21.

47. Emile Deschanel, *Pascal, La Rochefoucauld, Bossuet* (Paris, 1885), p. 13. Bourdeau writes: "Elle . . . voulait la guerre. L'ennui la ron-geait" (*La Rochefoucauld,* p. 58). A similar statement is to be found in Gleichen-Russwurm with regard to Marie de Medici: "Marie de Medici, the Queen Mother, . . . was bored in all her powerful glory and wanted once more to influence the business of State" (*Das galante Europa,* p. 67). We frequently see a linking of boredom and war, in which the latter figures as an antidote for the former: "Wars are probably first of all a means to fight boredom." See Alain (Emile Auguste Chartier), *Propos sur le bonheur* (Nimes, 1925), entry dated 29 January 1909.

48. Letter from La Rochefoucauld to Lenet, 23 October 1652, in *Oeuvres complètes,* p. 593. There is a reference to this letter in Misch, "Die Autobiographie," p. 211. Compare La Bruyère: "Un homme qui a vécu dans l'intrigue un certain temps ne peut plus s'en passer: toute autre vie pour lui est languissante." La Bruyère, *Les Caractères* (Paris, 1957), p. 244.

49. "Whatever Port Royal may have taught him about election, one is left with the strong impression that in his heart La Rochefoucauld was convinced that in Paradise his name would win him the *tabouret* he had been denied at the Louvre." A. J. Krailsheimer, *Studies in Self-Interest: From Descartes to La Bruyère* (Oxford, 1962), p. 97. See also Saint-Simon, *J'ai lu l'essentiel,* pp. 44f.

50. Saint-Simon, *J'ai lu l'essentiel,* p. 139.

51. Ibid., p. 142.

52. "Or, le Roi détestait les gens malades ou mélancoliques" (ibid., p. 142).
53. Mme de Sévigné to her daughter, Mme de Grignan, 30 May 1672. Quoted in Marcel Braunschvig, *Notre littérature étudée dans les textes*, vol. 1 (Paris, 1955), p. 457.
54. Bourdeau, *La Rochefoucauld*, p. 129.
55. Claude de Seyssel, *La Grande Monarchie*, vol. 1, p. 11. Quoted in J. W. Allen, *A History of Political Thought in the Sixteenth Century*, 2nd ed. (London, 1941), p. 277.
56. Leopold von Ranke, *Französische Geschichte vornehmlich im XVI. und XVII. Jahrhundert*, 2 vols., introduction by Otto Vossler (Stuttgart, 1954), p. 49. Elias adopted this description. See also Dieter Claessens, "Weltverlust als psychologisches und soziologisches Problem," *Archiv für Rechts- und Sozialphilosophie* (1963–64), pp. 513ff., reprinted in *Angst, Furcht und gesellschaftlicher Druck und andere Aufsätze* (Dortmund, 1966), pp. 61–69.
57. Claessens, "Weltverlust," p. 529 (p. 67 in reprint edition).
58. "Elle [Mme de Sablé] avait eu pour illustre servant M. de Montmorency, l'homme à la mode que les femmes s'attachaient, celui-là même auquel Richelieu fit couper la tête en 1632 . . . Elle se détacha de son Polydamas (c'était le nom romanesque de Montmorency) parce qu'elle souffrait de sa médiocrité d'esprit." Quoted in Bourdeau, *La Rochefoucauld*, p. 91. See also Ivanoff, *La Marquise de Sablé et son salon*, pp. 18ff.
59. Quoted in Nicolson, *The Age of Reason*.
60. "The Salon, always a purely French growth, came to its fullest efflorescence in Paris during the third quarter of the eighteenth century. There were at that time, as said Lady Hervey, 'societies to suit one in every humour, except a melancholy one.'" Janet Aldis, *Madame Geoffrin: Her Salon and Her Times, 1750–1777* (London, 1905), p. xi.
61. Nedd Willard, *Le Génie et la folie au dix-huitième siècle* (Paris, 1963), p. 21. On boredom and melancholy in Chateaubriand, see Friedrich Sieburg, *Chateaubriand*, tr. V. M. Macdonald (London, 1961).
62. This designation is that of Roger Charbonnel, who strictly opposes seeing any religious influences—for example, of a Jansenist nature—at work in La Rochefoucauld. Charbonnel, "Les Tendances philosophiques et religieuses de La Rochefoucauld," *Annales de Philosophie Chrétienne*, 144 (1903), pp. 493–505. For the opposite view, see Grandsaignes-d'Hauterive, who says: "Chez Mme de Sablé son pessimisme se précise; il se jansénise" (*Le Pessimisme*, p. 131).
63. "On pleure pour avoir la réputation d'être tendre; on pleure pour être pleuré, et on pleure enfin de honte de ne pas pleurer." La

Rochefoucauld, "Maxime 58 des Manuscrit Liancourt," in *Oeuvres complètes*, p. 354.

64. Ivanoff, *La Marquise de Sablé et son salon*, p. 160. (This was the reason for Georg Lukács' admiration for La Rochefoucauld—he opposes him on the one hand to Pascal and, on the other, to Schopenhauer and Nietzsche!) By contrast, compare Grandsaignes-d'Hauterive: "Le trait le plus intéressant de cette mélancolie de La Rochefoucauld, c'est qu'elle affecte un certain air romantique. A la manière d'un Werther, d'une René, ou d'un Obermann, sans doute avec plus de discrétion [!], de dignité et d'élégance, le gentilhomme du temps de Louis XIII paraît se complaire dans sa tristesse" (*Le Pessimisme*, pp. 35–36).

65. Krailsheimer, *Studies in Self-Interest*, p. 83.

66. "L'impuissance d'être gais nous fit prendre le parti d'être sensibles et philosophes." Grimm, *Correspondance littéraire* (1776); quoted in Helmut Hatzfeld, "Rokoko als literarischer Epochenstil in Frankreich," *Studies in Philology*, 35 (1938), p. 538. The statement by Mme de Motteville is similar, if in a different context: "Nul ne doit être si bon chrétien, ni si bon philosophe qu'un courtisan détrompé." Quoted in Grandsaignes-d'Hauterive, *Le Pessimisme*, p. 117.

67. Christian Garve comments on La Rochefoucauld's change from a life at court to a military life: "Concerning La Rochefoucauld's maxims: his bourgeois air is shed sometimes in the Army, but never at Court." Garve, *Versuche über verschiedene Gegenstände aus der Moral, der Literatur und dem gesellschaftlichen Leben* (Breslau, 1801), part 1, pp. 263–402. Garve emphasizes that the bourgeoisie's assimilation was facilitated by entering the army.

68. Hatzfeld, "Rokoko," p. 541.

4. On the Origins of Bourgeois Melancholy

1. Karl Marx and Friedrich Engels, *The German Ideology* (London, 1965).

2. Ibid.

3. Elias, *The History of Manners*, pp. 8–9. First emphasis added.

4. Ibid., pp. 18–19.

5. Mannheim's essay was found in his estate and was published under the title "Towards a Sociology of the Mind: An Introduction," in *Essays on the Sociology of Culture* (London, 1956). According to the editors, it was conceived in Germany in the early 1930s. The German original of Elias' book *The Civilizing Process* first appeared in 1939.

6. Adorno, *Prisms*, tr. Samuel and Shierry Weber (London, 1967), p. 35.

7. Mannheim, "Towards a Sociology of the Mind," p. 16.

8. Ibid., pp. 27, 28, 31, and 32.

9. This line of thought corresponds to Theodor Geiger's insistence that "what is wished for can itself never be an ideology; what is ideological is, rather, the thought generated by a wish." Theodor Geiger, "Kritische Bemerkungen zum Begriff der Ideologie," in *Arbeiten zur Soziologie* (Neuwied and Berlin, 1962), p. 422.

10. Leo Balet and E. Gerhard, *Die Verbürgerlichung der deutschen Kunst: Literatur und Musik im 18. Jahrhundert* (Strasbourg, Leipzig, Zurich, and Leiden, 1936), p. 30.

11. *Der junge Dilthey: Ein Lebensbild in Briefen und Tagebüchern, 1852–1870*, collected by Clara Misch, née Dilthey (Leipzig and Berlin, 1933), pp. 2–3.

12. See Rudolf Unger, *Hamann und die Aufklärung: Studien zur Vorgeschichte des romantischen Geistes im 18. Jahrhundert*, 2nd ed. (Halle, 1925), pp. 22 and 35. With his statement that "the importance of eudaemonism for the German literature of the eighteenth century is still greatly underestimated," Franz Schultz does more than just challenge our sharp portrait of the age both as resigned politically and as melancholy with respect to individuals. For Schultz, like Uz, links eudaemonism with the "certainty of the trouble-free and nonrebellious adaptation to the order and harmony of the world as a whole, overseen only by God." This already reflects the result of power being withheld from people and their resigned acquiescence to the distribution of power which has already been effected, and which has left the bourgeoisie out in the cold. Thus, eudaemonism appears—as does the specific individual psychology of the eighteenth century—to be a consequence of the state of resignation and also to amplify it. Franz Schultz, "Die Göttin Freude: Zur Geistes- und Stilgeschichte des 18. Jahrhunderts," *Jahrbuch des Freien Deutschen Hochstifts* (Frankfurt am Main, 1926), pp. 3–38; the quotations are from pp. 12 and 17.

13. Hauser, *The Social History of Art*, pp. 597–598.

14. Gustave Flaubert, *The Letters of Gustave Flaubert, 1830–1857*, ed. Francis Steegmuller (London, 1980), p. 197: Letter to Louise Colet of 21 August 1853. It must be said, if only to prevent a dichotomy from arising at the outset, that Emerson's argument in delineating society and solitude is similar to the approach taken by Flaubert: "Solitude is impracticable and society fatal. We must keep our head in the one and our hands in the other." Ralph Waldo Emerson, *Society and Solitude,* in *Complete Works*, vol. 7 (Boston, 1898), p. 20.

15. Wilhelm von Humboldt, "Das achtzehnte Jahrhundert," *Gesammelte Schriften*, vol. 2 (Berlin, 1904), pp. 1–112, esp. pp. 12, 70, and 84.

16. Compare William Rose, "Die Anfänge des Weltschmerzes in der deutschen Literatur," *Germanisch-Romanische Monatsschrift*, 12 (1924), p. 143.

17. Max Wieser, *Der sentimentale Mensch: Gesehen aus der Welt holländischer und deutscher Mystiker im 18. Jahrhundert* (Stuttgart, 1924), p. 7.

18. Ibid., p. 9.

19. Donald Brinkmann, "Der einsame Mensch und die Einsamkeit: Ein Beitrag zur Psychologie des Kontaktes," *Psychologische Rundschau*, 3 (1952), p. 21.

20. Karl Vossler, *Poesie der Einsamkeit in Spanien* (Munich, 1950), p. 45. Vossler provides an interesting etymological pointer linking solitude and melancholy when he discusses the derivation of the Portuguese word *saudade* from the Arabic *saudá*, meaning "a complaint of the liver, a pain of the heart, gloom, melancholy." (!) On the pervasiveness of the syndrome in modern-day Portugal, whose "national neurosis" is the discrepancy between minimal political significance and colonial hybris in foreign policy, see the unsigned article "Aus den Hauptstädten der Welt: Winter in Lissabon," *Die Zeit* (16 December 1966), p. 21. Here, the *saudade*, which is still widespread, is described as "an enjoyment of suffering, an enjoyment of pain, because pain provokes lamentation and lamentation gives the opportunity to express one's deepest feelings."

21. This sequence is given in Ernst Bloch, *The Principle of Hope*, tr. N. Plaice, S. Plaice, and Paul Knight (Cambridge, Mass., 1986), vol. 3, p. 958. This is one of the sources of the German ideology, as described, for example, by Adorno when attacking Heidegger and by Hans G. Helms when criticizing Max Stirner and his successors. See Theodor W. Adorno, *The Jargon of Authenticity*, tr. K. Tarnowski and F. Will (London, 1973); and Hans G. Helms, *Die Ideologie der anonymen Gesellschaft: Max Stirners "Einziger" und der Fortschritt des demokratischen Selbstbewusstseins vom Vormärz bis zur Bundesrepublik* (Cologne, 1966).

22. Johann Georg Zimmermann, *Solitude Considered, with Respect to Its Influence upon the Mind and the Heart*, tr. J. B. Mercier (London, 1796). Hereafter, page numbers are given in the text.

23. For a critique of such conceptions of boredom, see Leo Kofler, who distinguishes sharply between the boredom of the worker and that of the bourgeois in his *Zur Theorie der modernen Literatur: Der Avantgardismus in soziologischer Sicht* (Neuwied and Berlin, 1962). See especially the section entitled "Zur Soziologie des Arbeiters, Kleinbürgers und Bürgers als möglicher Gegenstände realistischer Kunst."

24. Zimmermann and Obereit, both Swiss, provided important contributions on the problem of solitude in the eighteenth century. Obereit

was the son of a Lindau adjudicator of law. He became a "healer of wounds" in 1740 (that is, a barber without any academic training), attended the universities of Halle and Berlin in 1746 and 1747, and was active for twenty-seven years in Lindau as a surgeon, and, as Milch puts it, an "avid reader and a tireless muser." In 1781 his book *Die Einsamkeit der Weltüberwindung* was published in Leipzig, and in 1786 the Duke of Meiningen offered Obereit the position of "cabinet philosopher" at his court.

Zimmermann, a student of Albrecht v. Haller, succeeded Werlhof as Royal Surgeon to George II, King of Great Britain and Grand Elector of Hanover. In 1786 he treated Frederick II of Prussia and in 1788 published in Leipzig his *Über Friedrich den Grossen und meine Unterredungen mit ihm kurz vor seinem Tode,* in which he claimed that the great Frederick's melancholy derived from the latter's conflicting feelings toward religion.

The difference in social station shapes the two men's conceptions of melancholy: Zimmermann endeavors to convey the sense of a man of the world even in his conception of melancholy, whereas Obereit remains entrenched in a religious conception of solitude that seems to prevent him from admitting that it may be linked to melancholy or boredom—a result of the Church's condemnation of "acedia."

On the debate between Zimmermann and Obereit, see Werner Milch, *Die Einsamkeit: Zimmermann und Obereit im Kampf um die Überwindung der Aufklärung* (Frauenfeld and Leipzig, 1937). See also Rudolf Ischer, "J. J. Rousseau und J. G. Zimmermann," *Neues Berner Taschenbuch* (1898), pp. 249–266.

25. A collection and ironic presentation of such landscape themes can be found in Karl Markus Michel, "Die Mulde: Etüde mit Zitaten," in *Zeugnisse: Theodor W. Adorno zum sechzigsten Geburtstag,* ed. Max Horkheimer (Frankfurt, 1963), pp. 183ff.

26. Milch, *Die Einsamkeit,* p. 77.

27. Helmut Rehder, "Johann Nicolaus Meinhard und seine Übersetzungen," *Illinois Studies in Language and Literature,* 37 (1953), p. 1.

28. Ibid., p. 5.

29. Christian Garve, "Über Gesellschaft und Einsamkeit," in *Versuche über verschiedene Gegenstände aus der Moral, der Litteratur und dem gesellschaftlichen Leben,* part 3 (Breslau, 1801), p. 66.

30. Ibid., pp. 296 and 368. Garve has, as a consequence, been justifiably linked with the beginnings of German sociology. See Lutz Geldsetzer, "Zur Frage des Beginns der deutschen Soziologie," *Kölner Zeitschrift für Soziologie und Sozialpsychologie,* 15 (1963), pp. 529ff.

31. See Georg Steinhausen, "Das achtzehnte Jahrhundert: Das Jahr-

hundert des Briefes," in *Geschichte des deutschen Briefes: Zur Kultur-geschichte des deutschen Volkes* (Berlin, 1889), pp. 245–410.

32. Karl Korn, *Studien über "Freude und Trûren" bei mittelhochdeutschen Dichtern: Beiträge zu einer Problemgeschichte* (Leipzig, 1932), pp. 20, 21, 99, 100, and 126.

33. Fr. Nick, *Die Hof- und Volks-Narren samt den närrischen Lustbarkeiten der verschiedenen Stände aller Völker und Zeiten: Aus Flögels Schriften und anderen Quellen* (Stuttgart, 1861), p. 27.

34. Karl Friedrich Flögel, *Geschichte der Hofnarren* (Liegnitz and Leipzig, 1789), p. 5.

35. Blaise Pascal, *Pascal's Pensées*, tr. M. Turnell (London, 1962).

36. Quoted in Günter Zehm, "Der Hofnarr und seine Nachkommen," *Die Welt* (28 August 1965), p. iii. On the whole issue of court jesters, see Wolfgang Promies, *Der Bürger und der Narr oder das Risiko der Phantasie* (Munich, 1966).

37. W. H. Bruford, *Germany in the Eighteenth Century* (Cambridge, 1935). Aristocracy and bourgeoisie converge in a "bourgeois-courtly compromise" when the *idea* of the human as the measure of all things is also accepted by the aristocracy—in other words, when an abstract concept gains the upper hand. See Hans Mayer, *Von Lessing bis Thomas Mann: Wandlungen der bürgerlichen Literatur in Deutschland* (Pfullingen, 1959), p. 15.

Hegel, by linking nature and boredom, had already forsaken the bourgeois standpoint that prevailed in the eighteenth century: "Changes in the natural world, no matter how great their variety, exhibit only an eternally recurring cycle; for in nature, there is nothing new under the sun, and in this respect its manifest play of forms produces an effect of boredom." *Lectures on the Philosophy of History*, tr. H. B. Nisbet (Cambridge, 1975), p. 124.

38. Otto Mann, *Der Dandy: Ein Kulturproblem der Moderne* (Heidelberg, 1962), pp. 48 and 57. See Jules Barbey D'Aurevilly, "Du Dandysme et de George Brummell," in *Oeuvres complètes* (Paris, 1927), vol. 9, pp. 205–278.

39. Simone François, *Le Dandysme et Marcel Proust: De Brummell au Baron de Charlus* (Brussels, 1956), p. 17.

40. Walter Benjamin, "Zentralpark," *Illuminationen*, in *Ausgewählte Schriften* (Frankfurt am Main, 1961), p. 258.

41. Florine Kalkühler, "Die Natur des Spleen bei den englischen Schriftstellern in der ersten Hälfte des achtzehnten Jahrhunderts" (diss., Münster and Leipzig, 1920), p. 3. When Kalkühler speaks of the French Academy's 1798 definition of *spleen* as "ennui de toutes choses, maladie hypocondriaque propre aux Anglais," we encounter

the interesting example of mutual accusations of boredom, since the English speak of "French boredom"! See Robert Herrlinger, "Die Milz und die Melancholie: Kulturgeschichte eines rätselhaften Organs," *Die Welt* (29 January 1966), p. iii.

42. On these links in Benjamin's work, see, in particular, "Der Flâneur" (prepublication of a text from the Passagen-Werk, edited by Rolf Tiedemann), in *Neue Rundschau*, 58 (1967), pp. 549ff. See also idem, "Die Moderne" (another prepublication edited by Tiedemann), in *Das Argument*, 10 (1968), pp. 44ff. In the first of these two texts, Benjamin speaks of the means Poe uses in describing a group of players whose behavior expresses the isolation of human beings in terms of their private interests: "They stem from the clown's repertoire." *Neue Rundschau*, 58 (1967), p. 564.

43. Charles Baudelaire, "Mon coeur mis à nu," in *Oeuvres complètes* (Paris, 1958), p. 1226.

44. "In the Middle Ages the court fool was an entertainer and his services were in demand to add amusement to an otherwise dull monotonous life." Gordon C. Hanson, "The Normal and Abnormal in Behavior," in *Modern Abnormal Psychology*, ed. W. H. Mikesell (New York, 1950), p. 3.
    Perhaps we should see both opera and operetta as modern institutions meant to banish melancholy and boredom, for the opera was originally intended to "dispel 'tedio,' namely boredom." See Joseph Gregor, *Kulturgeschichte der Oper: Ihre Verbindung mit dem Leben, den Werken des Geistes und der Politik* (Vienna, 1941), p. 53. We cannot determine here to what extent the stage does provide such "relief" in the broadest sense of the word. This is, after all, a basic question of aesthetics as a whole. Film entails something categorically new in this context, providing relief for the masses for the first time. This again leads us to suspect the presence of an ideology: relief in leisure time only stabilizes existing relations of labor and dominance.

45. Benjamin, "Zentralpark," p. 247. The quotation from Engels comes from *On the Condition of the English Working Class* and is quoted in Benjamin, "Der Flâneur," p. 568.

46. Karl Mannheim, "Das konservative Denken: Soziologische Beiträge zum Werden des politisch-historischen Denkens in Deutschland," in *Wissenssoziologie* (Neuwied and Berlin, 1964), p. 450. On this point see Ralf Dahrendorf, "Der Intellektuelle und die Gesellschaft: Über die sozial Funktion des Narren im zwanzigsten Jahrhundert," *Die Zeit* (29 March 1963), p. 9.

47. Theodor W. Adorno, "The Sociology of Knowledge and Its Consciousness," in *Prisms*, p. 35.

48. Ralf Dahrendorf, *Die Soziologie und der Soziologe: Zur Frage von Theorie und Praxis* (Constance, n.d.), p. 1.

49. Michael Landmann, *Pluralität und Antinomie: Kulturelle Grundlagen seelischer Konflikte* (Munich and Basel, 1963), p. 28.

50. Quoted in Wilhelm Josef Revers, *Die Psychologie der Langeweile* (Meisenheim a G., 1949), p. 20.

51. Rudolf W. Meyer, *Leibniz und die europäische Ordnungskrise* (Hamburg, 1948), pp. 259–260.

52. Helmuth Plessner, "Immer noch Philosophische Anthropologie?" in *Zeugnisse,* p. 66. A similar statement is to be found in Camus, "Frenzy Is the Reverse of Boredom . . . ," in *The Rebel,* tr. Anthony Bower (Harmondsworth, 1971), p. 45.

53. Balet and Gerhard, *Die Verbürgerlichung,* p. 185. See also Odo Marquard, "Zur Geschichte des philosophischen Begriffs 'Anthropologie' seit dem Ende des 18. Jahrhunderts," in *Collegium Philosophicum— Studien: Joachim Ritter zum 60. Geburtstag* (Basel and Stuttgart, 1965), pp. 214 and 217.

54. Wilhelm Dilthey, "Die Funktion der Anthropologie in der Kultur des 16. und 17. Jahrhunderts" in *Werke,* 4th ed. (Berlin and Leipzig, 1940), vol. 2, pp. 435 and 487.

55. Balet and Gerhard, *Die Verbürgerlichung,* p. 307.

56. Ibid., pp. 316, 318, and 319.

57. Martin Greiner, *Die Entstehung der modernen Unterhaltungsliteratur: Studien zum Trivial-Roman des 18. Jahrhunderts* (Reinbek bei Hamburg, 1964), pp. 48–49. On "resignation" in light novels, see also Marion Beaujean, "Der Trivialroman im ausgehenden 18. Jahrhundert" (diss., Cologne, 1962), esp. p. 172.

58. The title of Bernd's autobiography is given here in full because it clearly exhibits that proclivity for melancholy which stemmed from Pietist influences. Adam Bernd, *Eigene Lebens-Beschreibung, samt einer / Aufrichtigen Entdeckung, und deutlichen / Beschreibung einer der grössten, obwol grossen Theils / noch unbekannten / Leibes- und Gemüths-Plage, / welche Gott zuweilen über die Welt-Kinder, und auch wohl / über seine eigene Kinder verhänget* [Personal Description of My Life, Together with a Sincere Discovery and Clear Description of One of the Largest, Though as Yet Unknown Physical and Emotional Ailments Which God Has Imposed on the World's Children, and Assuredly on His Own Children] (Leipzig, 1738). The quotation is on p. 117.

59. Helmuth Plessner, *Lachen und Weinen: Eine Untersuchung nach den Grenzen menschlichen Verhaltens,* 2nd ed. (Munich, 1950).

60. Max Wieser, *Der sentimentale Mensch,* p. 169.

61. Helmut Rehder, *Die Philosophie der unendlichen Landschaft: Ein Beitrag zur Geschichte der romantischen Weltanschauung* (Halle, 1932), p. 3.

62. Friedrich H. Tenbruck, "Freundschaft: Ein Beitrag zu einer Soziologie der persönlichen Beziehungen," *Kölner Zeitschrift für Soziologie und Sozialpyschologie*, 14 (1964), p. 441. For a characterization of the bond of friendship in terms of contemplation, introversion, and a "metaphysics of suffering," see Peter Christian Ludz, "Ideologie, Intelligenz und Organisation: Bemerkungen über ihren Zusammenhang in der frühbürgerlichen Gesellschaft," *Jahrbuch für Sozialwissenschaft*, 15 (1964), pp. 82ff.

63. Tenbruck, "Freundschaft," p. 448.

64. Hegel, *Lectures on the Philosophy of History*, p. 79.

65. Friedrich Schelling, "Immanuel Kant," in *Werke*, vol. 3, *Schriften zur Identitätsphilosophie, 1801–1806*, ed. Manfred Schöner (Munich, 1927), p. 588. See also the emphasis on Kant's progressiveness, linked with a sharp critique of Lukács' "sociological schematism," in Günter K. Lehmann, "Die Ästhetik Kants und die ideologische Funktion seines Geniebegriffs," *Deutsche Zeitschrift für Philosophie*, 11 (1963), pp. 1138ff. For similar remarks, see Leo Kofler, *Zur Theorie der modernen Literatur*, esp. p. 603.

66. Max Horkheimer, "On the Concept of Man," in *The Eclipse of Reason* (New York, 1947).

67. Immanuel Kant, *Observations on the Feeling of the Beautiful and the Sublime*, tr. J. T. Goldthwait (Berkeley, 1960), p. 63. Other quotations are from the *Akademie* edition of Kant's *Collected Works*. Roman numerals refer to the respective volume. The only exception consists of quotations from the *Critique of Judgment*, which are taken from the J. H. Bernard translation (London, 1951). Page numbers will be given in parentheses in the body of the text.

68. The concept of an "aristocratic behavioral ideal" does not mean that such an ideal can be clearly assigned to one stratum of society. When Erich Auerbach emphasizes in his book *Das französische Publikum des 17. Jahrhunderts* (Munich, 1933) that the concept of the *honnête homme* was an "ideal for a personality," we should not disregard the fact that such an ideal could arise only with the pacification of spaces as described by Norbert Elias, for this made possible speculative thought and the chance for a stabilization and refinement of affects in protected interior domains. This amounts to a process of feudalization, and the patterns that emerge in it are initially of an aristocratic nature. Indeed, they never lost this trait. Auerbach also describes the salon of the Hôtel Rambouillet as "aristocratic" (ibid., p. 32), although bourgeois members were already granted access to it.

Honnêteté was and remained an aristocratic ideal pursued by the bourgeoisie for reasons of prestige. Herder's translation of *honnêteté* as "inner honesty" conveys less the genetic meaning of this behavioral maxim than the bourgeois wish to derive it from a "concept" of humankind and not from a particular social stratum. That the aristocracy in Germany and France later concurred with this "fundamentalization" of the concept only shows the extent to which the "aristocratic-bourgeois" compromise was desired by both sides. Herder's translation is in his *Adrastea I*, vol. 9, p. 35. For the transition of *honnête homme* from a courtly to a bourgeois notion, see Emil H. Maurer, *Der Spätbürger* (Berne and Munich, 1963), p. 20.

69. Friedrich Kaulbach, "Weltorientierung, Weltkenntnis und pragmatische Vernunft bei Kant," in *Kritik und Metaphysik: Studien Heinz Heimsoeth zum 80. Geburtstag* (Berlin, 1966), p. 62, n. 3.

70. Ibid., p. 63. Leo Lowenthal emphatically highlights the differences between Kant and bourgeois ideology on this point. See his "Knut Hamsun: Zur Vorgeschichte der autoritären Ideologie," *Zeitschrift für Sozialforschung*, 6 (1937), pp. 295–345. This essay appears in *Literature and the Image of Man* (Boston, 1957).

71. Jürgen Habermas, *Strukturwandel der Öffentlichkeit: Untersuchungen zu einer Kategorie der bürgerlichen Gesellschaft*, 2nd ed. (Neuwied and Berlin, 1965), p. 120.

72. Kaulbach, "Weltorientierung," p. 74.

73. Habermas, *Strukturwandel*, pp. 120–121.

74. This dichotomy is to be found in *Anthropology from a Pragmatic Point of View*. See K. P. Kisker, "Kants psychiatrische Systematik," *Psychiatrica et Neurologia*, 133 (1957), pp. 17ff. On the question of melancholy in Kant's work see Tim Klein, "Hamlet und der Melancholiker in Kants 'Beobachtungen über das Gefühl des Schönen und Erhabenen,'" *Kant-Studien*, 10 (1905), pp. 76ff.

75. Helmut Plessner, "Das Identitätssystem," *Verhandlungen der Schelling-Tagung in Bad Ragaz vom 22. bis 25. September 1954*, in *Studia Philosophica*, 14 (1954), p. 84.

76. Johann Wolfgang von Goethe, *The Sufferings of Young Werther*, tr. B. Q. Morgan (London, 1957). This is not to say that Goethe himself offers an example of this sort of compatriotism, and it is not the issue here. On Werther, see Engels' sarcasm concerning the "Jammergeschrei eines schwärmerischen Tränensacks," in "Deutscher Sozialismus in Versen und Prosa," quoted in Karl Marx and Friedrich Engels, *Über Kunst und Literatur*, vol. 1, p. 470. For the opposite view, which maintains that *Werther* is the work of bourgeois emancipation, see Lukács, *Goethe and His Age*, tr. Robert Anchor (London, 1968).

77. Quoted in Karl Jaspers, *Schelling—Grösse und Verhängnis* (Munich, 1955), p. 270. See also Jaspers' reply to Emil Staiger's lecture "Schellings Schwermut," in *Verhandlungen der Schelling-Tagung*, pp. 112ff and 134ff. Perhaps unconsciously, Staiger pinpoints the interconnection of the syndrome described above with the ideology of "depth": "below, depth, heaviness, origin, bottom: these words are repeatedly to be found in Schelling's later works" (ibid., p. 126). Adorno states the following on this point: "A dreadful German tradition equates profound thought with thoughts that are ready to swear by the theodicy of death and evil. A theological *terminus ad quem* is tacitly passed over and imputed, as if the value of a thought were decided by its outcome, the confirmation of transcendence, or by its immersion in introversion, its sheer being-for-itself; as if withdrawal from the world were flatly tantamount to consciousness of the origin of the world" (*Negative Dialectics*, p. 17, amended translation).

78. Jaspers, *Schelling*, p. 269.

79. Hermann Zeltner, "Der Mensch in der Philosophie Schellings," in *Verhandlungen der Schelling-Tagung*, p. 211.

80. Ibid., p. 220.

81. Ibid., p. 213.

82. Johann Fichte, *The Characteristics of the Present Age*, tr. W. Smith (London, 1847), p. 73.

83. Johann Fichte, *The Vocation of Man*, tr. W. Smith (Chicago, 1906), p. 32.

84. Ibid., p. 29.

85. Fichte, *The Characteristics*, p. 170.

86. Ibid., p. 72.

87. Werner Milch, *Die Einsamkeit*, pp. 66 and 84. The reference to Rousseau is in a letter written by Zimmermann to Heller. See also Friso Melzer, "J. G. Zimmermanns 'Einsamkeit' in ihrer Stellung im Geistesleben des ausgehenden 18. Jahrhunderts" (diss., Breslau, 1930), pp. 46–47. See also Ischer, "J. J. Rousseau und J. G. Zimmermann."

88. J.-J. Rousseau, *A Discourse upon Whether the Revival of the Arts and Sciences Has Contributed to Render Our Manners Pure? Proving the Negative* (London, 1760).

89. Ibid.

90. Fichte would appear to have had a stronger sense of the danger posed by boredom. "The notion [of perfection] first becomes a problem of humankind's vocation for Fichte when he finds himself confronted with the question of the actual purpose to be served by the final generation. Fichte is overcome with the fear that seizes every

sensitive person when contemplating what absolute prevalence of the boredom of cultural philistinism would be like, or, to put it another way, the predetermined form of concrete totality of absolute values. The regular one-and-the-sameness, this 'infallible mechanism,' would render all independence impossible and unnecessary." Eckart von Sydow, *Der Gedanke des Ideal-Reichs in der idealistischen Philosophie von Kant bis Hegel im Zusammenhange der geschichtsphilosophischen Entwicklung* (Leipzig, 1914), p. 62. Admittedly, Fichte's notion of an ideal state of ethical life in which every person submits "to the same obligations" and his concept of a Closed Commercial State, to be described below, unintentionally prejudge boredom as an institutional component of the future society that remains to be created. See von Sydow, pp. 41 and 46.

91. Arthur Schopenhauer, *The World as Will and Representation*, tr. E. F. J. Payne (Colorado, 1958), p. 350.

5. Spaces of Boredom and Melancholy

1. Ludwig Marcuse, *Unverlorene Illusionen: Pessimismus—Ein Stadium der Reife* (Munich, 1966), p. 117. (This is the second, slightly altered edition of his book on pessimism.) See also Walter Benjamin, "Zentralpark," p. 264. It seems wrong to suggest that melancholy achieved primacy in one particular epoch. See N. Paulus, "Die Melancholie im 16. Jahrhundert," *Wissenschaftliche Beilage zur Germania: Blätter für Litteratur, Wissenschaft und Kunst*, 18 (1897), pp. 137–141.

2. Jacob and Wilhelm Grimm, *Deutsches Wörterbuch*, ed. Moritz Heyne (Leipzig, 1885), vol. 6, p. 173. Here, one also finds the Bavarian word for boredom, *Langweil*, defined as "ongoing or great distress," and *langweilen* as "to be bored," or "to feel longing" (p. 184). The link here to the syndrome of melancholy is as clear as it is in the sixteenth-century French usage of *ennuy*.

3. Franz Dornseiff, *Der deutsche Wortschatz nach Sachgruppen* (Berlin, 1959), entry 11.26 *(Langeweile)*. It is worth noting that boredom appears here in the same category as conservatism!

4. Sören Kierkegaard, *Either/Or*, tr. D. F. and L. M. Swanson (London, 1944), p. 235.

5. Sören Kierkegaard, *Die Tagebücher, 1834–1855*, selected and translated into German by Theodor Haecker, 4th ed. (Munich, 1953), p. 199.

6. Sören Kierkegaard, *Fear and Trembling: Repetition*, tr. H. V. and E. H. Hong (New Jersey, 1983), pp. 132–133.

7. Sören Kierkegaard, *The Point of View for My Work as an Author*, tr. W. Lowrie (New York, 1962), p. 100, emphasis added.

8. Ibid., pp. 91 and 95. The image of an inverted world persists when Kierkegaard declares that "everything must be done back-to-front in reflexion" (p. 95).

9. Gessner, quoted in Willi Flemming, *Der Wandel des deutschen Naturgefühls vom 15. zum 18. Jahrhundert* (Halle a.d. Saale, 1931), p. 84.

10. Emmanuel Hirsch gives this in the German translation of *Either/Or: Entweder-Oder*, in Kierkegaard, *Gesammelte Werke* (Düsseldorf, 1956), vol. 1, p. 132, n. 89.

11. Theodor W. Adorno, "Kierkegaard noch einmal: Zum 150. Geburtstag," in *Neue Deutsche Hefte*, 95 (1963), p. 6.

12. Kierkegaard, *Either/Or*, p. 236.

13. Maurice Halbwachs, *Das kollektive Gedächtnis* (Stuttgart, 1967), p. 127. See also Maurice Halbwachs, *Das Gedächtnis und seine sozialen Bedingungen* (Neuwied and Berlin, 1966), pp. 142–143.

14. Ernst Bloch, *Freiheit und Ordnung: Abriss der Sozial-Utopien* (New York, 1946), p. 11.

15. As a consequence, writers find fault with paradise, with the perfect order of such a state, which creates boredom. See Jean Cazeneuve, *Bonheur et civilisation* (Paris, 1966), pp. 17–18; and George Steiner, "A Note on Literature and Post-History," in *Festschrift zum 80. Geburtstag G. Lukács*, ed. Frank Benseler (Berlin and Neuwied, 1965), pp. 502–511.

16. Bloch, *Freiheit und Ordnung*, p. 15.

17. Ibid., pp. 81–82.

18. Theodor W. Adorno, "Zum Verhältnis von Soziologie und Psychologie," in *Sociologica: Aufsätze, Max Horkheimer zum 60. Geburtstag gewidmet*, eds. Theodor W. Adorno and Walter Dirks (Frankfurt, 1955), p. 43.

19. Ralf Dahrendorf, "Pfade aus Utopia: Zu einer Neuorientierung der soziologischen Analyse," in *Gesellschaft und Freiheit: Zur soziologischen Analyse der Gegenwart* (Munich, 1963), pp. 85ff. and 92–93.

20. George Orwell, *1984* (Harmondsworth, 1972), p. 38. Subsequent references to this work are given in parentheses in the text.

21. Dahrendorf, "Pfade," p. 87.

22. See B. F. Skinner, *Walden Two*, 10th ed. (New York, 1962), esp. pp. 49, 83, 93, 96, 135, and 161.

23. Johann Gottlieb Fichte, *Der Geschlossne Handelsstaat: Ein philosophischer Entwurf als Anhang zur Rechtslehre, und Probe einer künftig zu liefernden Politik* (Tübingen, 1800), p. 275.

24. Ibid., p. 277.

25. Ibid., pp. 277–278.

26. On this point see Huguet, *Dictionnaire de la langue française* (Paris, 1932), vol. 2, p. 477: "Mais ce nom de *contenances* commence à se perdre en la cour, voire est perdu: et ne se retrouve qu'en villes."

27. Stendhal, quoted in D. Brauchlin, "Das Motiv des 'ennui' bei Stendhal" (diss., Zurich, 1930), p. 52. See also Frank Paul Bowman, "Melancholy in Stendhal," in *L'Esprit créateur*, 2 (1962), pp. 5ff.

28. Stendhal, quoted in D. Brauchlin, "Das Motiv," pp. 92 and 72.

29. Emile Magne, *Voiture et L'Hôtel de Rambouillet*, 7th ed. (Paris, 1929), vol. 1, pp. 59 and 61.

30. Aldis, "Madame Geoffrin," p. 9.

31. Edmund and Jules de Goncourt, *The Woman of the Eighteenth Century*, tr. J. Clercq and R. Roeder (London, 1928), pp. 41–42.

32. Ibid., p. 61.

33. I am thinking of the passage in Marx's *German Ideology*, tr. C. Dutt (Moscow, 1964), pp. 44–45: "For as soon as the distribution of labour comes into being, each man has a particular, exclusive sphere of activity, which is forced upon him and from which he cannot escape. He is a hunter, a fisherman, a shepherd, or a critical critic, and must remain so if he does not want to lose his means of livelihood; while in communist society, where nobody has an exclusive sphere of activity, but each can become accomplished in any branch he wishes, society regulates the general production and thus makes it possible for me to do one thing today and another tomorrow, to hunt in the morning, fish in the afternoon, rear cattle in the evening, criticise after dinner, just as I have in mind, without ever becoming hunter, fisherman, shepherd or critic."

34. Max Scheler, "Das Ressentiment im Aufbau der Moralen," in *Vom Umsturz der Werte: Abhandlungen und Aufsätze*, 4th ed. (Bern, 1955), pp. 36 and 41.

35. Ibid., p. 65.

36. Jean-Jacques Rousseau, *Emile*, tr. B. Foxley (London, 1911), p. 5.

37. Halbwachs, *Das kollektive Gedächtnis*, p. 53.

38. Aynard, *La Bourgeoisie française*, p. 243.

39. Ibid., p. 262.

40. Robert Minder, "Deutsche und französische Literatur: Inneres Reich und Einbürgerung des Dichters," in *Kultur und Literatur in Deutschland und Frankreich* (Frankfurt, 1962), pp. 5–6. See also Robert Minder, "Das Bild des Pfarrhauses in der deutschen Literatur von Jean Paul bis Gottfried Benn," ibid., pp. 44ff.

41. Theodor W. Adorno, *Kierkegaard: Construction of the Aesthetic*, tr. Robert Hullot-Kantor (Minneapolis, 1989), p. 47.

42. Ibid., p. 41.

43. Ibid., pp. 42 and 59. See in this context the chapters on Schopenhauer and Kierkegaard in Georg Lukács, *The Destruction of Reason*, tr.
   P. Palmer (London, 1980); and Marguerite Grimault, *La Mélancolie
   de Kierkegaard* (Paris, 1965).
44. Paul Scheerbart, *Glasarchitektur* (Berlin, 1914). Subsequent references
   to this work are given in parentheses in the text.
45. Alexander Rüstow, "Vereinzelung: Tendenzen und Reflexe," in
   Gegenwartsprobleme der Soziologie, ed. Gottfried Eisermann on the
   occasion of Alfred Vierkandt's eightieth birthday (Potsdam, 1949),
   pp. 45–78. Rüstow provides a few amusing examples of the mirror
   motif: "It was *rumored* of Friedrich Carl von Savigny (1779–1869),
   the famous lawyer, that he could not go past a puddle without looking at his reflection in it. Numerous anecdotes in a similar vein are
   told of August Wilhelm von Schlegel (1767–1845). And Henrik
   Ibsen (1828–1906) had a mirror built into the stiff crown of his hat
   so that he could admire himself at any time" (p. 57).
46. In *Zeitschrift für philosophische Forschung*, 20 (1966), pp. 471–495.
47. Kaulbach, "Weltorientierung," pp. 484–485.
48. Ibid., p. 490. Kaulbach refers to his own book, *Die Metaphysik des
   Raumes bei Leibniz und Kant* (Cologne, 1960).
49. Leibniz, quoted in Glockner, *Die europäische Philosophie*, p. 476. On
   the symbol of the mirror in Leibniz and Herder's reliance on his
   predecessor's notion, see also August Langen, "Zur Geschichte des
   Spiegelsymbols in der deutschen Dichtung," *Germanisch-Romanische
   Monatsschrift*, 28 (1940), pp. 269–280, esp. p. 271, n. 2.
50. Lucien Goldmann, *Towards a Sociology of the Novel*, tr. A. Sheridan
   (London, 1975), p. 9.
51. Maine de Biran, *Journal I: Février 1814–Décembre 1816* (Neuchatel,
   1954), p. 39. Littré understands *langueur* primarily as the "état d'une
   personne affaiblie, malade" (vol. 3, p. 249) and *ennui* as "tourment
   de l'âme" (vol. 2, p. 1406).
52. Ibid., p. 417. The phenomenon of "isolation *in* the world" appears
   particularly to attract the sociologist because here he can comfortably
   dissect the social structure and the "social retreat into an inner world,"
   as they are neatly adjacent. However, to derive a "modern sociological
   disease" from this (Rüstow, quoting A. Löwe, "Vereinzelung," p. 62)
   would seem to be somewhat over-hasty, at least with regard to the
   term "modern." Montaigne had sensed enough in this regard to be
   able to write: "Laissons à part cette longue comparaison de la vie
   solitaire à l'active . . ." (*Oeuvres complètes* [Paris, 1962], vol. 14, p. 232).
53. Proust is quoted from *Remembrance of Things Past*, tr. C. K. Scott Mon-
   crieff and T. Kilmartin, 3 vols. (Harmondsworth, 1981). Subsequent

references are given in parentheses in the text. Unless another source is given, biographical information has been taken from André Maurois, *The Quest for Proust*, tr. G. Hopkins (Harmondsworth, 1962). On the manner in which Proust's novel and his life coincide, see G. D. Painter, *Marcel Proust: A Biography* (Harmondsworth, 1983).

54. Maurois, *The Quest for Proust*, p. 133.

55. Proust wrote in 1910 that he had "read quite a lot of Bergson," and in 1912 informed Prince Antoine Bibesco that "my novels are not Bergsonian, for they are written under the sign of a distinction which not only has no place in Bergson's philosophy but directly contradicts it." Marcel Proust, *Briefe zum Werk* (Frankfurt, 1964), pp. 188 and 232.

56. Georges Poulet, *Proustian Space*, tr. E. Coleman (London, 1977). An indication of this can be found in Benjamin's thought on the subject when he writes: "The eternity which Proust opens to view is convoluted time, not boundless time. His true interest is the passage of time in its most real—that is, *space-bound*—form, and this passage nowhere holds sway more openly than in remembrance within and aging without." Walter Benjamin, "The Image of Proust," in *Illuminations*, tr. Harry Zohn (Glasgow, 1979), p. 213, emphasis added.

57. Hannah Arendt, *The Origins of Totalitarianism* (London, 1986), p. 80.

58. Benjamin, "The Image of Proust," p. 208. On boredom in Proust see ibid., p. 206.

59. Robert Dreyfus, "Marcel Proust au Lycée Condorcet," *Revue de France* (December 1925), p. 609; quoted in Poulet.

60. Proust, *Briefe zum Werk*, p. 292.

61. All quotations are from Poulet, *Proustian Space*.

62. See also Theodor Adorno, "Standort des Erzählers im zeitgenössischen Roman," in *Noten zur Literatur* (Frankfurt, 1958), vol. 1, pp. 61–72; in this essay Adorno links the *intérieur* and monologue, p. 67.

63. Written by Valéry for the second English translation of *Monsieur Teste*, tr. J. Mathews (London, 1951), pp. 6–7, emphasis added. Subsequent references to this work are given in parentheses in the text.

64. Niklas Luhmann, "Reflexive Mechanismen," *Soziale Welt*, 17 (1966), p. 3.

65. Ibid., pp. 17 and 23.

66. Dieter Claessens, "Rationalität revidiert," pp. 471, 473, and 474.

67. The great significance that now accrues to the *intérieur* in contemporary literature can be shown nowhere more clearly than in the French avant-garde novel, the *nouveau roman*. It is present even in the themes chosen: examples would be the house in Alain Robbe-Grillet's *Jealousy*

and the tenement block in Michel Butor's *Passage de Milan*. In the *nouveau roman*, also termed "novel of things," everything is transformed into an interior, for the novel-like analysis rests on absolute precision: things are moved closer both to the reader's field of vision and to one another. In the final instance, the world itself becomes *intérieur*—and this is the major difference between this conception and that of the nineteenth century. Originally, the *intérieur* was regarded as a haven from the world; now both are identical. The *intérieur* no longer offers an opportunity to live to the full in the interior, which would have been subjected to control if it has been in "the outside world." And if the world becomes an *intérieur*, then societal compulsions are also totally transposed onto the individual; people in the *nouveau roman* thus themselves become things. What emerges here is a dialectical relationship of melancholy and boredom: the person's individual affects disappear, as does psychology in the novel—what remains is boredom. (In his critique of Camus, Robbe-Grillet accused his colleague of resorting to the stock of "classical metaphors," among them that of evening as a "melancholy pause for breath.") The succession of the ever-identical and the renunciation of change create objective boredom—Hegel and Kierkegaard both perceived this. And what are "presence outside time" and "spatial permanence" other than indicators of boredom? If they do not already point beyond this. Roland Barthes states of the *nouveau roman* in connection with Robbe-Grillet's books that it is marked by a "continued attempt to commit suicide." It also certainly constitutes the effort to regain spontaneity by forcing boredom to its conclusion. Just as Barthes explains this *présuicide* in terms of the situation at the time, so should we here hunt out the social movements which suggested to the avant-garde that it should resort to boredom and no longer to eccentricity, whose counterpart is introversion. One can assume that the *nouveau roman* is the vanguard of "outer-directed literature," in which the point of reference is not other people but things outside of humankind. See above all Gerda Zeltner-Neukomm, *Das Wagnis des französischen Gegenwartsromans* (Reinbek, 1960); and Ludovic Janvier, *Literatur als Herausforderung: Die neue Welt des Nouveau Roman* (Munich, 1967).

68. These are Valéry's words in a letter to Gide dated 22 February 1897; the expression *testisme* is used by Valéry on 5 October 1896. See *Self-Portraits: The Gide/Valéry Letters*, tr. J. Guicharnand (Chicago, 1966), pp. 168 and 171.

69. Theodor W. Adorno, "Über einige Schwierigkeiten des Komponierens heute," in *Aspekte der Modernität*, ed. Hans Steffen (Göt-

tingen, 1965), pp. 129–149; the quotation is from page 131. Adorno's essay is laden with implications for the issues we are treating here.

70. Horst Enders, "Marginalien zur Theorie und Literatur der Texte," *Sprache im technischen Zeitalter*, 16 (1965), p. 1327.

71. Ibid., p. 1335.

72. Susan Sontag, "Notes on Camp," in *A Susan Sontag Reader* (Harmondsworth, 1982), p. 117.

73. Ibid., p. 115. Sartre refers to Genet's gloss that "the only criterion for measuring a deed is its elegance."

74. Ibid., p. 107.

75. Halbwachs, *Das kollektive Gedächtnis*, p. 87.

76. Georg Simmel, "Soziologie des Raumes," in *Schmollers Jahrbuch*, 27 (1903), p. 29.

77. See the essay by Hans-Joachim Lieber and Peter Furth, "Zur Dialektik der Simmelschen Konzeption einer formalen Soziologie," in *Buch des Dankes an Georg Simmel*, ed. Kurt Gassen and Michael Landmann (Berlin, 1958), pp. 39–59.

78. Kisker, "Kants psychiatrische Systematik," p. 18.

79. Hoff, "Das veränderte Erscheinungsbild der Melancholie," p. 731.

80. Ibid., p. 732.

81. Ibid., p. 723. It should again be pointed out that the interruption of lactation uncovered in psychiatric and medical terms as the cause of melancholy appears in the iconography as the "motif of dried-out breasts." See on this issue Günter Bandmann, *Melancholie und Musik: Ikonographische Studien* (Cologne and Opladen, 1960), p. 105, as well as the examples in Klibansky et al., *Saturn and Melancholy*.

82. Dieter Claessens, "Ein Theorem zur Struktur der Psyche," in *Angst, Furcht und gesellschaftlicher Druck und andere Aufsätze* (Dortmund, 1966), p. 79. See also Claessens, *Familie und Wertsystem*, 2nd ed. (Berlin, 1967).

83. See Michel Foucault, *Madness and Civilization: A History of Insanity in the Age of Reason*, tr. R. Howard (London, 1971), as well as his *Maladie mentale et psychologie* (Paris, 1966).

84. Sigmund Freud, "Trauer und Melancholie," in *Gesammelte Werke*, 3rd ed. (Frankfurt, 1963), vol. 10, pp. 446, 429, and 431. The English translation by James Strachey is in the *Standard Edition* (London, 1917), vol. 14, pp. 243ff. [Since the translations of Freud's work have been the subject of much criticism, we have chosen to translate the passages ourselves.—*Translators*.] See also J. O. Wisdom, "Die psychoanalytischen Theorien über die Melancholie," *Jahrbuch der Psychoanalyse*, 4 (Bern and Stuttgart, 1967), pp. 102–154.

85. Ludwig Binswanger, *Melancholie und Manie: Phänomenologische Studien* (Pfullingen, 1960), pp. 9 and 140.

86. Hubert Tellenbach, "Die Räumlichkeit der Melancholischen: Über Veränderungen des Raumerlebens in der endogenen Melancholie," *Der Nervenarzt*, 27 (1956), pp. 12ff. See also idem, "Zweite Mitteilung: Analyse der Räumlichkeit melancholischen Daseins," *Der Nervenarzt*, 27 (1956), pp. 289ff.

87. Hubert Tellenbach, *Melancholie: Zur Problemgeschichte—Typologie— Pathogenese und Klinik* (Berlin, Göttingen, and Heidelberg, 1961), p. 13.

88. Ibid., p. 50. Page numbers are henceforth given in parentheses in the text.

89. Tellenbach, "Analyse der Räumlichkeit," p. 290.

90. Ibid., p. 293. Tellenbach italicizes the whole passage.

91. "Something that lags behind the state it has itself reached." Tellenbach, *Melancholie*, p. 125.

92. Hubert Tellenbach, "Hiob und das Problem der Selbstübersteigung: Einübung um Transzendieren als Prinzip einer psychotherapeutischen Melancholie-Prophylaxe," in *Werden und Handeln: Festschrift für v. Gebsattel* (Stuttgart, 1963), pp. 420ff.

93. Ibid., p. 430. On the differences between inclusive and residual melancholy see also Hubert Tellenbach, "Gestalten der Melancholie," *Jahrbuch für Psychologie, Psychotherapie und medizinische Anthropologie*, 7 (1960), esp. pp. 11–12 and 15–16.

94. Georges Dumas, *La Tristesse et la joie* (Paris, 1900), pp. 30, 34, and 99. See also Georges Dumas, *Les Etats intellectuels dans la mélancolie* (Paris, 1895); and, on the concept of coenesthesis, Gordon W. Allport, *Becoming: Basic Considerations for a Psychology of Personality* (New Haven, 1955).

95. Norman Cameron, *The Psychology of Behavior Disorders: A Biosocial Interpretation* (Boston and New York, 1947) has a section, pp. 495–539, entitled "Manic and Depressive Disorders." Page numbers are henceforth given in parentheses in the text. See also Norman Cameron, "The Paranoid Pseudo-Community," *American Journal of Sociology*, 44 (1943–44), pp. 32–38, for a description of the conflict between "supposed community of response" and "actual community."

96. See also Sigmund Biran, *Melancholie und Todestriebe: Dynamische Psychologie der Melancholie* (Munich and Basel, 1961), in which the "mode for extinguishing stimuli" (p. 71) is of great interest for the issue at hand. Biran also goes into the "reference to space"; paraphrasing Heine, he speaks in the context of this mode, a reference which reminds one of the "loss of world," of the "mattress grave" of

the melancholics! [Heine used these words to refer to his bedridden state at the end of his life.—*Translators.*]

97. Alexander Mitscherlich, "Über die Vielschichtigkeit sozialer Einflüsse auf Entstehung und Behandlung von Psychosen und Neurosen," in *Krankheit als Konflikt: Studien zur psychosomatischen Medizin* (Frankfurt, 1966), vol. 1, p. 89. Italicization of "interpersonal relationships" added.

98. Binswanger, *Melancholie und Manie*, p. 10.

99. Bombast von Hohenheim, *Werke*, ed. von Sudhoff, vol. 8, p. 273. Quoted in Werner Leibbrand and Annemarie Wettley, *Der Wahnsinn: Geschichte der abendländischen Psychopathologie* (Freiburg and Munich, 1961), p. 209.

100. Sándor Radó, "Das Problem der Melancholie: Vortrag auf dem X. internationalen Psychoanalytischen Kongress zu Innsbruck am 1. September 1927," *Internationale Zeitschrift für Psychoanalyse*, 13 (Vienna, 1927), p. 453.

101. Albert K. Cohen, "The Study of Social Disorganization and Deviant Behavior," in *Sociology Today: Problems and Prospects*, ed. Merton, Broom, and Cottrell Jr. (New York, 1959), p. 463.

102. Ibid., p. 462.

103. August de Belmont Hollingshead and Frederick C. Redlich, "Social Stratification and Psychiatric Disorders," *American Sociological Review*, 18 (1953), pp. 163ff.

104. Robert J. Kleiner and Seymour Parker, "Goal-Striving, Social Status, and Mental Disorder: A Research Review," *American Sociological Review*, 28 (1963), pp. 189ff. See also John A. Clausen, "The Sociology of Mental Illness," in Merton et al., *Sociology Today*, pp. 485ff.

105. Kleiner and Parker, "Goal-Striving," p. 191.

106. Ludwig Stern, *Kulturkreis und Form der geistigen Erkrankung* (Halle, 1913).

107. On Hollingshead and Redlich in particular, see Adorno, "Zum Verhältnis von Soziologie und Psychologie," p. 42. The article in question is Hollingshead and Redlich, "Social Stratification and Schizophrenia," *American Sociological Review*, 19 (1954), p. 302. See also Theodor W. Adorno, "Postscriptum," *Kölner Zeitschrift für Soziologie und Sozialpsychologie*, 18 (1966), pp. 37ff.

108. Herbert Marcuse, *Eros and Civilization* (London, 1969). See also idem, "Das Veraltern der Psychoanalyse," in *Kultur und Gesellschaft II* (Frankfurt, 1965), pp. 85–100; and idem, *Psychoanalyse und Politik* (Frankfurt, 1968). This, of course, allows us only a cursory treatment of what Caruso terms the "social aspects of psychoanalysis."

109. Marcuse, *Eros and Civilization*, p. 21.

6. *Arbitrariness and Bindingness*

This chapter is based on a seminar paper presented in a course led by Prof. Helmut Schelsky. I would like to thank him and the other participants for their encouragement.

1. Duveau, *Sociologie de l'Utopie,* p. 18.
2. Eckart von Sydow, *Die Kultur der Dekadenz,* 2nd ed. (Dresden, 1922), pp. 196 and 197.
3. Jorge Luis Borges, "Of Exactitude in Science," in *A Universal History of Infamy* (Harmondsworth, 1981), p. 131.
4. Gaspard Guillard de Beaurieu, *L'Elève de la nature* (Amsterdam, 1764), pp. 5 and 7.
5. Dieter Claessens, "Rationalität revidiert," *Kölner Zeitschrift für Soziologie und Sozialpsychologie,* 17 (1965), pp. 465–476. Reprinted in idem, *Angst, Furcht,* pp. 116–124. The quotation is from the original.
6. Claessens, "Rationalität revidiert," p. 474.
7. The inscription Burton designed for his own grave in Christ Church Cathedral in Oxford reads: "Paucus notus / paucioribus ignotus, / Hic jacet / Democritus junior / Cui vitam dedit et mortem / Melancholia." See Klibansky et al., *Saturn and Melancholy.*
8. Georg Stieler, *Nikolaus Malebranche* (Stuttgart, 1925), pp. 4ff. See also Karlo Oedingen, "Der Ursprung des europäischen Rationalismus," *Zeitschrift für philosophische Forschung,* 12 (1958), pp. 218–241.
9. Karl A. Wittfogel's "comparative study of total power" is eminently useful for an analysis of systems of bindingness with a radical monopoly of control. See Wittfogel, *Oriental Despotism* (New Haven, 1957).
10. Arnold Gehlen, *Man: His Nature and Place in the World* (New York, 1987).
11. If philosophical orientation were to weigh more heavily in the present study, then the concept of intentionality would have to be discussed more thoroughly. Husserl speaks in this connection of the type of *"universal perception of the world";* this means *"truly being,* whether real or ideal . . . i.e., *meaning only as a particular correlate in my own* current and potential *intensionality."* Edmund Husserl, *Cartesianische Meditationen und Pariser Vorträge,* in *Husserliana* (The Hague, 1950), vol. 1, pp. 21 and 23. See also Husserl, *The Paris Lectures,* tr. Peter Koestenbaum (The Hague, 1970). More fundamentally, a distinction would have to be made between Brentano's intentionality of the object and Husserl's intensionality of an act; Husserl refers in this context to Brentano's "empirical psychology," demonstrating how close this is to the position of Gehlen, who wished to create an empirical philosophy.

12. See Claessens, "Rationalität revidiert," p. 475.

13. See Dieter Claessens, "Weltverlust als psychologisches und soziologisches Problem," *Archiv für Rechts- und Sozialphilosophie* (1963–64). Reprinted in idem, *Angst, Furcht,* p. 67.

14. Hence the strong affinity between the eccentrics and the aristocracy: "And Baudelaire and the decadents of 1880—more than a century of rebellion was completely satiated by the audacities of 'eccentricity.' If they all were able to talk of unhappiness it is because they despaired of ever being able to conquer it, except in futile comedies, and because they instinctively felt that it remained their sole excuse and their real claim to nobility. That is why the heritage of romanticism was not claimed by Victor Hugo, peer of the realm, but by Baudelaire and Lacenaire, poets of crime." Camus, *The Rebel,* p. 48.

7. *Reflection and the Inhibition of Action*

1. Karl Vossler, *Poesie der Einsamkeit in Spanien,* p. 171. There is no guarantee that Luis de Léon actually spoke these words; scholars have assumed that they were invented by the Italian Nicolás Crusenio in 1623. Even if invented, they are nevertheless suited to give a vivid portrayal of a behavioral proclivity. See *Enciclopedia universal illustrada europeo-americana* (Barcelona, no date), vol. 29, p. 1675, s.v. "Luis de Léon."

2. In addition, we must not forget that one's education may aid one in becoming an "aristocrat of the mind": Luis' parents were "nobles y limpios" and his father, a lawyer ("abagado de Corte"), ensured that Luis received the proper education ("le proporcioné la educación correspondiente á la clase distinguida á que perteneciá"). *Enciclopedia universal,* p. 1673.

3. Dobrolyubov, "What is Oblomovitis?" in *Essential Writings: Belinsky, Chernyshevsky and Dobrolyubov* (Bloomington and London, 1976), pp. 133–175; the question is posed on p. 140. Dobrolyubov mentions other literary models, namely Lermontov's *Hero of Our Time,* Herzen's *Who is to Blame?,* Turgenev's *Diary of a Superfluous Man, Rudin,* and *Hamlet from Shtshigry,* and Pushkin's *Eugene Onegin.*

4. Wilhelm Goerdt, "Oblomowerei und Philosophie in Russland," in *Collegium Philosophicum: Studien Joachim Ritter zum 60. Geburtstag* (Basel and Stuttgart, 1965), pp. 43 and 47. See also Walter Rehm, *Experimentum Medietatis: Studien zur Geistes- und Literaturgeschichte des 19. Jahrhunderts* (Munich, 1947), pp. 96ff: "Gontscharow und die Langeweile"; and idem, *Gontscharow und Jacobsen, oder Langeweile und Schwermut* (Göttingen, 1963).

5. Walter Hilsbecher, "Versuch über Oblomow," in *Merkur*, 20 (1966), p. 843.
6. Günter Bandmann, *Melancholie und Musik*, p. 48.
7. Ernst Freiherr von Feuchtersleben, *Ausgewählte Werke* (Leipzig, 1907), p. 172.
8. Paul Valéry, *Mauvaises Pensées et autres . . .* (Paris, 1942).
9. Karl Birnbaum, "Grundzüge der Kulturpsychopathologie," *Grenzfragen des Nerven- und Seelenlebens*, 116 (Munich, 1924), p. 39.
10. Joachim Ritter, "Über das Lachen," *Blätter für deutsche Philosophie*, 14 (1940–41), p. 1.
11. Paul Radin, *The World of Primitive Man* (New York, 1953).
12. Heinisch, *Der utopische Staat*, p. 225.
13. Duveau, *Sociologie de l'utopie*, p. 6.
14. Ibid., p. 14.
15. Ibid., p. 17.
16. Mühlmann, *Der revolutionäre Umbruch*, p. 337.
17. Quoted in Duveau, *Sociologie de l'utopie*, p. 14.
18. Ibid., p. 22.
19. Hans Freyer, *Theorie des gegenwärtigen Zeitalters* (Stuttgart, 1963), p. 65. See also Krauss, "Geist und Widergeist," p. 347; he claims that in utopia "the spatial image . . . as always . . . precedes the temporal image."
20. Freyer, *Theorie des gegenwärtigen Zeitalters*, p. 65; and idem, *Die politische Insel*, p. 35. See also Duveau, *Sociologie de l'utopie*, p. 9: "The suspension of time in the utopian city is one of the points that should be of particular interest to sociologists."
21. Ivanoff, "La Marquise de Sablé," p. 162.
22. Bourdeau, *La Rochefoucauld*, pp. 82–83.
23. Félix Hémon, *La Rochefoucauld* (Paris, 1896), p. 122.
24. Frantz Funck-Brentano, *La Cour du Roi Soleil* (Paris, 1937), pp. 194 and 197.
25. Pierre Deniker, "A propos du suicide mélancolique de Vatel," *La Vie médicale*, special no. entitled *Humeur et angoisse* (December 1962), p. 38. The incident was first described in a letter Mme de Sévigné wrote to her daughter.
26. Hémon, *La Rochefoucauld*, p. 198. Grandsaignes-d'Hauterive differentiates in like manner with regard to La Rochefoucauld, namely between a "période d'action" and a "période mondaine." *Le Pessimisme*, pp. 7–8.
27. Wilhelm von Humboldt, "Das achtzehnte Jahrhundert," pp. 70 and 84.
28. Immanuel Kant, *Reflexionen zur Anthropologie*, ed. Benno Erdmann from Kant's handwritten notes (Leipzig, 1882), pp. 68 and 168.

29. Goethe, *The Sufferings*, p. 91.
30. Ibid., p. 97.
31. Hans R. G. Günther, "Psychologie des deutschen Pietismus," *Deutsche Vierteljahresschrift für Literaturwissenschaft und Geistesgeschichte*, 4 (1926), pp. 158, 166, and 167.
32. Georg Lukács, *The Theory of the Novel*, tr. Anna Bostock (London, 1978).
33. Ibid.
34. Bruford, *Germany in the Eighteenth Century*, pp. 80–81.
35. Ibid., p. 11.
36. Ibid., p. 10.
37. Kierkegaard, *Either/Or*, p. 238.
38. Robert Musil, *Tagebücher, Aphorismen, Essays und Reden*, ed. A. Frisé (Hamburg, 1955), p. 113.
39. Pierre Janet, "The Fear of Action," *Journal of Abnormal Psychology and Social Psychology*, 16 (1921–22), p. 152.
40. Pierre Janet, "Fear of Action as an Essential Element in the Sentiment of Melancholia," in *Feelings and Emotions: The Wittenberg Symposium* (Worcester, Mass., 1928), pp. 303 and 309.
41. Sigmund Freud, Letter to Martha Bernays, Paris, 21 October 1885, in *Letters of Sigmund Freud*, tr. T. and J. Stern (London, 1961), p. 186.
42. Freud, "Trauer und Melancholie." See also Hoff, who mentions inhibition as a third symptom of the melancholic syndrome, an inhibition that expresses itself psychologically "in a slowing down of all processes of experience." Hoff, "Das veränderte Erscheinungsbild," p. 730. On this point, see also Wisdom, "Die psychoanalytischen Theorien."
43. Freud, "Einige Charaktertypen aus der psychoanalytischen Arbeit," in *Gesammelte Werke*, 3rd ed. (Frankfurt am Main, 1963), vol. 10, p. 371.
44. Hoff, "Das veränderte Erscheinungsbild," p. 730.
45. Th. Ribot, *Les Maladies de la volonté*, 8th ed. (Paris, 1893), p. 37: "Il ne faut jamais oublier non plus que vouloir c'est agir." See also Harald Schultz-Henke, *Der gehemmte Mensch: Entwurf eines Lehrbuchs der Neopsychoanalyse*, 2nd ed. (Stuttgart, 1947), p. 13.
46. N. R. F. Maier, *Frustration: The Study of Behavior without a Goal* (New York, Toronto, and London, 1949), pp. 113 and 133; emphasis added.
47. Georges Dumas, *Les Etats intellectuels dans la mélancholie* (Paris, 1895), p. 42. The book is dedicated to Ribot!
48. Ibid., p. 9: "mélancolie avec conscience, mélancolie dépressive, mélancolie anxieuse, mélancolie avec stupeur."

49. Dumas, *La Tristesse*, p. 30.

50. Ibid., p. 34.

51. Ibid., p. 79.

52. H. Völkel, *Neurotische Depression: Ein Beitrag zur Psychopathologie und Klinik* (Stuttgart, 1959), p. 6; emphasis added. Page numbers are henceforth given in parentheses in the text.

53. Emil Kraepelin, *Psychiatrie: Ein Lehrbuch für Studierende und Ärzte*, 8th ed. (Leipzig, 1909), vol. 1, p. 362.

54. Emil Kraepelin, *Einführung in die psychiatrische Klinik*, 4th ed., 1st series (Leipzig, 1921), vol. 2, p. 5. Page numbers are henceforth given in parentheses in the text.

55. Richard von Krafft-Ebing, *Die Melancholie: Eine klinische Studie* (Erlangen, 1874), p. 7. Page numbers are henceforth given in parentheses in the text.

56. Richard von Krafft-Ebing, *Text-Book of Insanity*, tr. C. G. Chaddock (Philadelphia, 1904), p. 289. Page numbers are henceforth given in parentheses in the text.

57. Georges L. Dreyfus, *Die Melancholie: Ein Zustandsbild des manisch-depressiven Irreseins* (Jena, 1907), p. 22. Page numbers are henceforth given in parentheses in the text. On p. 10 Dreyfus specifically addresses the question of inhibition as presented by Kraepelin.

58. Tellenbach, "Die Räumlichkeit," pp. 12 and 290.

59. Tellenbach, "Gestalten," pp. 11 and 12.

60. Ibid., p. 24. Page numbers are henceforth given in parentheses in the text.

61. Tellenbach, *Melancholie*. Page numbers are henceforth given in parentheses in the text. See also Tellenbach, "Hiob," and "Zur Klinik der Oralsinn-Störungen."

62. Ludwig Binswanger, *Melancholie und Manie*, p. 10. See also idem, *Being-in-the-World*, tr. J. Needleham (London and New York, 1963); and idem, "Über die manische Lebensform," in *Ausgewählte Vorträge und Aufsätze* (Bern, 1955), vol. 2.

63. Nikolaus Petrilowitsch, "Zur Psychologie und Psychopathologie der Blasiertheit," *Jahrbuch für Psychologie, Psychotherapie und medizinische Anthropologie*, 7 (1960), pp. 55–56.

64. On autistic thought in connection with inhibition and reflection, see E. Bleuler, "Das autistische Denken," *Jahrbuch für psychoanalytische und psychopathologische Forschungen*, 4 (1912), pp. 1ff. On the phenomenon of pain in this context see Hans Bürger-Prinz, "Zur Psychologie des Schmerzes," in *Zur Psychologie der Lebenskrisen*, ed. Ch. Zwingmann (Frankfurt, 1962), pp. 280 and 276. Bürger-Prinz takes up Pradines' work. See also Walter Schulte, "Kopfschmerz und Persönlichkeit:

Gestaltung, Resonanz, Raum, Spannung und Sinn," *Der Nervenarzt*, 26 (1955), pp. 154ff.; and Hanns Ruffin, "Melancholie," *Deutsche medizinsche Wochenschrift*, 82 (1957), pp. 1080ff.

65. Viktor von Gebsattel, "Die depressive Fehlhaltung," in *Imago Hominis: Beiträge zu einer personalen Anthropologie* (Schweinfurt, 1964), pp. 201ff. See also Gebsattel, "Zur Frage der Depersonalisation: Ein Beitrag zur Theorie der Melancholie," *Der Nervenarzt*, 10 (1937).

66. Felix Schottlaender, "Über Einsamkeit, Polarisation und dramatisches Bedürfnis," *Psyche*, 1 (1947–48), pp. 24ff.

8. Melancholy and the Search for Legitimation

1. Klibansky et al., *Saturn and Melancholy*, pp. 256–257.

2. This is the procedure which Gehlen regarded as typical for modern times, a procedure that focuses on "incorporating and portraying a theory of the soul by making a detour of the rational mind." Gehlen, *Urmensch und Spätkultur*, 2nd ed. (Frankfurt and Bonn, 1964), p. 108.

3. Klibansky et al., *Saturn and Melancholy*, p. 247.

4. Peter Schönbach, "Dissonanz und Interaktionssequenzen," *Kölner Zeitschrift für Soziologie und Sozialpsychologie*, 18 (1966), pp. 253–270. Page numbers are henceforth given in parentheses in the text.

5. Gershom Scholem, *The Messianic Idea in Judaism* (New York, 1971), pp. 32 and 35. See also Gershom Scholem, "Die Metamorphose des häretischen Messianismus der Sabbatianer in religiösen Nihilismus im 18. Jahrhundert," in *Zeugnisse*, pp. 20–32; and Robert Alter, "Sabbatai Zewi and the Jewish Imagination," *Commentary*, 42 (1967), pp. 66ff.

6. Scholem, *The Messianic Idea*, p. 290. Scholem's psychiatric assumptions are based on the work of Bleuler and Lange. When he writes that for Nathan "from the outset the figure of Job . . . is the prototype of the Messiah's person," this also proves Sabbatai's orientation toward the "melancholic." See also Tellenbach, "Hiob."

7. Siegmund Hurwitz, "Sabbatai Zwi: Zur Psychologie der häretischen Kabbala," in *Studien zur analytischen Psychologie C. G. Jungs*, vol. 2, *Beiträge zur Kulturgeschichte* (Zurich, 1955), p. 253. On Saul see Rikwah Schaerf, "Saul und der Geist Gottes: Ein Beitrag zum Problem der Melancholie," ibid., pp. 209ff.

8. Hurwitz, "Sabbatai Zwi," p. 259.

9. Ibid., p. 261.

10. Romano Guardini, *Vom Sinn der Schwermut* (Zurich, 1949), p. 7.

11. Ibid., p. 50.

12. Superficially, Bloch's conception cannot be referred to by such a

statement, *"because the world-process itself is a utopian function, with the matter of the objectively Possible as its substance"* (*Principle of Hope*, p. 177). Yet here the process is both total and preformed, in that it brings utopia with it. To unite the notions of process and of utopia makes heavy demands on utopian thought. If we remind ourselves of the link between homesickness and melancholy, then Bloch's utopia reveals its antimelancholic character; "something arises in the world, something which no one yet has inhabited" (*Freiheit und Ordnung*, p. 190).

13. Maine de Biran, *Journal*, vol. 1, p. 247.

14. Benjamin, *The Origin of German Tragic Drama*, tr. and ed. John Osborne (London, 1977), p. 146.

9. The Climate of Melancholy and Anthropological Reduction: The Philosophy of Arnold Gehlen

1. Arnold Gehlen, *Der Mensch: Seine Natur und seine Stellung in der Welt*, 1st ed. (Berlin, 1940), pp. 449–450. The quotations are all from chapter 55, "Supreme Leadership Systems." From now on I shall make continual use of my essay "Handlung und Reflexion: Aspekte der Anthropologie Arnold Gehlens," *Soziale Welt*, 18 (1967), pp. 41–66.

2. Arnold Gehlen, *Der Mensch*, 8th ed. (Frankfurt and Bonn, 1966), p. 394. The two subsequent quotations also come from this edition.

3. Gehlen, *Urmensch und Spätkultur*, 2nd ed. (Frankfurt and Bonn, 1964), pp. 9 and 89. What is decisive here is that historical differentiation is juxtaposed with phenomena of *consciousness*.

4. We shall forgo criticism of Gehlen here. We could, first of all, note his striking neglect of the Other, of the "companion," and secondly the fact that he fails to take the opportunity to outline a theory of "finding friendship with the world." For such a step would severely weaken the "melancholy" of his point of departure. As we shall see, however, Gehlen needs the theory for the sake of his conception of institutions. See also Dieter Claessens, *Familie und Wertsystem*, 2nd ed. (Berlin, 1967); and idem, *Instinkt, Psyche, Geltung* (Cologne and Opladen, 1968).

5. Gehlen, *Urmensch*, pp. 157 and 42.

6. Arnold Gehlen, "Probleme einer soziologischen Handlungslehre," in *Soziologie und Leben*, ed. Carl Brinkmann (Tübingen, 1952), p. 44.

7. H. Klages, *Technischer Humanismus: Philosophie und Soziologie der Arbeit bei Karl Marx* (Stuttgart, 1964), p. 16.

8. Gehlen, *Der Mensch*, 7th ed. (1962), p. 349.

9. In *Merkur*, 106 (1956), quoted in *Studien zur Anthropologie und Soziologie* (Berlin and Neuwied, 1963), p. 330. We shall return, via reference to the work of Klaus Heinrich, to the hidden link between cynicism and melancholy.

10. Gehlen, *Man in the Age of Technology* (New York, 1980), p. 83. This interconnection is presented in too compressed a form in Gehlen's work. We have already discussed the sociological importance of the fact that people were not ashamed to describe "sentimental" modes of behavior and attitudes as "melancholy," indeed saw this rather as providing additional legitimation. See also Helmut Schelsky, *Auf der Suche nach Wirklichkeit* (Düsseldorf and Cologne, 1965), pp. 391ff.

11. Gehlen, *Man in the Age of Technology*, p. 102; emphasis added.

12. Gehlen, *Der Mensch*, p. 203.

13. Arnold Gehlen, "Über kulturelle Kristallisation," in *Studien zur Anthropologie und Soziologie*, p. 321.

14. Ibid., p. 323. For criticism of this conception see Jacob Taubes, "Kultur und Ideologie," lecture presented to the Sixteenth German Sociologists' Congress, 1968, unpublished.

15. Hendrik de Man, *Vermassung und Kulturverfall: Eine Diagnose unserer Zeit* (Bern, 1951), p. 136.

16. Gehlen, *Studien*, p. 81.

17. Klibansky et al., *Saturn and Melancholy*, p. 120.

18. Arnold Gehlen, "Das gestörte Zeit-Bewusstsein," *Merkur*, 17 (1963), p. 320.

19. See Franz Stenderhoff, "Zur Psychologie des Pessimismus," *Zeitschrift für angewandte Psychologie und Charakterkunde*, 42 (1941), pp. 257–327; and 43 (1942), pp. 1–37, esp. p. 259.

20. See on this point Arnold Gehlen, "Über die Geburt der Freiheit aus der Entfremdung," *Archiv für Rechts- und Sozialphilosophie*, 40 (1952), p. 3; and idem, *Deutschtum und Christentum bei Fichte* (Berlin, 1935).

21. Arnold Gehlen, "Die Struktur der Tragödie" (1934), quoted in *Theorie der Willensfreiheit und frühe philosophische Schriften* (Berlin and Neuwied, 1965), p. 246.

22. See Martin Greiffenhagen, "Das Dilemma des Konservatismus," in *Gesellschaft in Geschichte und Gegenwart* (Berlin, 1961), pp. 13ff.

23. Gehlen, *Urmensch*, p. 69.

24. Gehlen, *Der Mensch*, p. 382.

25. Gehlen, *Urmensch*, p. 41. With respect to the "melancholy climate," Gehlen did not need to correct himself via this pragmatic turn. William James's "continuous indecision with reference to what is world and can be world," the difference between "a diseased mind (melancholy) on the one hand and a healthy mind on the other," fit a

scheme of order and dis-order and permit one to devise a concept of action that works against dis-order. John Dewey similarly describes the interrelation of reflection and action-inhibition when viewing mournfulness as disturbed (defective) action. See Eduard Baumgarten, *Die geistigen Grundlagen des amerikanischen Gemeinwesens,* vol. 2, *Der Pragmatismus: R. W. Emerson, W. James, J. Dewey* (Frankfurt, 1938), esp. pp. 132 and 257. See also William James, *The Varieties of Religious Experience: A Study in Human Nature,* 4th ed. (London, New York, and Bombay, 1904), pp. 127ff: Lectures 6 and 7, "The Sick Soul."

26. Klaus Heinrich, "Antike Kyniker und Zynismus in der Gegenwart," *Das Argument,* 8 (1966), p. 118. The essay is reprinted in Heinrich, *Parmenides und Jona* (Frankfurt, 1966).

27. Quoted in the introduction to Gehlen, *Theorie der Willensfreiheit,* p. 7.

28. Hermann Zeltner, "Dilemma der Freiheit: Zur Philosophie Arnold Gehlens," *Soziale Welt,* 18 (1967), p. 75.

29. Gehlen, *Theorie der Willensfreiheit,* p. 8.

30. Quoted in the introduction to Gehlen, *Studien,* p. 9.

31. Gehlen, "Wirklicher und unwirklicher Geist," p. 232n.; quoted in Friedrich Jonas, *Die Institutionslehre Arnold Gehlens* (Tübingen, 1966), p. 1. Jonas takes up where Gehlen left off in 1931.

32. The following page numbers in parentheses in the text refer to the 1931 Leipzig *Habilitationsschrift.*

33. Also important here is the concept of "situation" which Gehlen employed above all in the treatise "Der Idealismus und die Lehre vom menschlichen Handeln" (1935), and from which he later explicitly distanced himself (see *Theorie der Willensfreiheit,* p. 340).

34. Gehlen presumes (p. 127, n. 82) that putting the negative into practice—for example, by suicide—rests "on the evidentiality of access to a true form of being," and he continues: "As a consequence, the drive to suicide seems to me to belong to endogenous melancholy: life lies in wait for the first, slightest chance to destroy itself—a great exception, given that it is otherwise so concerned with itself. One should not try and prevent this." On the anthropological foundation as a constitutive moment in melancholy, see also Karl Mannheim, "Contributions to a Theory of the Interpretation of World Views," in *Wissensoziologie,* p. 131.

35. Alwin Diemer, in the *Fischer Encyclopedia of Philosophie,* ed. Alwin Diemer and Ivo Frenzel (Frankfurt, 1958), p. 229, s.v. "Ontologie."

36. Gehlen's statement that "the conviction of this book is that the ontological conditions of humankind change historically" (*Habilitationsschrift,* p. 31) is no modification of an ontology, for the talk is of

conditions and not of *stages* of being. This is, nevertheless, the basis for cultural critique, which must be founded on historically determined differences. These first permit the retrospective-reactionary thrust Gehlen takes; critique of immutable elements would not only be a waste of energy but would also miss the chance for "heroic" subjection, "dissolution" in the negative, and so on.

37. In *Der Mensch* Gehlen concerns himself with attempts to explain institutions in terms of rational purposive action (Malinowski) or primary, subjective purposiveness (Scheler, Bergson). He states: "Both faulty constructs are dangerous to the extent that they seem to compromise teleological thought as such, which is, however, indispensable in a third *(ontological)* form, as we shall presently see." *Der Mensch*, pp. 392–393, emphasis added. Ontology thus persists precisely in the decisive category of secondary objective purposiveness and finds its legitimation in the "origins" (ontology) and from "above" (metaphysics).

38. Theodor Adorno, *Eingriffe: Neun kritische Modelle* (Frankfurt, 1963), p. 14. Subsequent page numbers are given in the text.

39. "Meinung Wahn Gesellschaft," in *Eingriffe*, p. 165.

40. Jürgen Habermas, in the *Fischer Encyclopedia of Philosophie*, pp. 18–35, s.v. "Anthropologie." For a comparison of Adorno and Gehlen, see the discussion between the two in *Die Philosophie und die Frage nach dem Fortschritt*, ed. Kuhn and Wiedmann (Munich, 1964), pp. 326ff; also Karl Markus Michel, *Die sprachlose Intelligenz* (Frankfurt, 1968), pp. 117–118.

41. In his *Destruction of Reason*, Lukács uses this term as a derogatory label for critical theory as practiced by the Frankfurt School.—*Translators.*

Index

Bourgeois escapism, 55–58
Bourgeois ethics, 156–157
Bourgeois flight from the world, 72–73
Bourgeoisie, 37–38, 50–52, 101, 103, 104, 157
Bourgeois literature, 59, 158
Bourgeois melancholy, 55–86, 138–139, 141, 153–154, 174, 183
Bourgeois psychology, 102, 137–138, 152
Bourgeois sentimentality, 152. *See also* Sentimentality
Brainwashing, 132
Breton, André, 27
Bright, Timothy, 19–20
Bruford, W. H., 155, 156
Brummell, Beau, 69
Bürgerlichkeit, 103
Burton, Robert, 9, 10–22, 134, 146
Bussy-Rabutin, Count, 42
Byron, Lord, 11

Cameron, Norman, 127, 129–130
Campanella, Tommaso, 23, 24, 92, 146, 206n84
Camp movement, 118–121
"Catalogue of vices," 9, 18
"Changed Image of Melancholy, The" (Hoff), 123
Characteristics of the Present Age, The (Fichte), 83–84
Chateaubriand, François René de, 51, 52
Church, bindingness and arbitrariness in, 134
Citizens, active versus passive, 76
City of the Sun, 17, 23–24, 92, 206n84
Civilizing Process, The (Elias), 20
Claessens, Dieter, 116–117, 133
Class, 101, 206n79
Clergy, melancholy and, 206n81
Closed Mercantile State (Fichte), 84, 94
Cockaigne, 91
Coenesthesis, 126
Cognitive dissonance, 168–173
Cohen, Albert, 10, 129–130
Color symbolism, melancholy and, 23–24

Comic opera, 71
Communication, boredom and, 118–119
"Compatriotism with the world," 81–82
Complexio temperata, 19
"Concept of Reality in Idealism, The" (Gehlen), 179
Conformity, 4
Conservative thought, cyclical nature of, 187
Constitutional depression, 179, 180. *See also* Depression
"Constitutional mourning," 173
Cosmology, dis-order and, 19
Court, 36–46, 67, 96, 149
Court etiquette, 38, 48, 50. *See also* Etiquette
Court games, 96–97
Court jesters, 66–71
Courtly rationality, 52–53
Courtly society, nature and, 74
"Court sociologist," 71
Criterion of immanence, 48–49
Critique of Judgment (Kant), 78
Cult of introversion, 54
Cults of friendship and letter writing, 66, 75, 102, 152–153
Cultural critique, 182–184, 243n36
"Cultural crystallization," 183

Dahrendorf, Ralf, 4, 92–93
Dandyism, 69–70, 105, 119
Decision making, action and, 135
De Concordantia Catholica (Nicholas of Cusa), 184–185
Deffand, Madame du, 51
Democritus, 13, 134, 202n33
"Democritus to the Reader," 12
Depression, 171–172, 173, 178, 179, 180, 181
Dermenghem, Emile, 21
Detachment, 119
Deviance, 8, 132–133
Deviant behavior, 4–5, 6
Dialogue on the Novel (Jens), 11
Dilthey, Wilhelm, 59
Disburdening, 140, 150, 152